Oileáin

A Guide to the Irish Islands

David Walsh

Pesda Press

www.pesdapress.com

First published in Great Britain 2004 by Pesda Press
'Elidir', Ffordd Llanllechid
Rachub, Bangor
Gwynedd
LL57 3EE
Wales

Editor: Des Keaney

Photo Editor: Séan Pierce

Distributed by Cordee
3a DeMontfort Street
Leicester
LE1 7HD
UK

Printed by Cambrian Printers - Wales

Dedication

I could never have been out there on the Atlantic, doing all this so much, in my kayak, on the water, among the islands, without a special kayaker. I pay tribute to my main paddling partner through much of the last 12 years or so, Fred Cooney.

He never once let me down or failed to look out for me on my bad days. I can truthfully say I was never unnecessarily afraid when he was around. I dedicate this publication of Oileáin to my friend of a hundred islands. Thank you, 'Dark One'.

Acknowledgements

Oileáin would never have been possible without the help and assistance of its many supporters. At the risk of giving offence I single out Des Keaney and Seán Pierce for their endless assistance putting it all together, and my wife Sheila for tolerating and encouraging. Des and Seán have not only greatly assisted in the concept over the years, they each put in enormous effort in the recent push to publication. They handed in photos, edited, judged, criticised, and steered me through it all. Sheila gave me a long leash always. She prefers me at home with the family "most of the time happy, and not all of the time unhappy".

I pay special tribute (in chronological order) to Robin Ruddock, Pat Ewen, Kevin O'Callaghan, Stephen Hannon, Seán Connor, Phil Beattie, Matt Corbett, Mike McClure, Trevor Fisher, Dave Kavanagh, and Josie & Máire UíGhiobúin. *Maith sibh go léir agus buíochas.*

There were others, John Hussey, Rory Walsh, Mary T. Butler, Eadaoin Healy, Paddy Barry, Dave Carraher and John O'Connor.

Photographs

A special thanks is due to Séan Pierce for making the initial selections and scanning all the photographs used in this book.

Thanks is also due to all those who sent us photos, they are:

Fred Cooney, Josie Gibbons, Des Keaney, Mike McClure, Kevin O'Callaghan, Séan Pierce, Alex Ritsema, Alyn Walsh and David Walsh.

Front Cover: Tearaght Sunset. Co. Kerry - Séan Pierce
Back Cover: Saint McDara's Island, Connemara - Séan Pierce
                     Cross on Caher Island, Co. Mayo - Séan Pierce

Introduction

Oileáin is a detailed guide to almost every Irish offshore island. The guide is comprehensive, describing over 300 islands, big and small, far out to sea and close in by the shore, inhabited and uninhabited. *Oileáin* tells it as it is, rock by rock, good and bad, pleasant and otherwise. It concentrates on landings and access generally, then adds information on camping, drinking water, tides, history, climbing, birds, whales, dolphins, legends or anything else of interest.

Oileáin will, I hope, appeal to all who go to sea in small boats, divers and yachtsmen as well as kayakers. The sheer level of detail contained in *Oileáin* must surely throw new light on places they thought they knew well. It is not a book about kayaking. It so happens that a practical way of getting to islands is by kayak, and that is how the author gets about. Scuba divers and RIBs get in close too. Yachtsmen get about better than most, and they too enjoy exploring intensively from a dinghy. With the increasing availability of ferries, boatless people will also enjoy *Oileáin*.

Offshore islands are the last wilderness in Ireland. Hillwaking is now so popular that there are few untrampled mainland hills. Ninety per cent of offshore islands are uninhabited outside of the first fortnight in August, and eighty per cent even then. You won't meet many other people, if any at all, out beyond an Irish surf line. It is a time of change though, and holiday homes are very much the coming thing in some offshore areas. Sea going will never stop being a great adventure. Therefore, offshore islands are still the preserve of the very few. Now is a golden era for exploration.

The Author

David Walsh is a Dublin solicitor, where he lives in Ranelagh with his wife Sheila. He has four children: Justin, Daire, Sarah and Orla. He was always a keen climber, with a wide general interest in outdoor pursuits, particularly birding, river canoeing, and some scuba diving. On a sailing and climbing trip to Spitzbergen in 1990, he saw four sea kayaks glide between icebergs in a remote frozen fiord. He knew he just had to have a piece of the action, and the activity has consumed his life since then. David began exploring and documenting Ireland's islands in 1991 and has personally visited almost 300 of those in the text. He is a founder member of the Irish Sea Kayaking Association and held the position of Chairman from 1995 to 2003.

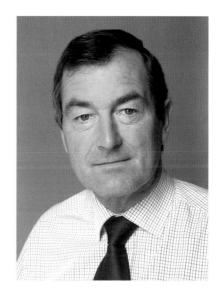

Using This Book

There are a couple of things it is useful to know when using *Oileáin*.

First, Grid References

Oileáin is unique among books describing seafaring matters in that it uses grid references in preference to latitude and longitude, to describe position. This results from the peculiarly intimate relationship kayaks enjoy with the land. Any modern yacht or RIB has GPS that copes perfectly well with the translation. Nevertheless there is a detailed description of how grid references work in the Glossary of Terms.

Second, Special Terms

Kayakers have always found it useful to attempt to classify the whole logistical issue of places and methods to put boats into the water and take them out again, how to get conveniently to and from those places by land, with or without large or small numbers of cars. Different concepts, used sometimes in combination, have emerged, throwing up the following words with specific meaning in the text that might not otherwise be appreciated:

Embarkation	Quality mainland place which is handy for vehicles, sheltered, easy launching at all tides, maybe useful for multiple excursions.
Landing	Mainland place from which logically to launch for a trip, but other virtues may be very limited.
Landing Place	Logical place to land, usually on an island, with the emphasis on the quality of use of the place, e.g. good camping, sheltered, easy landing at all tides, convenient to a point of interest.
Landing Point	Landing is handy, but the place is of limited interest.
Landing Possible	Emphasis on the "it can be done, but …"
Waystop	Emphasis on absence of land access, but may be lovely for a picnic.
Pitstop	Unsatisfactory waystop. Leg stretching and similar activities only.
Escape	Unsatisfactory or emergency stopping only.

Thus an embarkation place is more than an embarkation point, e.g. you could drive to an embarkation point but maybe not leave a car/cars there, or the put-in is tricky, or tidal, or exposed. Similarly a landing place is more than a landing point. In the one you could land and stay overnight, in the other maybe land and / or only picnic or explore. In turn "landing possible" is worse again, and "escape" rates poorest of all. One might choose to lunch at a waystop, but one stretches one's legs at a pitstop, and little more.

Deep Water Landing	Involves landing from deep water onto solid rock. This includes landings onto anything from exposed rocks, to harbour steps, or very steep slips. Many harbours will have only a deep water landing, and these can be awkward. Kayakers don't like deep water landings much.

Contents

Contents

The Mid-West 102
Shannon Estuary to Galway City including the Aran Islands

Connemara South 123
Galway City to Slyne Head

Contents

The North-West
Sligo to Malin

The North East
Lough Foyle to Carlingford Lough

The writing of this section of the guide was greatly assisted by referring to 'A Sea Kayaker's Guide to the Causeway Coast', by Robin G.Ruddock. It is an excellent publication and worth reading if you are visiting the area from Lough Foyle in the W to Torr Head and Cushendun in the E.

County Derry

Lough Foyle

C660-390   Sheet 3/4

Embarkation

The logical embarkation point for the outer regions of Lough Foyle is Magilligan Point, by the Martello Tower. Access is by the B202 past the prison and rifle range. Do not block roads. Park by the hotel. The whole region is a security area, frequently patrolled. Especially beware of the military zone on the beach immediately to the E of the point, Benone Beach, on which it's better not to land (certainly not while firing is going on).

Further to the E, beyond the military zone, there is public access at about C716-363. There is a concrete slip across the beach. However, the beach surfs and there is a strong tidal drift. This may have relevance for launching. Expect caravans, lifeguards, and beach casting anglers.

Military installations on both sides show the importance of the lough in such terms.

The whole lough is less interesting inwards to the SW. There are large areas of mudflats on the E side. That said, it is a busy, well marked and well lit area. It is excellent for night navigation, sheltered but with strong tides. If paddling up into the city, it is possible to take out at Prehen Boat Club upstream of the Craigavon Bridge on the E bank.

Road access is better on the Donegal side and there are nice secluded beaches. Greencastle at C648-400 lies directly across from Magilligan

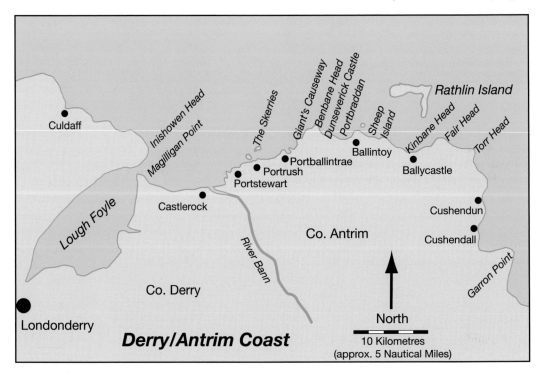

Derry/Antrim Coast

Point. The Donegal shore gets the more interesting up towards Inishowen Head at C685-438. The sea is much more exposed beyond the head.

Tides

Fierce tides push through the narrows. Rates of 3.5 knots should not be treated lightly. Eddies on the Donegal side are more pronounced and more usable in the latter half of flood and ebb. The ingoing stream is from about HW Belfast +0330 and the outgoing from HW Belfast -0230.

Downhill

C753-362   Sheet 4

There is public access at the extreme E end of Benone Beach at a point called Downhill Strand. The Downhill Hotel is now closed and awaiting demolition. Parking and toilets are by the hotel and access is by a stream through an archway under the railway. This spot is popular with anglers. The rocky area to the E of the prominent Mussenden Temple at C758-363 is loose basalt, eroded to provide caves and arches. Fulmar and Kittiwake thrive on the sewerage outfall.

There is good access and parking at Castlerock village itself at C766-365, where there is parking and toilets at the beach access point.

County Antrim

River Bann

C783-367   Sheet 4

To the E of Castlerock village is the Bar Mouth, where the River Bann flows into the sea. Turbulent water can be experienced quite a distance offshore. The flood at the mouth is weak by comparison to the ebb. Especially when the river is up, the ebb and the flow of the river combine to produce mighty standing waves. The flow of the river is controlled by floodgates well upstream. Powerful rip currents either side of the mouth are dangerous enough. The mouth artificially narrows the stream and this projects the fresh water out with great force. The fresh water is easily distinguished in the sea water and gives a good guide as to tide direction and strength off the beaches. The river is marked as far up as Coleraine. The area is a noted birding spot in winter.

Portstewart

C815-386   Sheet 4

The area behind Portstewart Strand to the W of the town is part golf course and part National Trust. There is fee-paying access to the NT section, where there are toilets and parking. There is a powerful rip each end of the strand. When the strand is dumping, it is better to launch off a slip at Portnahapple at C813-376, which is usable in most conditions.

The harbour at C815-386 can be difficult to enter or exit in heavy seas, with multi-directional reflected waves. The slip is exposed to surge. There is good parking and this is the access of choice in calm conditions.

There is some interesting rock hopping locally, clapotis almost always and some small caves and a blowhole that performs well in good swell. The tide can run fast around Portstewart Point.

Portstewart to Portrush

C815-386 to C856-407 Sheet 4

The coastline here is basalt and reasonably interesting, low lying at first. Rinagree Point at C833-397 is the halfway point. To its W is Black Rock and just off it lies Lawson's Rock, which breaks even in a moderate swell. It is possible to shelter in the lee of Black Rock. There is a tiny storm beach accessible from landward just E of Rinagree Point. Boomers may be expected hereabouts. Rock hopping and narrow channels are best enjoyed in calmer conditions and at about HW.

Portrush

C856-407   Sheet 4

Portrush West Bay is easily accessed under the railway line. The slipway in the harbour is awkward in swell, being quite close to the entrance and is quite busy. Consider using Portandoo Harbour at C857-412 instead, though the parking is a little more remote. There is also good parking at the W end of Curran Strand with parking at C863-406.

Ramore Head is interesting exploring in calm conditions. Skerries Sound often kicks up and is best avoided by the inexperienced. The ebb sets up powerful standing waves.

The Skerries - Portrush

C875-427   Sheet 4

These rocky islands lie about 2km NE of Portrush. The islands are basalt and the N side is 'steep to' and usually has unsettled sea conditions as the tide and swell often work in opposition. They are mostly grassy and low on the S side. Strong tide races set between the islands and associated rocks to their N. The sheltered S side is usually settled, and the best landing on the large skerry is towards the E end where there is almost a gap in the island. The Skerries are privately owned so get permission to land from Mr Metson in Portrush at 028 70857412, especially if intending to camp. There is a small brackish lake on the large skerry. Large numbers of birds nest and some rabbits survive. The best embarkation point is at Portandoo Harbour at C857-412 on the NE part of the headland, which is well sheltered. The rocks S of the harbour are a nature reserve and of interest to the geologist for its ammonite exposures. There are Grey Seal and a small colony of Common Seal.

The Storks at C897-425 are rocks lying 2km ESE of the Skerries, and 1km NNW of Dunluce Castle. They are marked by a tall, unlit red beacon. Fishing is good hereabouts.

Portrush to Portballintrae

C856-407 - C930-424   Sheet 4

White Rocks Beach at C899-411 is accessible from the road and there are good toilet and parking facilities. Calm conditions are necessary as the surf can be quite powerful with large dumping waves in heavy seas. The rips are strong and the tide flows strongly just beyond the break line. The rips are easily read from above on the road.

It is mainly cliffs eastwards to Portballintrae. There are a number of interesting caves in the first section along under prominent Dunluce Castle at C905-415. One such cave is directly under the castle. Exploration of some of the other caves hereabouts requires a torch. There is good rock hopping eastwards to Portballintrae, with at least one good sheltered deep water landing in a channel about the halfway mark. Another cave just W of Binbane Cove is 40 to 50m long. Beware of a choke point halfway in, where the surge can catch the unwary.

In Portballintrae Harbour, there is a public slipway at C926-423. There are toilets and a car park which can become quite congested in summer. Local kayakers prefer the larger car park at C930-424 overlooking Bushfoot Strand to the E of the town. Access to the beach is just W of the car park.

Portballintrae to Dunseverick

C930-424 to C999-447 Sheet 5

The rocks between the harbour and Bushfoot Strand can be fun at HW. On passage however, give them plenty of clearance. Stay at least 200m clear of the E harbour entrance to avoid a boomer called the Blind Rock. Bushfoot is named for the River Bush which flows in here at the SW corner. Upriver 2km is the town of Bushmills, famed globally for its Black Bush whiskey. The beach tends to surf and should be used with caution. After rain, a brown tongue of water enters the sea and what happens to it is a good guide to what the tide is doing just then. The E part of the beach is irregularly rocky and not a good place for small boats. There is a small slip below Runkerry House at C934-435.

The coastline eastwards is the Giant's Causeway section. It is committing and there are no easy landing places. It is also one of the most beautiful sections of the entire Northern Ireland coastline.

Just SE of the off-lying rock, the Mile Stone at C934-440, is the massive and beautiful Runkerry Cave at C935-439, complete with boulder beach and long dry passage. There are other caves hereabouts, most notably in a small cove 0.5km E of Runkerry called locally Portcoon, with a dry side entrance.

There is a slip in Portnaboe, the last cove before the Causeway proper. Visitors once walked from this point, before the access from above was organised.

The Causeway section itself is 5km around Benbane Head (C965-461). There are many exposures of geological features; dykes, sills and the various layers of volcanic activity are easily seen. The Causeway itself and all the related geology are far better seen from seaward. In strong off-

Causeway Coast, Co. Antrim - Mike McClure

shore winds there are vicious down draughts and each of the bays can funnel the wind to strong gusts. The wreck of a Spanish Armada ship, the Girona, is at Lacada Point at C952-455. It is easy to understand how only a handful survived the wrecking.

Formidable tides run off Benbane Head and great seas can build up off it and off Bengore Head 1km E. Relief and shelter can be had further E in Port Moon at C979-451, where landing is possible. The coastline eastwards towards Dunseverick Castle falls away, but is bouldery. There is a small, well-sheltered harbour at Dunseverick at C999-447, with a small maritime museum and good enough parking. Camping is possible here but forbidden, except in emergency. There are some lovely rock pools just W of the harbour, suitable for swimming and diving.

Dunseverick to Ballintoy
C999-447 - D039-456   Sheet 5

The rocky area immediately E of Dunseverick is cliffy with caves hidden from view by raised beaches. White Park Bay to the E is particularly beautiful. Portbraddan is a small harbour at the W end of the beach at D008-444. It boasts the smallest church in Ireland. Access and parking are poor. It is possible to launch off a boulder beach. Very pretty. The salmon fishery, as with all those on the N coast, is closed.

There is a youth hostel set high above the beach itself, behind the official car park. It is a long carry to the beach and not really suitable for kayak launching. The beach gives good surf though. Boulders and a dyke called the Long Causeway obstruct the E end. The rocky islets E of the beach towards Islandoo at D038-457 are NT and give good sport in the right conditions.

Ballintoy - Ballycastle
D039-456 - D121-415   Sheet 5

Inside Islandoo lies the wonderful Ballintoy harbour at D039-456, a splendid embarkation place for this area generally, or for just a lunch stop. The tides are really powerful through the channels, even right outside the harbour mouth. The harbour has a strand for landing, two slips, toilets and even a coffee shop. It gets congested

Sheep Island, Co. Antrim - David Walsh

in summer. Take care towing a trailer down to the harbour, as the road is steep and twisty. Good facilities, great views. Lovely.

The tides set so strongly and eddy so fiercely in the main offshore current that it is possible to surf the deep water eddies in Boheeshane Bay eastwards towards Larry Bane Head at D049-452.

Sheep Island

D048-458   Sheet 5

Sheep Island lies ENE of Ballintoy Harbour and was bought by the National Trust in 1967. The rats on the island were exterminated by 1970 and it again became an important nesting site for Puffin and Cormorant. The large numbers of the latter indicate healthy fish stocks in the rivers of the NE coast. The island is flat topped with steep cliffs on all sides, essentially a large sea stack.

There is a strong eddy between the island and Larry Bane Head at D049-452. The power of the eddy gives only a hint of the strength of the tide races in the main current on the N side.

Landing

Landing can be made at two points. On the N of the island is an obvious bay. A boulder beach at the head of the bay gives access to a corrie-shaped area whose southern side is a narrow ridge linking the higher points of the SW and NE sides. The climb from the boulder beach is firstly on easy grassy slopes but then onto steeper rock. An exposed climb leads onto high grassy slopes. The climb should not be underestimated as the rock is loose and the slope steep.

A second landing, with easier access and support holds, is located on the SE corner.

SPA

Cormorant

Carrickarede Island

D062-449   Sheet 5

Carrickarede Island is about 2km E of Ballintoy Harbour and is worth visiting by sea. It is owned by the National Trust and can be visited by land across its famous rope bridge, in place from Easter to the end of October to serve salm-

Salmon fisherman's cottage, Carrickarede, Co. Antrim - David Walsh

on fishermen. The tide race off the NW corner is powerful, but can often be avoided by going under the rope bridge. The sand bar here is covered on the top two thirds of the tide. The rock strata is interesting, giving good nest sites for Kittiwake, Razorbill and Guillemot. There is a wonderful cave on the outside, visible only from the sea.

Carrickarede to Ballycastle

The cliff scenery now becomes quite majestic. The small wooded area at Port More is very unusual. Buzzards are common hereabouts. Landing may be had by an old winch on the W side of a forest. It is possible to escape here, but it is a long scramble to the nearest road.

Watch for the splendid through-cave in Kinbane Head at D088-438. Tides set strongly at the head, and a very defined line separates the eddy from the flow. This is an excellent teaching area. Landing is possible on the W side of the head. A long steep path leads up the cliff to a car park on the E side.

Nice cliffs join Kinbane Head to Ballycastle, with dramatic caves. The cliff structure hereabouts is liable to rock fall, the slips evident by lack of vegetation. One such is directly above an inviting cave entrance, so do take care.

Ballycastle has a number of options for landing. The large breakwater has a concrete slip. The old pier has a slipway beside it. Car parking abounds, except in summer congestion. There is also a car park at the E end of the beach at D132-416 by Pans Rocks.

Rathlin Island

Chart 2798 covers the general area, as does OSNI Sheet 5. The information in the Pilot and the Sailing Directions is essential on this challenging section of coastline.

Rathlin lies just over 10km N of Ballycastle, where there is a good embarkation place at the pier at D122-415. The island is served by regular ferry, and boasts a stable population. Most of the habitation and services are at Church Bay. Camping with water and toilets is possible amongst old caravans at D148-506, just S of the harbour. There is a hostel in the Old Manor House at the harbour, and some guest houses,

Rathlin Island, S coast, Co. Antrim - Séan Pierce

the most convenient of which is just beside the large pier at D147-510. More remote camping spots can be had along the shore by Rue Point at D151-473 and along the E coast in the many secluded bays. Camping is convenient at Portawillin at D161-512 where there is a small pier with steps. The rest of the island is generally steep with cliffs towering above boulder beaches and landing is impossible or uninviting except in an emergency.

The island, steeped in history, has a distinct character all its own. Wallace Clark's book 'Rathlin - Disputed Island' gives a lot of information about its history from the earliest settlers to modern times. In earliest times porcellainite, or flint (as in stone age axes) was mined here and exported. The island was successively conquered and reconquered by the Vikings, Scots, Normans and the English. Most famously, it was litigated over between Ireland and Scotland, and found to be Irish because there were no snakes (Saint Patrick is said to have banished all snakes from Ireland in the 5th Century).

Circumnavigation

For the sea canoeist, this is one of the most committing of paddles, which is best done clockwise as the shape of the island sets up eddies to one's advantage. The E side is the only part where progress could be made against the tide. The island is 'L' shaped and at each of the headlands there are major tide races, which are always active except at slack water, though it is generally possible to stay inshore and avoid their full force. The MacDonnell Race at the NE corner is particularly fearsome.

The cliffs on the N side are high and dark and the feeling of exposure is greatest here. There are caves in the NE corner near the E lighthouse, the most famous of which is said to have been used by Robert the Bruce, where he met his spider. The S facing cliffs W of Church Bay are chalk overlaid with basalt, and very picturesque. There are some interesting shapes and stacks as one nears the W end of the island. There is an old pier at D102-509 in Cooraghy Bay, which gives a chance of a rest before tackling the committing part of the paddle.

SPA

Peregrine, Guillemot, Razorbill.

The island, and the NE corner of Ireland generally, is splendidly situated for passage migrants in spring and autumn. Puffin, Buzzard and Eider are amongst the birds abounding in summer.

A large colony of Common Seal may be found in Mill Bay, just S of the main harbour.

Embarkation and Tides

The most obvious embarkation place is from Ballycastle, and the best time to start the crossing is just before slack water Dover (approx Belfast). There are very informative diagrammatic chartlets showing tidal movements, hour by hour, in the Irish Coast Pilot, Causeway Coast Guide and the Sailing Directions of the Irish Cruising Club, N and E Coasts volume. Alternatively, embark from Dunseverick Harbour at D000-445 or Ballintoy Harbour at D038-456 if wishing to travel to the island on the last few hours of the flood or back on the ebb. Tides reach 6 knots in Rathlin Sound so Ballycastle is more or less impossible except on the slack. 4.5 knots are experienced off Torr Head at D234-407 and 4 knots off Cushendun at D253-327, the flows beginning at HW and LW Belfast. Rathlin is a challenging paddle even for the experienced, and careful planning is required.

Ballycastle - Cushendall

D121-415 - D263-256   Sheet 5

There is a good view of Ballycastle Bay and Fair Head from the car park at the harbour. The strand all along Ballycastle Bay shelves steeply, and any swell produces powerful dumping waves onto the coarse sandy beach. The tides are powerful close inshore, and with rain, the outflow from the river by the harbour gives a good indication of what is happening.

The shore from Pans Rock at D133-417 to Murlough Bay 6km E is unrepentant. Initially there are large boulders after a cable or so. There is but the one landing, at Carrickmore at D164-427, the most secluded campsite in Northern Ireland. Around Fair Head, the tide races, off big boulders without shelter, backed by enormous climbing cliffs. There can be vicious downdraughts from winds from the S. Fierce tide

races may be expected, and even the eddies close inshore are vicious.

These cliffs were discovered for climbers by a sea kayaker on passage, Keith Britton. In 1964, Geoff Earnshaw and Calvert Moore put up the first climb - Earnshaw's Chimney. By 2003, there were 363 routes at Fair Head cliffs, the finest in the land, bar none. This was the first recorded of many such interactions between these symbiotic outdoor pursuits, kayaking and climbing.

Murlough Bay requires landing onto the rocks, but is sheltered, near the bottom of the NT car park. At LW a beach appears E of the cottages. The road here is private.

Eastwards, the shoreline changes to steep and unstable grass slopes, intermingled with loose cliff and scree. There is a small landing E of Torr

Coast near Cushendun, Co. Antrim - Séan Pierce

The Maidens, Co. Antrim - Séan Pierce

Head at D234-408. Have a look at the interesting stone shelter in the mouth of the cave. The local fishermen are particularly informative. Have a fair tide hereabouts, or suffer.

The coastline S is much the same, steep grass eroded to provide exposed rock on the shore. The lack of distinct features makes judging progress difficult. There are some pleasant shingle beaches N of Cushendun.

At Cushendun, land at the S end where a lane gives access to a car park, near the outflow of the Glendun River at D251-334. There is a paying campsite up in the village, too far away to be convenient.

The coastline S to Cushendall is similar. There is a car park in Cushendall at the N end of the beach, with easy access at D263-256.

The Maidens

The Maidens or Hulin Rocks are two small lighthouse islands located 9km ENE of Ballygalley. The West Maiden is also known as the Northern Rock, its lighthouse is called the West Tower. The East Maiden is known as the Southern Rock and holds the East Tower. Both were active lighthouses until the West Maiden was abandoned in 1903. The East Tower was modernised, automated and went electric in 1977.

Embarkation

The most convenient is from a large car park with a slipway and access to a small shingle beach at D378-080 between Ballygalley and Ballygalley Head.

Shipping:

The safest route to the island means staying N of Ballygalley Head. The port of Larne just S is busy with very fast cross channel ferries and shipping. Most take a line from Larne to Scotland that passes S of the Maidens, but some do pass N and then inside the Maidens when awaiting berthing space in Larne.

West Maiden

D450-115   Sheet 9

The West Tower Lighthouse and its attendant three storey cut-stone buildings dominate the island. The lighthouse tower can still be climbed internally, as the old stairway steps are still in reasonable condition. Access to the flat unprotected roof is through a narrow opening in the top floor. The view is worth the effort. An interesting iron walkway bridge links the tower to the accommodation block. The keepers' quarters are now quite ruined and their layout compares interestingly with those on the more modern East Maiden.

Landing

Landing on the West Maiden is more difficult than on the East Maiden. The most suitable area for deep water landing onto rock shelves is located on the W side, N of the old pier under some large rocky outcrops. No beach was found but several cuts may be usable at HW. There is an old pathway that leads NW from the main building to NW corner but no steps or obvious landing was located. The old pier at the SW corner is not suitable for kayak landings.

East Maiden

D457-114   Sheet 9

This is a small but attractive low-lying rocky island dominated by the East Tower Lighthouse and its attendant buildings. Space is at a premium but the lighthouse buildings are well maintained and their layout invites one to explore.

Landing

Landing is at either the NW or SE corner onto steps or onto rock shelves at lower tides. Landing should not be underestimated as tides run strongly around the island and through the sounds and channels that separate the lighthouse islands from a series of outlying skerries. An older disused pier is located at the S end.

Muck Island

D465-025   Sheet 9

A medium sized island, about 1km N/S, located 300m off the mainland near the beautiful little harbour of Portmuck at D460-024. The island is interesting and has a nice mixture of wilderness habitats. Coastal grasses dominate the central part and the island rises steeply from W to E. There is a beach of mixed sand and shingle on its western side and a rocky bar extends shorewards off its southern point. This dries and is a problem for kayakers attempting to pass inside, especially at LW, when it is possible to walk out to the island. The island increases in height on its eastern flank to give quite attractive steep basalt sea cliffs and holds breeding populations of Kittiwake, Razorbill, Black Guillemot and Guillemot. Three small rocky stacks lie off the northern end. The National Trust owns the island and information signs on the mainland do not encourage visitors.

Muck Island is off Island Magee which, despite its name, is not an island. However, it does have some excellent paddling, particularly in the section known locally as 'The Gobbins'. The best part starts after Heddles Port at D479-991 and continues to Hills Port at D485-972. It boasted a great Victorian walkway, the remains of which are still visible from the sea. Unfortunately it was closed years ago due to disrepair. There are also seven caves in this section.

County Down

Copeland Islands

Sheet 15

Embarkation

Donaghadee is the logical embarkation point for a day trip to the Copeland Islands. There used to be a ferry which allowed 2 hours wandering about Copeland Island itself. It is not running at present but may again. For kayaks, there is a small car park and slipway just W of the harbour at J588-803.

Copeland Island is the innermost of the group, with Lighthouse Island next and Mew Island on the outside. Donaghadee Sound lies inside Copeland Island. Copeland Sound lies between Copeland Island and Light House Island. Given the strong tides, this is an excellent proficiency training and testing ground. Any trip around the group can be challenging, as the tides do run hard in the sounds. Grey and Common Seals are both found, the former on Copeland itself and the latter favouring the more exposed channels between Mew and Lighthouse.

Tides

There are strong tide races through the sounds. The tide floods SE from Belfast HW +0500 to

HW -0100, about an hour ahead of the tide on the rocks by the shore. The streams through Donaghadee Sound achieve 4.5 knots in places, and through Copeland Sound achieve 2.5 knots, so great care is necessary.

Off the islands, the tide turns about an hour later. The infamous Ram Race forms just at the E tip of Mew, and extends for up to 2km SSE on the flood and NNW on the ebb. On the S going flood a huge eddy forms behind Mew. This loops back on itself, along the coast from about Ballyferis Point, 7km S of Donaghadee, and then out E of the islands. The race to the SSE of Mew is at its worst where the two re-join, on the second half of the flood, from about HW Belfast -0215 to +0030 (i.e. about local HW). The NNW race occurs on the last half of the ebb from HW Belfast +0345 to +0615 (i.e. about local LW).

SPA

Arctic Tern, Brent Goose, Ringed & Golden Plover, Turnstone.

Copeland Island

J590-834   Sheet 15

Copeland Island is the largest island of the group and closest to the shore. It lies 3km N of Donaghadee. There are a number of holiday homes on Copeland and sandy beach landings are possible in Chapel Bay at J591-834 on the SW and Deer Bay at J596-838 on the NE. The population was evacuated in 1946. Bleak enough, grassy, and bracken covered in parts. Ask permission to camp.

Lighthouse Island

J597-856   Sheet 15

Lighthouse Island (sometimes referred to as John's Island) lies 2km N of Copeland Island, is owned by the National Trust, and has a bird observatory on top, used by the NT. Landing is at the SE corner at J597-856 onto sand at LW but stones on higher tides. Originally the lighthouse was here, but a later light was lit on the better placed Mew Island. Apparently, many wrecks were caused by the light on Lighthouse Island being clearly seen but the low lying Mew being totally overlooked. Hence the lighthouse was moved to the more logical position.

Mew Island

J602-861   Sheet 15

Mew Island is owned by the Commissioners of Irish Lights, and has a number of small associated islands on its SW side, all linked and walkable. The lighthouse (built in 1884) is reminiscent of an airport control tower. Apparently, this lighthouse was only automated in 1996, and until then the keepers even maintained a golf course for their entertainment! Landing is possible at the lighthouse jetty tucked into the channel, or into a cut in the NW, both deepwater landings.

Before the lighthouse was built on Mew, a spectacular wreck was that of the 'Enterprise' in 1801. Then, in 1833, Alexander Graham Bell used a new fangled invention called a diving apparatus to retrieve its valuable cargo.

A great tragedy was played out here on 31st January 1953 when the ferry 'Princess Victo-

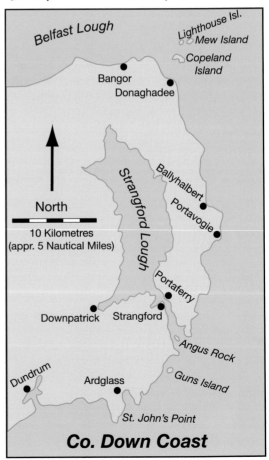

Co. Down Coast

ria' got into trouble en route from Stranraer to Belfast in a severe NW gale. Heavy seas stove in the car deck doors, just after leaving the Scottish port. As the ferry slowly listed and began to sink, it drifted. The 'Princess Victoria' thought it was drifting down the Scottish coast, so the rescue services were sent to the wrong place. Only when the Copeland lighthouse was sighted was their correct position transmitted. The order was eventually given to abandon ship, and the life rafts were launched. The women and children were all in the first two rafts, both of which capsized. All drowned in sight of the men still on board.

When the rescue services finally came on the scene, the seas were truly mountainous. Great heroism later merited several gallantry awards of the highest level available to non-military personnel. Captain Ferguson (brother of Harry Ferguson, inventor of the modern tractor) and his radio operator David Broadfoot stayed at their posts to the end and went down with the ship. 121 died. There were 44 survivors, all adult males.

The same storm peaked in the North Sea that night. A combination of low pressure, a spring tide surge, and sustained NW winds raised the sea level more than 3m, flooding Holland over its dykes, and 1,600 were drowned.

Bangor to Strangford Lough

Sheet 21 / Sheet 15

The paddling from Donaghadee at J691-802 to Ballyquintin Point at J624-454 at the mouth of Strangford Narrows - a distance of about 40km - is a straightforward but interesting enough piece of coastline. The Ards Peninsula has almost an island feel to it because of its remoteness by road and the ferry service which operates at the southern end at Portaferry.

The coastline from Donaghadee to Ballyhalbert Point at J664-630 is less interesting than further S, being of shingle and sand beaches.

Next comes Portavogie at J663-595, a busy fishing harbour often congested with trawlers. North Rock at J674-561 with its breeding Grey Seals, lies 3km SSE. South Rock at J677-531 lies 2km offshore and 3km N of Kearney

Mew Island, Co. Down - Mike McClure

Point. The rocky shoreline of Kearney Point at J645-511 is owned by the National Trust and is a good place to go 'rock pool peering' for marine invertebrates such as Dog Whelks, Mussels, and Starfish. It is a very enjoyable day trip to catch the ebb tide from Strangford out to the mouth, then N to the Rocks, and back on the flood. The South Rock lightship, fully automated, lies 2km ENE of the South Rocks. There is a spit of land between the North Rocks and Ringboy Point at J650-574 to the WNW. Occasionally the sea can become steep and untidy here, particularly when the swell is against the tide.

Tides

The tidal stream decreases as one travels southwards towards Ballyhalbert from 4.5 knots in Donaghadee Sound to about 2.5 knots off Skullmartin Rock at J649-687. Further S, from Ballyhalbert Point at J664-630 to Ballyquintin Point at J624-454, the tides run along the coast and reach 1.5 knots in springs.

Strangford Lough

Sheet 21

Strangford Lough is one of the largest sea loughs in Britain and Ireland. In ecological terms it is unique and the jewel in Northern Ireland's coastline. It has a great deal to offer sea canoeists at every level, from sheltered backwaters for introducing novices, to powerful tide races, overfalls and whirlpools for the more experienced at the narrow entrance, called the Narrows. The old name for Strangford was 'Cuan' (meaning safe harbour) but the Vikings renamed it Strangford or 'The Violent Fjord'.

SPA

Arctic, Common and Sandwich Tern, Bartailed Godwit, Golden Plover, Knot, Brent Goose, Redshank, Shelduck.

Strangford is the premier autumn arrival site for the Brent Goose. Some remain on for the winter but most disperse to other sites throughout Ireland.

There are 2 species of seal to be found around our coasts. They are the Common (or Harbour) Seal and the Grey Seal. They are quite distinctly different. The Common has a spaniel dog type of head and is considerably smaller than the Grey, which has a flat head with a large obvious nose. There are about 400 Common Seals and 80 Grey Seals in the lough.

The Common Seal give birth in June and it is most entertaining to watch the antics of the pups from the quiet position of a sea kayak. The greys give birth in October and it is a rare and beautiful sight to see the white furry pups of these much larger seals.

Chart 2156 and OS sheet 21 each covers the lough in detail.

Angus Rock

Sheet 21   J610-453

Angus Rock is the first point of note entering the Narrows, near the mouth. It is just a rock, virtually covered at HW, but on it stands a small lighthouse, white with an unusual red top band. At HW, there is just a concrete ramp proud of the water which can take a few kayaks at picnic time. At lower water, quite an extensive area of rock gets exposed. This is an important waystop, a most useful journey breaker on local day trips.

There are overfalls and broken water around Angus Rock, both on the flood and ebb tide. See the tidal stream atlas for details. On spring tides, from the 1st to 3rd hour of the ebb, an interesting grade 2 rapid occurs on the N side of the Angus Rock. This can get up to about a grade 3 with a diagonal stopper during very big equinoctial springs. There is a drop in sea level across the rocks of about 3 feet and it is possible to get good surfing on the stopper wave.

On the last hour of the ebb, an enjoyable set of waves often form, again on the N side of the Angus Rock, where you can join the seals for some surfing. On the flood tide, again just N of the Rock, another small set of overfalls is formed. There is an obvious drop in the sea level followed by small boils and whirlpools.

The Narrows

Sheet 21

Strangford Lough covers 150km² of sea and contains 1650 million m³ of sea water at high tide. HW at Portaferry is at least 2 hours later than at the mouth of the Narrows. It takes approximately 350 million m³ (or tonnes) of water to fill the lough from LW to HW. All this water can only get into the lough by passing through the Narrows which is 9km long and at its narrowest point, only 600m wide. Hence a vast river of water rushes through at speeds of up to 7.5 knots.

Tides

At the entrance to the Narrows, the ingoing flood tide begins at HW Belfast -0330. Passage is straightforward and fairly safe on the flood. However, during the ebb, a heavy breaking sea can be encountered. This is particularly dangerous with any form of wind from the S/SE/E creating a swell. Breaking seas of up to 8m have been seen (from a car along the shore!). For the more experienced and confident only, excellent deep-water surf waves are formed at the entrance, where it is advisable to play only on the last hour or two of the ebb.

The next point of interest is the Routen Wheel, just SW of Rue Point. The Wheel is on the E side of the channel. It is quite easy to avoid by closely hugging the coast along the E side. A good viewing point is from the wee island called Isle O'Valla at J593-488.

The Wheel is characterised by short-lived but heavy and violent boils, whirlpools and stoppers. It is caused by an underwater ridge of rock only 4.6m below the surface, rising suddenly either side from 18m below, sticking diagonally out from the shallower E side of the main channel into the main flow. The NE/SW ridge that creates the Wheel is situated along a line 200m SW of Rue Point at J597-487 to J599-489. This is no ordinary rapid. A boil forms, then another beside it swivelling the other way, and soon a whirlpool forms on the boundary. Admire it as pretty, but then you are in it, sinking ever lower, pointing upstream, to the side, down again, then the whirlpool stops and away you go again. Paddling back up through the Wheel is an experience too as you try to read the water, the way boils are pushing and so on. A good eddy exists S of Rue Point on the E side, as far as Gowland Rock at J603-485, so that a number of runs of the Wheel can be enjoyed.

The Wheel occurs during both the flood and ebb tide although it tends to be more violent during the ebb. The turbulence lasts for about 400m and any capsizes can easily be dealt with beyond the turbulence. Rescues need to be swift as the speed of the current reaches 7.5 knots. It is safer to play during the flood.

There is a rapid beside a beacon to one side, Gowland Rock at J603-485, where a surf wave forms, just like on a river. The area around here is used a lot by seals to haul out on the rocks. Care should be taken not to disturb them from their haul outs as it can cause injury.

One of the greatest dangers on the Narrows is the potential for being run down by the ferry which runs between Strangford and Portaferry. This ferry has to contend with a 6 knot tide and does a remarkably efficient 'ferry glide' across the flow. The Captain does not appreciate having to contend with dodging canoeists as well. The ferry departs Strangford on the hour and half hour and departs Portaferry every quarter past and quarter to the hour. The crossing time is about 5 minutes.

'Exploris', an excellent aquarium, is situated within a minute's walk from the main slip at Portaferry and is well worth a visit as it has displays of the marine wildlife of the lough and the Irish Sea.

Another place well worth a visit is the Barn at Castleward, owned by the National Trust, in Castleward Bay at J575-497. Access from the water is best gained during HW as there are extensive mud flats in the bay. The Barn has excellent audio visual displays of the marine wildlife, particularly the bird and mammal life found in the lough. They also have a number of very good videos on the wildlife of the lough. Entry is free.

Audley's Castle, built in the 16th Century, lies on the W side of the Narrows about 1km N of Strangford and is worth a visit. It is possible to land at the little beach and jetty beside it at J589-501 and climb to the top where there is an excellent view of the Narrows and the towns of Portaferry and Strangford.

Inner Strangford Lough
Sheet 21
Tides

Inside the lough, the tidal strength decreases from 6 knots between the two towns to 4 knots at Ballyhenry Island at J575-520, 2km NW, as the water disperses into the lough. It further reduces to about 1.5 knots at Dunnyneill Islands at J547-539, a further 3km NW.

The E coast of the lough has a lot less of interest to the canoeist than the W due to the lack of islands etc. However, at 'The Dorn' at J593-568, there is a reasonable tidal flow from an enclosed bay of up to 2.5 knots, especially on the ebb and a spectacular marine waterfall about an hour to two after high water.

The W side of the lough is a fascinating maze of submerged drumlin hills forming over 100 islands and rock pladdies. Chapel Island at J562-513 and Jackdaw Island at J557-510 are the first to be reached when paddling W out of the Narrows. In the spring, Jackdaw is an important nesting site for terns and should be avoided. Many of the islands have large colonies of Irish Hares which can often be seen running along the beach.

Audley's Castle, Strangford Lough, Co. Down - Mike McClure

In the SW corner, Salt Island at J532-500 lies within the Quoile Estuary, and is one of the many islands owned by the National Trust. The Trust have built a bothy on the SE side of Salt which was an absolutely superb facility for the canoeist looking for a bit more comfort than a tent. The Bothy slept 12, had an open fire, gas cooker, running water and a couple of WCs. However, due to stringent new health and safety laws, it cannot be used at present. Camping is permitted on Salt Island.

To the SW of Salt Island lies the Slaney River where St. Patrick landed in 432 A.D. He must have landed here during HW or he would have had to slog through the stinking mud to reach the shore. He went to Salt and was confronted by the local Chieftain who became Patrick's first convert to Christianity in Ireland.

Heading N from the barrage which protects Downpatrick from tidal flooding, lies Gibbs Island at J509-496 which is one of the few islands within the lough to have trees. There are some mature Scots Pines on Gibbs. Further N, the first major island outside the Quoile estuary

is Island Taggart at J533-545. This is one of the largest islands in the lough and used to support two small farms. These belong to the National Trust and are well worth a visit as they show what life on the island was like. Look out for the coffin in the barn! They were also used for the film 'December Bride', a story of life in the area in the early 1900s. Foxes, badgers and otters are all resident on Taggart, meriting an overnight camp and exploration. Camping is permitted.

Between Taggart and Mahee Island at J530-636, almost 10km N, lie the 'basket of eggs' - dozens of little islands which are excellent for night navigation as they are sheltered and safe. Tides can run at about 1-2 knots during springs in a N/S direction between some of the islands and particularly through Ringhaddy Sound at J537-582.

Green Island Rock at J545-602 is a haul out for Common Seal and is very accessible to allow a group of novices to experience canoeing with seals.

To the W and N of Rainey Island at J527-630, there are two channels where the tide runs either side of the island at up to 5 knots in its rush to fill or empty Reagh Bay to the NW. Again, this is an excellent area for introducing novices to moving water. HW in the area is at approximately HW Dover +0220.

Mahee Island at J530-636 has an early Celtic Monastery. The monks are believed to have occupied the area from the 5th to the 10th Centuries. The area N of Mahee Island holds little of interest to the canoeist, unless you're into mud wrestling in a big way, as large expanses of mudflats cover the area. The mudflats do support vast numbers of waders. During the winter, the statistics of birds using the lough demonstrates the international importance of Strangford as a wildlife sanctuary:

Swans   290+

Geese   13,500+ (including 1,300 Pale-bellied Brent Geese, more than 75% of the world population)

Ducks   9,000+

Waders   50,000+

The lough has areas renowned for their beauty or scientific importance and legislation protects this valuable and unique area. Access is unrestricted in the lough and conservationists rely heavily on the goodwill of recreational users. The National Trust has produced 'The Castaways Code' and map for those using the lough for recreational boating. This should be consulted before paddling in the lough during the nesting season (April-June) and the islands marked 'Birds Welcome' should be avoided.

Guns Island

J596-415   Sheet 21

Guns Island lies 2km S of the entrance to Strangford Lough. The SE side of Guns Island is a mass of nesting Kittiwake, Guillemot and Cormorant on the cliff ledges and paddlers should keep a reasonable distance offshore to avoid disturbance during the nesting season (April-June). The N side is favoured by a large colony of gulls that nest on the tussock grass just above the shore. A reasonably strong tide runs between Guns Island and the mainland – up to 2 knots. At extreme low water springs, it is possible to walk or wade across to the island.

Strangford Lough to Carlingford Lough

Sheet 21/Sheet 29

Killard Point at J613-435, a National Nature Reserve, is well worth a visit, especially in June to see the abundance of butterflies and wild flowers growing on the sand dunes. Among these can be found the beautiful Bee Orchid, Spotted Orchid, Wild Thyme and Yellow Rattle. Butterflies include the Common Blue, Small Heath and Meadow Brown.

The 14km from the entrance of Strangford Lough to St.John's Point is a lovely paddle along small cliffs and a rocky shore of siltstones and shales believed to be formed during the Silurian period, 435 million years ago. This area is known as the Lecale and shortly after the last ice age would have been a large island with the sea connecting Dundrum inner bay with Strangford Lough.

Banderg Bay at J605-432 followed by Ballyhornan Bay at J594-420, are pleasant sandy beaches with clay cliffs behind, where there are nesting Fulmar. Never disturb these birds at their nest as they have the ability to douse you with an extremely evil smelling mucus from their nostrils which sticks better than any glue known to man! Portnacoo at J589-406, 200m SW of the southern tip of Guns Island, has a 2m wide gap in the rocks which opens out into a cove with a 15m wide pebbly peach, an ideal lunch stop.

At Legnaboe, on the mainland about 600m S of the southern tip of Guns Island, there is a narrow sea cave which appears safe to enter at all states of the tide, provided there is little swell.

Along this piece of coast lie the villages of Ardglass at J563-373 and Killough at J540-363. Although Killough was an important fishing port, the harbour is now derelict, whilst Ardglass has taken over as a principal fishing port, famous for its herrings, pronounced locally as 'hearns'. A new marina has been built at Ardglass and there is easy access to the sea from both Killough and Ardglass.

SPA

Brent Goose (Killough Harbour)

From St. John's Point at J526-333 to Newcastle (a distance of 15km as the crow flies or as the canoeist paddles), the scenery is dominated by the beach and sand dune systems of Murlough National Nature Reserve (NNR).

Within the inner bay at Dundrum, there is a causeway and bridge at J402-356. This connects the farms and houses within Murlough NNR to the main Dundrum to Newcastle road. The tide flows through this bridge at up to 6 knots on springs in its rush to fill or empty the southern half of the inner bay. Good eddies are created by the bridge stanchion and this is used almost constantly at HW by local paddlers to teach and practise moving water techniques. HW at the bridge is +0030 HW Dover. The best fun is to be had during springs. This occurs every second weekend when the tide is usable from approx. 1000hrs until 1500hrs, HW being around midday.

During the ebb from Dundrum inner bay, tremendous deep water surfing waves can be formed at the entrance if there is even a little swell from the S or E. However, once the tide has finished ebbing, the only practical course of action is to paddle to Newcastle 5km away as the inner bay will be dry.

For 2km to the S and 3km to the N of the entrance to Dundrum inner bay, care must be taken due to the rifle range at the army camp at Ballykinler. There are 3 yellow marker buoys marked DZ and the paddler should keep to the seaward side of these when the red flag (day) or red lights (night) are visible over the base just N of the entrance to the inner bay. However, tracers have been sighted by local canoeists doing a night paddle from St.John's Point to Newcastle that would indicate that they could travel more than 2km beyond these buoys. The Coastguard should be contacted before paddling this section of coast.

The tides along this section of coast to St.John's Point are weak. A trip from St.John's Point to Newcastle is a very popular paddle on a good moonlit night as you have the lighthouse flashing behind you, the twinkling lights of Newcastle to aim for and the foreboding outline of the Mournes dominating the paddle.

Newcastle is very much the seaside holiday tourist town and is usually thronged between Easter and September, especially at weekends. However, good access to the beach exists from various car parks in the town. Access is also available from the harbour where there is very limited parking. It should be noted that this dries out at low water. Access may still be gained over the wall to the stony beach to the S of the harbour at J382-296.

A sewage outfall pipe lies about 1 cable offshore to the S of the harbour and, although Newcastle's sewage works are meant to be one of the most sophisticated in the UK, the area surrounding the pipe should be well avoided! During S or E winds, good surfing can be had at the beach and a good break exists at the mouth of the harbour at lower water. During particularly strong winds, i.e. above Force 6, the surf is very broken and you can find yourself 500m offshore still looking for a way out through the soup. Having said that, this must be one of the most picturesque places to surf - 'Where the Mountains of Mourne sweep down to the sea'.

The scenery of the Mourne Mountains dominates the 25km from Newcastle to Cranfield Point at J270-099 on the northern side of the entrance of Carlingford Lough. It is made up of rocky beaches and small cliffs, a relic from the ice age that shaped the panorama of the Mourne scenery more than 10,000 years ago.

From Newcastle to Bloody Bridge at J389-269, the coastline is interesting. The small cliff scenery provides enjoyable rock dodging, particularly at high water, when many of the caves and channels become more accessible. The National Trust owns the section of coast between Bloody Bridge and the mouth of the Crock Horn Stream below Ballagh Bridge, 2km S at J388-249. After that, there is good access to the sea at Glassdrumman Port at J381-222, and a very pleasant little sandy beach from which to launch or enjoy your lunch.

There are a number of small but enjoyable caves in the area, one of which has a blowhole at the top. There are also two bigger caves, one of which involves a 50m squeeze, where hands are needed to get through. This cave is not obvious from the sea but it can be found with careful exploring and it's worth going through, especially in a plastic boat!. The other large cave has a small rocky beach at the back and if there isn't much swell, it's good fun landing and exploring on up the cave. A short trip from Newcastle to Bloody Bridge and back is ideal for introducing novices to spectacular sea canoeing.

The next principal port is Annalong which has a small harbour at J378-197, used mainly by small craft engaged in creeling (laying lobster pots). Further along the coast is a small rock called Selk Island at J359-176, which appropriately enough has a small colony of Common Seal.

Then, passing Lee Stone Point at J334-144, the large granite boulder (another relic of the ice age known as an erratic) is an obvious feature. The fishing port of Kilkeel lies 6km short of Cranfield Point. This is one of Northern Ireland's busiest fishing ports with up to 70 boats using the harbour at J317-140.

County Louth

Carlingford Lough

Carlingford Lough is the most dramatic sea lough on the E coast of Ireland with the Mourne Mountains to the N and the craggy Carlingford Mountain to the S. It has great variation, from pleasant, sheltered paddling within the lough to big races and overfalls at its mouth.

The S side of the lough is in the Republic of Ireland while the N side is in Northern Ireland. Up until the 1950's, a lucrative smuggling trade reputedly ran between Greencastle and Carlingford harbours.

The tidal streams within the lough are weak and a pleasant and undemanding crossing can be made from Killowen or Rostrevor Quays to Carlingford village. However, during strong WNW winds, squalls funnel down from the hills around Rostrevor and cause little cyclones and mini tornadoes on the sea. These are known locally as 'Kettles' as the water appears to boil and steam off the surface.

The Newry Canal can be accessed on the S side of the lough beyond Warrenpoint at J108-207. This is really only practicable during HW as the area surrounding the access to the canal dries to extensive mudflats. There are reports that the canal is going to be reopened. The canal goes to Lough Neagh but a passage, even by canoe, is exceptionally difficult, as it is heavily overgrown and silted.

SPA

Common and Sandwich Tern, Brent Goose

Blockhouse Island

J255-096   Sheet 29

Blockhouse Island (a guano pile in springtime) lies between Sheep Rock and Haulbowline Lighthouse, is bigger than either but is not named on the OS map. This small rocky islet guards the entrance to Carlingford Lough. A military building was erected here in 1602, now entirely ruined, and was known as Carlingford Fort. The island is small and worthwhile mainly as a waypoint on tour, as landing may always be had onto stormbeaches on the W or slabby limestone on the E side.

The lighthouse just to the E at J260-096 is 20m high with a white light flashing three times every ten seconds and an ancillary red light lower down continuously flashing. Landing at the lighthouse is not permitted and anyway can only be achieved in calm conditions. The main channel into the lough passes to the N of the island, where one must avoid commercial shipping. Navigation in the lough is very buoyage orientated so consider using Chart 2800.

Embark on the southern side of the lough from Greenore or from the pretty Carlingford Harbour. The best launching in Greenore is from behind the pier at J225-107, and in Carlingford launch just outside the E pier at J194-118, as the silted harbour exposes black mud at the bottom of the tide.

On Northern Ireland side, launch from Greencastle Point at J242-117, or a small car park and beach at J263-107, between Soldiers Point and Cranfield Point.

Tides

Tides run strongly in the lough entrance near the island, where the ebb and flow start with local HW and LW, which are much the same as Dublin. Onshore winds on the ebb throw up a fearsome sea state. The tide runs at 3.5 knots in springs in the dredged approach channels. The flow follows the main channels except for an eddy on the flood on the E side of Blockhouse Island.

Good overfalls and races occur during both the flood and the ebb around the Haulbowline Lighthouse. The most pleasant and relatively safe playing in these overfalls is on the flood tide. The area is regularly used by local clubs and centres for rough water training.

Kayaking under Fair Head, Co. Antrim – Des Keaney

The East Coast
Greenore Point to Wexford Harbour
County Dublin

Islands off Skerries

A group of three low-lying islands lie just off the coast at Skerries, with 'The Rock' further off. Taken together they form an interesting day trip with good wildlife interest. They are listed as areas of Scientific Interest by Duchás with SPA status. Camping is possible, but no water is available. The presence of a healthy population of rats on the inner islands may discourage an overnight. Rugged Rockabill further out is a lighthouse island rock.

SPA

Short-eared Owl (up to 7 in winter), Golden Plover, and Common, Sandwich and Roseate Tern.

Embarkation

The most convenient embarkation place is at the slipway beside the RNLI building at the pier in Skerries, where parking is generally convenient at O255-612. Do not, under any circumstances, block the access to or interfere with the operation of the lifeboat station, or of the working pier. The main catch at Skerries is prawn and shrimp. Accordingly, the local fishermen are benignly disposed to seals, which do not catch either. Seals are plentiful hereabouts. Launching may also be had less conveniently from the E facing South Strand, but only at HW to avoid a long carry.

Tides

Local HW/LW is the same as for Dublin.

Inshore amongst the inner islands, the flow starts at HW Dublin -0100. Tides flow strongly in the sounds.

Between the inner islands and Rockabill, the ebb starts an hour later, at Dublin HW. The flood runs N from -0615 to HW Dublin, and reaches 1.5 knots in springs.

Colt Island

O267-611   Sheet 43

A small, low-lying island lying just off the point at Skerries. Land easily on sand/shingle on SW side. The E side has reefs and breakers that should be avoided in strong NE - SE winds in spring ebb tides.

Saint Patrick's Island

O276-613   Sheet 43

A small island, outside Colt, known locally as Church Island. The accuracy as to whether St. Patrick ever landed here is a source of some debate. This is the jumping off point for Rockabill.

South Landing, St. Patrick's Island, Skerries, Co. Dublin - Séan Pierce

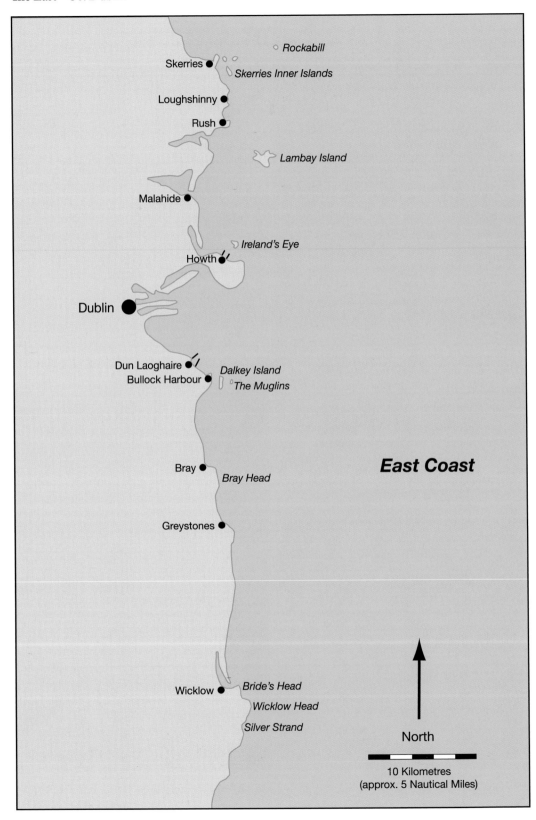

Rockabill

Skerries

Skerries Inner Islands

Loughshinny

Rush

Lambay Island

Malahide

Ireland's Eye

Howth

Dublin

Dun Laoghaire

Bullock Harbour

Dalkey Island

The Muglins

East Coast

Bray

Bray Head

Greystones

Wicklow

Bride's Head

Wicklow Head

Silver Strand

North

10 Kilometres
(approx. 5 Nautical Miles)

Early Christian church ruins, St. Patrick's Island, Co. Dublin - Séan Pierce

Land easily at a sheltered storm beach, just W of the S tip, in almost any conditions. Landing is also possible at higher tides at a shingle cove just further E. There is a further landing place on the N facing shore near a ruined house and marked by two metal poles - a small beachlet among the rocks, for when southerlies prevail.

There is the ruin of an Early Christian Church and a small monastery, which dates back to Viking times. It was important enough to merit a synod being held in 1148 in which fifteen bishops, two hundred priests, and several other clergy assisted. The church towards the eastern tip is still very much worth the visit.

St Patrick's Island has an internationally important breeding population of Cormorants (2001 Census) of 550 pairs. There are breeding gulls, Shags and Fulmars in summer, while geese, ducks and waders provide winter interest. There is a colony of 70-80 Grey Seals, especially during winter.

The NE and eastern sides of the island catch the full ebb tide over a rocky underwater reef. Overfalls can develop, especially in S to SE winds against a spring ebb tide. In the sound between St. Patrick's and Colt Islands, a lesser overfall can develop over a small bar that extends westwards off the corner of St. Patrick's.

Shenick Island

O267-598   Sheet 43

Shenick is the most southerly of the inshore group and is dominated by a Martello Tower at its northern end. This is a Birdwatch Ireland reserve since May 1987. Kayakers landing should be sensitive to the effects of disturbance in the breeding season (April / June). Ask Birdwatch Ireland at (01) 2819878 if in doubt. Land easily at the NW side onto a beach under the Martello Tower. This beach is on the N side of a spit reaching out westwards towards the mainland, and is usually sheltered. The island has both a geological and natural history interest. There are breeding Fulmar, gulls, Oystercatcher and Shelduck, while in winter the numbers of Brent Goose, Curlew, Purple Sandpiper, Ringed Plover and Short-eared Owl make the island a nationally important site.

The passage between Shenick Island and the mainland virtually dries out at LW.

Rockabill, Co. Dublin - Séan Pierce

Rockabill

O323-626   Sheet 43

Rockabill is the larger of two granite rocky islets, strictly called Lighthouse Island. The smaller islet is the Bill and they are connected at low spring tides. They have a total area of 0.9ha above the high water mark. The lighthouse was first constructed in 1860, and was rebuilt in 1900. It was automated in April 1989. The island was designated as a Special Protection Area in 1988 and as a Statutory Refuge for Fauna under the Wildlife Act 1976. The Roseate Tern Conservation Project began in May 1989 and prevents landing in spring and early summer. Ask Birdwatch Ireland at (01) 2819878 if in doubt. Resident wardens enforce the restrictions.

The Roseate Tern is an endangered species so do respect the rules. Ireland takes seriously its duty to Roseate Tern and Brent Goose, its two biggest contributions to international conservation. This conservation programme is one of the huge successes for Birdwatch Ireland. 90% of Ireland's Roseates breed here, which represents 35% of Europe's population, so it really is off limits in season.

Landing

Landing on Lighthouse Island is in the sound between the two islands onto a small pier with steps or onto rocks to the side, depending on circumstances. There is another pier with steps just further E, but which is usually more exposed. A narrow cut immediately right of this pier opens to give a convenient pool at low to half tide for landings. Beware of all landings at springs when considerable lift can occur.

The Bill

O323-628   Sheet 43

Landing is possible on the Bill at low water in calm conditions onto rock shelves on the western corner. At LW springs, it is possible to clamber across kelp-covered rocks between the two islands. The Bill is quite an enjoyable rock scramble, and holds breeding Arctic Tern, Common Tern and a small Kittiwake colony in season.

Roseate Tern - Séan Pierce

Lambay Island

O315-500   Sheet 43

Embarkation

The closest approach is from Donabate Martello Tower at O263-505 but this would only be suitable if travelling out and back on the flood. Rush Harbour at O274-543 is almost as near, and in calm conditions is handiest on the ebbing tide. In NE winds or a strong ebb tide, launch in Loughshinny Harbour at O273-568. Loughshinny is always dependable, sheltered, has good parking, and is the best choice with bigger groups. The best plan for a day trip is a slingshot from Loughshinny, lunching at the island during the LW slack.

Landing

The island is privately owned by the Revelstoke family and no landing should take place. This is particularly true of the W side of the island where the main harbour and housing is situated. If in distress, at least stay below the high water line, and out of sight. The owners value their privacy, the welfare of the nesting wild bird population, and the health of the most unusual domesticated animal population, marsupials included.

There are two satisfactory beaches on the N side, just E of the north-west point, one tucked into the point itself facing E at O310-515, and the other is just further E, below an unsightly rubbish dump, facing N at O312-512.

There are no beaches or landing sites anywhere on the eastern half of the island, but there are three excellent, small, sandy or stony beaches on the S side, in sheltered coves. One is in the middle in Bishops Bay at O315-500, one W of the middle, somewhat out of harm's way, and one tucked into the south-west corner.

Tides

Tidal races run strongly on all four corners. Local HW is the same as Dublin HW. The stream floods N from HW Dublin +0430 to -0130, and ebbs in reverse. Between Lambay and the mainland, 2 knots can be achieved in springs.

Fauna

The island is a significant wild bird habitat and holds internationally important numbers of breeding Cormorant, Shag, Razorbill and Guillemot. 59,000 breeding pairs of Guillemot were counted in 1995/1999, which makes it the second most important colony in Ireland after Rathlin Island (c.96,000 pairs). It is the most important colony for Herring Gull and Shag in the country. The 675 pairs (1999 census) of Cormorant qualify this as the largest colony in Ireland. In winter, there are up to 1,000 Greylag, and several other species of geese.

SPA

Barnacle Goose, Peregrine

History

The Romans never got to the Irish mainland that we know of, but they did get to Lambay, traded with it, and called it Limnios. In 795, the first ever raid by the Vikings on Ireland happened here. Lambay is a Viking word. After the Battle of the Boyne in 1691, a 15th Century castle was used as a concentration camp for the defeated Jacobite troops, and was converted into a mansion around 1900.

Shipwreck

The White Star Line lost the largest merchantman ever built in Britain, its biggest, best, and most modern passenger ship, on its maiden voyage, in a major tragedy with huge loss of life, trying to set a new record for the shortest ever sea passage for the British and Irish emigrants aboard. Sound like the Titanic?

Wrong. Long before the Titanic in 1912, it had all happened before.

The 'Tayleur' left Liverpool in January 1854. It was about the first ever ironclad clipper, huge at 1979 tons, with masts 45m high, and 650 passengers. Clippers were square-riggers, built for forward speed, not for manoeuvring. It had little in the way of sea trials. The ship was undermanned. The crew was inexperienced. No one had yet worked out how to use a compass aboard a metal craft. There were five different classifications of passengers, yet there was no mention of vegetables or fruit on any of its menus. Scurvy was just about becoming understood.

In thick weather, land was sighted ahead. It was misidentified, at terrible cost. Too late, remedial action failed. The ship struck the E point

of Lambay. In shallow water, the ship died slowly against the rocks. Some passengers scrambled ashore, others slid down a rope. Escape from the ship at this critical point favoured the able bodied, so women and children featured disproportionately among the dead. Bodies littered the shore for weeks after. 100 are buried on Lambay. 86 survived and eventually did make Australia.

Dublin North - Camping

For camping kayakers on passage, getting past Dublin is a challenge. On the N side, possibilities are few. Skerries town is perfectly possible and particularly along the beach S of the town, but it is a quite public promenade. The inner islands off Skerries offer an alternative choice, but all harbour rat populations for company, as does Ireland's Eye further S. There are two possibilities that are well secluded, or at least unobtrusive.

O198-660 - Balbriggan

2km NNW of the town. Known locally as Bell's Field, this headland area has some good sandy beaches located along its northern side with grassy areas for camping. No water available. The area is of archaeological interest and several burial mounds are present.

O270-545 - Rush - North Beach

Camping and caravan park, tel. 01-8437131. A short carry from HW mark. Land onto a safe sandy beach. Pub grub at 400m walk. Coming from Dublin by car, turn left in Rush along R128 for Skerries, then right after 150m, down to the beach and campsite.

Malahide Arches

O225-469   Sheet 50

Most of Malahide Estuary is separated from the open sea by a man-made embankment over which runs the Dublin to Belfast railway line. Under the middle arches, the waters fill the inner bay with great force on the higher spring tides.

The average Dublin spring tide is 4.1m. Conditions for good surfing exist from 4.0m upwards, and may exist in some conditions at lower levels. A Dublin HW of more than 4.2m gives seriously good surfing, in plastics, GP boats or sea kayaks. Spring tides occur every fortnight, but the heights of these vary enormously, and are generally highest around the summer and winter solstices. In the Dublin area, spring tides always occur when the tide reaches HW at about noon or midnight.

For the higher spring tides, playtime starts at Dublin HW -0200, and the best of the fun finishes at about Dublin HW or a little after. On lower spring tides, playtime begins a bit later at around Dublin HW -0130. In midsummer, it may well be possible to have a suitable daylight tide late in the evening, but for 95% of the year, all play will take place in the relatively early morning, what some may regard as the 'Crack of Noon'. Appropriate starting times vary, mostly between 0830 and 1130.

In bigger spring tides, it is best to arrive before the water begins to pour, as that is when the waves and stoppers are most friendly. As time progresses, the water force becomes much stronger. Although the surfing becomes more dramatic, the wave-acquisition needs that bit more energy, the eddies become less pronounced, and the penalty for error the more tiring as the length and power of the run-off increases.

On smaller spring tides, the run through begins as above, at Dublin HW -0200, but lacks power for half an hour or more. It achieves its best in the last hour before Dublin HW, and goes on a bit longer. Also, the eddies are not washed out as much, and though the surf waves are much less powerful, they are magic.

There are about twelve arches. The strongest flow, and where eddies are hardest to acquire, is in the middle. A wreck was jammed against the outside of the embankment until Christmas 1996. Its absence is still much regretted. It used to greatly lessen the flow to the three arches it immediately blocked, and send great forces of water to the arches on either side, creating huge variety in playing characteristics. Now the variation is somewhat less. However, there is still great variation, both from arch to arch, and from minute to minute as the tide builds, and the inner bay deepens.

The Arches also seem to be entirely hazard free, suitable for any group competent and willing to perform frequent X-rescues. Intermediate to Advanced standard or Proficiency Level 3/4

upwards is advised. Downstream of the actual stoppers and playwaves, the turbulent run-off stretches out 150m. In places, it is reminiscent of easier mega-volume Alpine rivers, with confused man-eating boils and eddy lines.

It is best to park inside or W of the railway line, on the Malahide side of the estuary. The road from the village runs along the inner bay, and parking is in lay-bys at O223-463. Starting on the seaward side would involve a carry across the railway line when finished, as playtime ends long before the flow under the arches starts going out.

Approaching Malahide from Dublin, turn left at the crossroads in the very centre of the village. Then turn left again immediately and go under a railway bridge where you will find the parking places on the right.

SPA

Bar-tailed Godwit, Golden Plover, Little Egret, Ruff, Kingfisher.

Ireland's Eye

O284-414   Sheet 50

Ireland's Eye is an interesting, small, uninhabited island off Howth Harbour. Circumnavigation is recommended as the cliff scenery is excellent. The island is most attractive and most popular in early summer. There is a regular ferry in season, from Howth East Pier.

The island is noted for its rock climbing on the tor at the NE corner, on the sea stack just off it, and also on the big cliff centred on the N side. Do please though exercise caution as regards bird life, and climb later in the season.

SPA

Peregrine. The island is a breeding ground for various auks, Fulmar, Kittiwake, Shag, Cormorant, gulls, and others. In particular, a Gannet colony started to breed here in 1989, and is now the only significant such colony between the Saltees to the S and Ailsa Craig in Scotland.

Embarkation and Landing

There is convenient access at a public slipway beside the Lifeboat Station at O285-394 in Howth Harbour. Landings can be had at various points, the best of which is at the sandy beach just SE of the Martello Tower. No water. The lusher parts of the island are rat infested, making camping unattractive.

The Round of Howth Head

The round of Howth Head is a popular trip for Dublin sea paddlers. Ireland's Eye is also attractive to take in as part of the excursion. Attractive for its scenery, and its handy shuttle, the only downside to this trip is a sewerage outlet operating just off the Nose of Howth at O301389 on the NE corner of the Head. However, the situation is much improved in 2003 as most of the sewage now goes to the modern treatment works in Ringsend.

Ireland's Eye, Co. Dublin - Séan Pierce

The put-in point to the N is at the public slipway at the RNLI station in Howth Harbour. There is plentiful parking. To the S of the Head, the launching point is the sandy beach at Sutton Sailing Club at O265-377, just NW of the Martello Tower. The Club is welcoming to small competent and considerate parties. Parking is limited so it is not suitable for large groups. Also, at LW, the tide goes a long way out. A shingle beach at O296-373, 1km N of the Bailey Lighthouse O297-363 offers a welcome break, and there is even a track upwards to the commonage above. Stopping is also possible in several places on the S side.

The round of Howth is usually done anticlockwise, on a rising tide, best in calm or gentle southerlies. An 'out and back' trip from Howth Harbour is also quite feasible and avoids the shuttle.

SPA

Fulmar, Cormorant, Shag, Herring Gull, Kittiwake, Guillemot, Razorbill, Black Guillemot.

Tides

The main E coast streams run N and S off the Bailey and the Nose, and on both sides of Ireland's Eye, where 2 knots can be achieved. There can be very bumpy water anywhere on the seaward side, especially with wind over tide. In particular the Bailey, where the tidal stream coming out of Dublin Bay meets the main stream, can be quite nasty. The Nose at the NE side of the head is often very bumpy, easing as one approaches Howth Harbour. The N/NE flood runs from Dublin HW +0430 to -0130, and the ebb the reverse.

The main E coast flood enters Dublin Bay on its S side heading NE, and circles around the inner bay to exit eastwards along the S side of Howth Head. To complicate matters, the main ebb, except when flowing at its strongest, in the middle three hours, eddies around the N part of the bay. Therefore, an outgoing stream runs E along the S shore of the Head for nine hours out of the twelve, from Dublin HW +0300 to Dublin HW. The ingoing W stream flows for only the other three, from Dublin HW to Dublin HW +0300.

In the first hour or two of the flood, from Dublin HW -0600 to -0400, paddlers often find that the stream exiting Dublin Bay E is stronger than the main coastal flood N. Thus the stream at the Bailey is E, and sets up a huge circular eddy, for about 2km to the N.

Dublin Bay

The inner part of the bay, with its city and industrial surrounds, holds little interest for sea kayakers, and is dealt with briefly. All the practical embarkation points are considered. The outer parts of the bay, from Dun Laoghaire to Dalkey Island on the S side, and from Sutton to Howth on the N side, are justifiably popular.

Tidal Overview

The tide floods N and ebbs S off the entrance to the bay, flooding from Dublin HW -0600 to HW, reaching 3.25 knots each way in springs. Inside the bay, the situation is more complex. Tides in the middle of the bay are stationary. The streams circulate around the edges. The effect of this is to constantly renew the waters of the bay which dissipates the worst polluting effects of the nearby population. Timings and strengths are very different on the two sides of the bay.

The flood enters the Bay through Muglins and Dalkey Sounds, past Dun Laoghaire Harbour, around the bay and out past the Bailey. The ebb flows past the Bailey towards Dun Laoghaire Harbour and out SE along the shore to Dalkey Island, and it also eddies around the N part of the bay.

Tides in the north

In the northern part of Dublin Bay, the E/NE outgoing stream runs for 9.5 hours from Dublin HW +0300 to the following HW, and the ingoing SW stream flows for only 3 hours from Dublin HW to +0300.

Tides in Dublin Harbour

The streams inside the harbour, under ordinary conditions, go with the rising and falling tide. Beware however heavy rainfall causing the river to flood. The overlying fresh water conditions favour short weak floods and long strong ebbs, and the outgoing stream can thus be very strong at the mouth, reaching 3.5 knots. This is typical of heavily freshwater-fed enclosed places.

Tides in the south

In the southern part of Dublin Bay, the NW flood runs from Dublin HW +0555 to -0030, and ebbs in reverse. In Dalkey Sound, this whole cycle begins and ends an hour earlier in neaps or an hour and a half earlier in springs.

Coastline

North Bull Island forms the entire inner, northern side of the Bay, involving a substantial LW carry. Landing, but without road access, is occasionally possible along the S shore of Howth Head.

Landing is possible all the way from the mouth of the Liffey to Sandycove, except for regulated areas inside the busy ferry port of Dun Laoghaire Harbour where some parts must be totally avoided. In particular, keep well away from the SE of the harbour. The closer to Dublin though, the less conducive it becomes to land. From Dun Laoghaire Harbour inwards, the shore is mostly sandy beach, with the tide receding long distances at LW. In addition, the railway runs all the way along here making road access only occasionally available.

From Sandycove at O257-281 to Sorrento Point at the S end of Dalkey Sound at O273-261, the ground is almost entirely small granite cliffs fronting impressive private property. Pretty, but landing is practical only at the three public harbours, Sandycove, Bullock and Coliemore.

Dublin Bay Embarkation Points

Sutton Sailing Club

O265-377   Sheet 50

This is an embarkation point for the round of Howth Head. Even here at LW, there is something of a carry, and the parking is very tight. So, if doing a shuttle, leave vehicles at Howth Harbour, irrespective of the direction of the kayak journey. The Club is welcoming, but realistically, the parking is inadequate. The Sailing Club is easily found by car, being well signposted. From Sutton Cross take the road to the Hill of Howth and, after 1km, turn right into Strand Road. Follow the signposts along the shoreline to the club.

Bull Island

O227-374   Sheet 50

N of Dublin Port is the North Bull Island, in the NW corner of the bay. It is connected to the shore by an ancient wooden bridge at O213-359 at its SW end, and a road/causeway at O225-374, midway along the island, built 1962. Much silting of the inner stretch of water has occurred since then, especially close to the causeway, which is now recognised to have been an environmental nightmare, and studies are underway to find a solution. The North Bull Wall which bounds the island on the S also delimits the N side of Dublin Port, and was built in 1825 on the advice of the famous cartographer and harbour builder, Captain Bligh, of Bounty fame.

SPA

Golden Plover, Bar-tailed Godwit, Great Northern Diver, Little Egret, Peregrine, Merlin, Short-eared Owl.

The significance of the Bull for bird watchers is in the huge numbers and the variety of species. It is popular because the birds may be easily watched. Living close to buses, cars, golfers, joggers and even dogs, the birds do not startle easily. In the channels, the rising tide concentrates the birds as it pushes them up the shore, and they can be watched from very close range. The Bull features prominently in the early stages of the education of all Dublin birders. It holds its interest for even the very advanced, because it is always throwing up surprises - rare migrants, and the odd mega-vagrant.

The Bull has internationally important numbers of Brent Goose, Knot, and many other winter species. Most of the centre of the island is taken up with two golf courses, which are fenced off from the outer rim. Birders are found mostly on the mainland side, and swimmers favour the open beach on the outer side. Hares abound on the golf courses and are tolerated with equanimity by the golfers. There is an Interpretive Centre near the causeway. It probably owes its existence to its timing, as it was built shortly before planning permission became necessary.

Dollymount Strand

O223-353   Sheet 50

Dollymount Strand runs the entire length of the outside of North Bull Island. The embarkation point is at the SW end of the beach. By car, cross the wooden bridge at O213-359 at Clontarf onto the island, and continue past the golf clubhouse into the dunes. There can be a modest carry.

Not a logical embarkation point for anywhere in particular, this put-in point is nonetheless popular for the surf. As well as getting small play-surf, in gentle westerlies in particular, this is where surfers embark to surf the wake of the incoming car ferries. If the ferry is late and hasn't slowed down to enter harbour (a regular occurrence), especially on lower tide levels, the second or third bow wave of the ferry can be large enough to run you all the way to the beach 1km away. Catch it just outside the North Bull Lighthouse. Not for novices.

Poolbeg

O214-336   Sheet 50

Should there be a reason to do so, embarkation is possible, with convenient parking, from the very end of the road leading to the South Pier wall of Dublin Harbour, known as Poolbeg. Launch E of the two red and white towers. It is recommended to launch at HW on the seaward side of the road. The tide recedes a considerable distance here. Circumstances may not allow this, as surf builds up in a sustained SE blow. The harbour side is available at all tide levels, but a sewerage plant discharges at this point and it's very close to the shipping.

Merrion Gates

O197-311   Sheet 50

One would have to be desperate. Launching and landing is only possible at HW. If so, this is the most convenient spot in terms of parking and launching on the entire S city area. Park and access where the Strand Road meets the Merrion Road and the railway, hence the name, Merrion Gates.

Seapoint

O227-290   Sheet 50

A popular swimming spot and parking is under extreme pressure. Go down a little

Poolbeg, Dublin Bay – David Walsh

cul-de-sac called Brighton Vale, off Seapoint Avenue. This spot is convenient for both Seapoint and Salthill Dart stations. From here inwards to Dublin, the LW 'carry' becomes increasingly prohibitive. Launch from the beach out of season. Lifeguards will probably ask you to use the eastern slipway during the summer, to protect swimmers.

Salthill

O233-287   Sheet 50

There is a pleasant beach giving access directly to the open water. It is situated just outside the West Pier of Dun Laoghaire Harbour, reachable by road via the harbour. By car, cross the railway bridge closest to the West Pier at O240-290. Turn immediately left, leaving the railway to the left and the water to the right. Follow the twisting road to its end, 200m further along, under a barrier, at a spacious car park.

This sheltered beach never inflicts too long a carry. Windsurfers and beginner boaters of all kinds use it. Swimmers prefer Seapoint, 600m further E. For kayakers, it is favoured as the em-

barkation point for starting and ending longer journeys, as parking here never comes under pressure and the length of absence is of no matter. Furthermore, it is just outside the Salthill/Monkstown Dart station.

Coal Harbour

O239-290   Sheet 50

Tucked into the SW corner of Dun Laoghaire Harbour are two inner harbours, collectively known as the Coal Harbour. There are public slipways in both, suitable for those windy days when straying outside would not be sensible. By car, cross the railway bridge as described above. The public car park and slipway are immediately obvious, and signposted.

D.M.Y.C.

O236-289   Sheet 50

Alternatively, also inside the Coal Harbour, but avoiding late night hours, the slipway of the Dun Laoghaire Motor Yacht Club is generally available to visiting boat people. The parking is safer, and the club is welcoming. The club is located at the base of the West Pier close by the railway footbridge.

Forty Foot - Front Harbour

O257-282　Sheet 50

At Scotsman's Bay, this W facing little harbour was once much used for the launching of rubber boats by scuba divers, but they ran into trouble with the authorities for their excessive enthusiasm. Now all speed craft are banned from using the slipway there, to the benefit of swimmers and others using the little cove. Kayakers should not attract attention to themselves as the rule may well be applied to all small boats. Be respectful of other water users, don't do a lot of shouting, and don't strap a big knife to your ankle.

Otherwise, this is a splendid, sheltered little harbour, mostly sand filled, with no boat carry at any stage of the tide. Parking is feasible except in heat waves or holiday times. The Forty Foot is at hand for a swim afterwards. Divers are barred there too, even on foot. This cove needs sustained N or NW winds before the sea gets lumpy.

Bullock Harbour

O263-278　Sheet 50

Bullock has ample parking and easy launching at all stages of the tide, although it is mucky on lower waters. It is the favoured put-in spot on all Dublin's S side. Bullock is a crowded harbour, with boat hiring facilities for the mackerel in season. Of interest is Western Marine, a chandlery that is as well appointed as any in Dublin. The sea just S of the harbour is often lumpy, due to tidal movement and cliffs. In a north-easterly, this can be the most challenging part of the outing. Bullock is the best embarkation place for Dalkey Island.

Maiden Rock

O273-269　Sheet 50

An important Roseate Tern colony has been established on the rock, 500m NW of Dalkey Island. Please give a wide berth during the breeding season from April to July.

Coliemore Harbour

O273-265　Sheet 50

Parking is very restricted at this attractive little harbour on the Coliemore Road. Small

pedestrian ferries ply to Dalkey Island on day trips. Much coarse bottom fishing goes on from the harbour walls. The harbour is very congested, and in swell, launching from the rather steep not-so-sheltered slip can be tricky. It is best on the bottom third of the tide when sand is exposed. Water and toilet are available. A pretty place.

Dalkey Island

O277-263　Sheet 50

An interesting small grassy island, it has a Martello Tower, a fort, goats and other furry creatures. No reliable water has been found but a well W of the church, just above the shore, is kept whitewashed. The views of Dublin Bay from both the Martello Tower and the ruined fort are well worth the trouble.

History

Archaeological excavations have revealed Mesolithic Bann flakes, Neolithic hollow scrapers and Bronze Age arrowheads on the island. In the early medieval period, the island was a base for sea-going traders, importing goods from the Mediterranean and western France.

The medieval church is dedicated to St.Begnet. The lintelled doorway is a feature of the period prior to the 12th Century. The bellcote high on the gable above is likely to have been added later, possibly in the 15th Century. The high side walls might also have been raised about then. The fireplace at the E end was added when the church was used as a residence by soldiers and masons in the early 19th Century.

The Martello Tower and the gun battery were built in response to the threat of invasion from French forces around 1804 and 1805. The tower is exceptionally large. The original entrance is high up and was reached by a ladder. The present entrance is an insertion and leads directly into the magazine. The gun platform on the roof mounted two 24-pounder guns.

The gun battery is built into the granite cliffs on the southern tip of the island. While it is unimposing from the mainland, ships sailing into Dublin Bay would have had three large guns trained on them.

Dalkey Island, Co. Dublin - David Walsh

Embarkation

Embark from Bullock Harbour at O263-277, 3km NW, rather than the nearer Coliemore Harbour. Launching and parking is easier.

Landing

Landing is best at a little beach on the landward side of the NW corner, W of the church. There is also a little cove just inside the nearby pier. The beach here is usable except on the bottom third of the tide. A regular ferry runs from Coliemore Harbour opposite to the pier.

Tides

The tide runs strongly inside and outside the island. Outside the island, in Muglins Sound, it turns as with the main coastal stream outside at Dublin HW. Inside, in Dalkey Sound, it turns much earlier. In neaps, it turns at Dublin HW and LW -0130 achieving 1.5 knots. In springs, it turns at Dublin HW and LW -0200 achieving 2.5 knots.

One stream of the main flood tide swings around Killiney Bay and divides with one part eddying through Dalkey Sound (hence the timing differential). The main part sweeps E out to sea past the southern tip of the island. Overfalls occur where the streams reconnect, just off Sorrento Point at O273-261.

Expect bigger overfalls on the flood tide at the southern tip of the island. These are particularly big with a S or SE swell. Paddlers prefer to circumnavigate anticlockwise, especially on the flood, to avoid being pushed up onto the rocks at this point. If in doubt about the conditions, have a look first from a safe distance at Sorrento Point. Following the coast of the island will ensure you are in the full flow before you see the overfalls. A decision to turn back at this stage will mean paddling against a 2-3kn flow.

The Muglins

O284-268   Sheet 50

Often visited in tandem with Dalkey Island, Muglins is a rock with a light beacon, 500m NE of Dalkey Island. Tides are the same as for the outside of Dalkey Island, i.e. the flow changes

The Muglins, Co. Dublin – David Walsh

with Dublin HW and LW. Landing is forbidden, and the tide flows strongly. Beloved of divers and anglers.

Killiney Bay

O260-246   Sheet 50

Between Dublin and Bray is a green belt which professional planners are determined to keep that way, and we wish their efforts well. Killiney Bay is where this green belt enters the sea. One of the prettiest bays around Dublin, road and place names fancifully reflect supposed Italian counterparts S of Rome. White Rock at O266-257 is 600m past Sorrento Point and has rocky outcrops with popular bathing places. A gravel beach runs the next 6.5km to Bray. The railway runs just inland of the northern part, the station being where the footbridge is visible at O260-242.

2km offshore at this northern end of the bay is the shallow Frazer Bank, which has an enormous effect upon the flood tide. One branch of the tide flows in a curve close along inshore and veers eastwards to meet the main tide flooding

northwards in the direction of Dalkey Island and the Muglins. The two streams collide just SE of Dalkey Island. A severe dose of bumpy water is thus set up. The spot is infamous, with wild but somewhat controlled conditions.

County Wicklow

Bray

O276-179   Sheet 56

Bray is a large town and was once a satellite of Dublin from where people came on holidays. Now it is virtually a suburb of the metropolis. As a legacy, a wide promenade runs the entire 1.5km length of the town front, from Bray Harbour at O270-193 in the N to Bray Head at O276-179 in the S. The entire promenade is given over to tourism, amusement arcades in the S with pubs and B&Bs at the other end.

The River Dargle enters the sea through the harbour. It dries out at LW and is not a particularly attractive embarkation point. The bottom of the harbour is very silted. There is a slipway and beach in the harbour, which is usable on the top two-thirds of the tide. There is another slipway on the outside of the N pier. A Martello Tower stands at the base of the S pier.

Bray Head

O286-170   Sheet 56

Bray Head is a mountain with twin peaks. The more northerly, 206m high peak has a prominent cross on top. The larger, 240m peak is to the S. At shore level, there are two roughly equivalent headlands, Bray Head at O286-170 and Cable Rock at O290-156. Cable Rock is a pronounced headland with an off-lying rock. There are large seabird colonies on the head in the breeding season.

Swell develops if there are sustained or strong winds from N, E or S, and gives difficult conditions all along the headland from the promenade in Bray to Cable Rock. The sea frequently breaks over Cable Rock, 80m off the headland. The tide flows strongly through the gap. Beware of a deeper rock, about 50m off the shore, which breaks the lower half of the tide in bad conditions. The sea state off Bray Head is almost always more severe than on the adjoining coast. Rogue waves are not unusual. This is not a place to go swimming, as the escape routes are tricky, the few storm beaches having dumping surf.

This whole 3km section is a fine paddle, very scenic, the slopes of Bray Head rising above, and the cliffs at the water's edge a modest rock-climbing haven. Look for the climbing cliffs just N of the Cable Rock headland. They are identified by the metal spikes in the steep ground in the first 20m above HW where the railway tunnel opens.

There are three landable storm beaches on the head, but they are exposed and steep, or even missing, at HW. Above them runs the railway line, which was engineered out of the cliff with great difficulty in the mid 19th Century. The most convenient embarkation point in Bray is at the extreme S end of the promenade at O276-179, closest to the head.

Tides

From Dalkey Island to Wicklow Head, 35km S, the N going flood runs from Dublin HW +0515 to -0045, achieving 3.5 knots in places, in springs. The S going ebb achieves 3 knots. N of

Greystones though, it is mostly possible to keep inshore, out of the way of an unfavourable tide.

Greystones

O296-128   Sheet 56

Greystones Harbour lies almost 3km S of Cable Rock. Greystones North Beach is mostly shingle, backed by quickly eroding mud cliffs.

The beach inside the harbour is the easiest embarkation point for kayaks, at any point of the tide. Close nearby is a chip shop, ice cream, pub, and all small modern town facilities. The walk on the shore above the cliffs along here up Bray Head is lovely, as is the walking southwards along the shore.

Greystones to Wicklow

O296-128 - T322-941   Sheet 56

For 20km S of Greystones, all the way to Wicklow, the coastline is uniformly flat and boring when seen from the sea. The backdrop however is the Wicklow Hills, known as the Garden of Ireland, always lovely. Landing can be achieved at any point but the shingle beach is mostly steep with dumping surf. On land, the going is anything but boring. The railway runs the entire length of the stretch, right on top of the beach, with pleasant perambulating pathways beside it. Four roads come down to the sea, so the section may be broken into smaller bits for more leisurely-minded strollers. The more determined can walk from Bray or Greystones to Wicklow and get the train back.

SPA

Bewick and Whooper Swan, Little Tern, Golden Plover, Bar-tailed Godwit.

1km of rocky coastline S from the harbour, the town ends and the long beach begins at O299-121. The hinterland along the entire stretch attracts rare bird species, especially waders, and particularly in winter. 6km S along the beach, the Kilcoole wetland system flows under a bridge at O315-061 and into the sea. This wetland system is unique in being so low-lying that it has been scantily mapped by the Ordnance Survey.

More to the naturalists' taste, there are two eco-systems in one, fresh water and salt water, side by side. The two are wonderfully different,

Greystones, Co. Wicklow - Séan Pierce

and the subject of much study as to their comparable flora and fauna. Barry O'Flynn of nearby Kilcoole carried out the first study in 1973.

About 3km further S is Six Mile Point at O318-038, the most easterly point on the route. In summer, there is a colony of Little Tern, which nest in the gravel, and are so splendidly camouflaged that it is truly inconsiderate to walk on the beach hereabouts at all. It is a Birdwatch Ireland reserve but only well marked from the land. Please therefore be careful if landing.

Camping

Pleasantly camp just about anywhere. Indeed this is probably the first grassy camping S of Dublin.

Tides

From Dalkey Island to Wicklow Head, the N going flood runs from Dublin HW +0515 to -0045, achieving 3.5 knots in places, in springs. The S going ebb achieves 3 knots. This stretch is unsheltered from ebb or flood, and is a sustained hard battle if against the tide.

Wicklow Town
T322-941   Sheet 56

Wicklow is a major town, where just about everything may be acquired.

Embarkation

Wicklow Harbour is by far the easiest access hereabouts for day trips to Wicklow Head, or journeys N. Use a stone beach just inside the W pier where there is plenty of parking. Alternatively, use a slipway beside the Lifeboat Station just inside the East Pier, where parking is more restricted.

Broad Lough

The Leitrim River, only 1km long, connects the Broad Lough to Wicklow Harbour. The Broad Lough is an expanse of fresh water, running N for 4 to 5km, just inside the shoreline. The Lough is bounded on its E by a thin spit of low-lying land down which runs the main Dublin to Rosslare railway line. On the W is Tinakilly House, and some of the finest reed beds a thatcher ever saw. This is a summer breeding place of Reed Warbler. It is a wild place, home to Greylag Geese and myriad other wintering species in the cold months. It can be shallow and muddy at anything but high water which is sometime later than at Wicklow town itself. The Leitrim River is tidal with a significant flow on the narrower stretches when the water level in the harbour is lower than that in the lough. Broad Lough is good to paddle when conditions are bad elsewhere.

SPA

Little Egret, Hen Harrier, Peregrine, Merlin, Ruff, Bar-tailed Godwit, Kingfisher.

Wicklow Head

T235-924   Sheet 56

Wicklow Head is a serious attraction to E coast paddlers in search of truly powerful sea forces in a full-blooded open water environment, yet with sanctuary nearby. On the head is a huge lighthouse, amongst the most powerful on the East coast. There are cliffs and caves on both sides. There is a pronounced eddy system either side of the head itself, and guaranteed playtime except for the shortest of slacks. On passage, err with caution to get past efficiently, as this is undoubtedly one of the most significant headlands of the southern part of the E coast.

Tides

At Wicklow Head, the N going flood starts earlier than on the Dublin/North Wicklow coast further N. The flood tide runs from Dublin HW +0345 to -0115 approximately. Downstream, expect long powerful run-offs. It is always possible to rest in eddies in the lee of the head, except when the wind is from the eastern quadrant.

Inshore tides all along the Wicklow and Wexford coasts generally follow the direction of the coast, and information on timing is unreliable. From Wicklow Head to Arklow, the flood is thought to run up to 3 knots in springs and the ebb at 1 knot.

Off Wicklow Head itself where big boats go, the flood is up to 4 knots, and the ebb 3 knots, but close by the rocks where kayaks go, the current gets seriously fast. Local paddlers say 6 knots, both ways. Bride's Head at T339-931 is 1km N of Wicklow Head, and on the ebb, the flow can be almost as strong there.

From Wicklow Harbour to Wicklow Head, the tide close inshore always runs SE. On the ebb, it runs strongly at up to 3 knots. On the flood, a major eddy system operates. Local paddlers report considerable struggles close inshore in springs. Going N, keep in the bumpy main flow for 1km at least and then keep at least 1km offshore until Wicklow Harbour.

Going S, on the other side of Wicklow Head, keep in the main flow as long as you can. A weaker eddy system operates, almost as far as Long Rock at Silver Strand at T338-910.

Embarkation

Access to the head is usually from Wicklow town as described above, but if a launching from S is preferred, there are several awkward choices. Public access is always available from Brittas Bay, but this is 10km to the S. Closer access points involve an awkward carry down steep steps to a beach. Magheramore beach at T330-884 is loved by surfers, especially on a low tide with a sustained wind from the S/SSE. Access by car is now disputed, though available, but please close the entrance gate at T324-886. The access at Silver Strand at T337-911 is the most reliable, at least in summer, and closest. The road access at T336-914 is through the more northerly of two paying caravan parks above the beach. It involves a cruelly steep carry down long steps and a (seemingly) much longer carry back up later. Camping is possible and the surroundings are pleasant. This is a famous fishing spot, and there is friendly surf on the beach for playing in. It may be closed in wintertime.

SPA

Peregrine, Merlin.

The South Coast
Wexford Harbour to Baltimore
County Wexford

Tuskar Rock

T227-072   Sheet 77

Ireland's most south-easterly island, this austere, 5m high rock is 9km off the coast across strong currents. The passage is 11km from the beach, and deserves respect. There is a very remote and exposed feel to this place, which is famous for its lighthouse.

Landing

The steps at the small quay on the ENE side are probably the best landing. There is a narrow channel behind the quay but it surges. There are steps on the WNW side, should sea conditions allow. There are possible exposed landings at the S, and some shelving slabs on the N side, either of which might work.

Fauna

The island has an impressive list of recorded bird species, largely documented by R. M. Barrington (1900). Successive light keepers assembled the records from detailed recording in the 1800s. The island is a magnet for migrant birds due to its strategic position as the main entry and exit point from Ireland to mainland Europe. Barrington records several occasions when over 3,000 birds were killed at the light in one night during poor weather conditions. Seal, Common Porpoise and Dolphin are frequently reported.

Tides and Trip Planning

The trip planning requires thought. The tides run at over 3 knots in the main channel on springs (see details later). A straight out-and-back ferry glide may be impractical. A slingshot approach is recommended, (setting off upstream of the rock so that the tidal stream carries you onto it). There is no suitable launching place to the SW. Anyway, the tide sets over a dangerous shallow area halfway out on that side. This area is called The Bailies (T177-060), a long, thin, N/S strip, which should be avoided.

The option of coming from the N avoids The Bailies, and means catching the last of the S going stream. The S going stream starts at Dublin HW -0230 and ends at Dublin HW +0430, so aim to be on the rock at the latter time. Launch 90 minutes before from the beach at T140-123 at the back (i.e. SE) of Rosslare Harbour pier. The harbour is the major passenger and cargo ferry terminal of the SE of Ireland. Make no mistake, get out from the land and come down onto the rock. On the return journey, make for

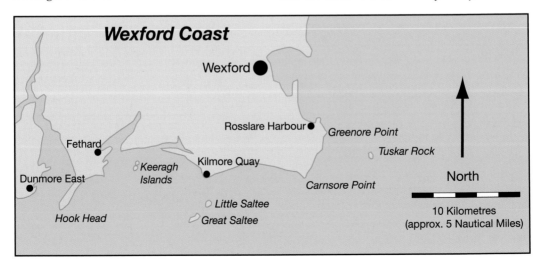

the mainland and then creep round Greenore Point. Tides speed up and overfalls occur at The Bailies and at Greenore Point.

Dangers

(a) Local paddlers report that the tide running past Greenore Point (as the tired paddler returns to land from the sea) can be the strongest encountered in the area. There is a report of a party seeing a lobster pot in this area, in mist, 1 or 2km out. Having decided to check the direction and speed of the current, they could not make it upstream to the pot! Consider that any slippage here shovels the paddler into the busiest part of the main shipping channel, and the need for care cannot be exaggerated.

(b) It is important to note that the shipping channel to France approaches Rosslare W of (i.e. *inside*) the Tuskar. The shipping channel to Wales, which includes the Lynx fast ferry, as well as all merchant shipping, lies *outside* to its N, and therefore should not concern this excursion. An enquiry as to French ferry times might be sensible.

History

The lighthouse was constructed in 1815 with 11 men losing their lives during construction. 10 were drowned when an October storm swept them away, leaving a further 14 hanging onto the rock for 3 days, one of whom died of his injuries later. It was also a dangerous place to be during World War 2, a light-keeper lost his life and a second was injured when a drifting mine exploded against the rock.

The Saltees

Sheet 77

Embarkation

Mainland launching is from the convenient, sheltered, pebbly beach immediately behind the W pier at Kilmore Quay. The beach is tucked in between the pier and Crossfarnoge (or Forlorn) Point at S965-032. Parking is generously available.

Parking is more limited at or near the harbour itself. Launching is possible off the slipway, but there is a per boat charge, rigorously policed. The beach on the E side of the harbour extends out a long way at LW, so is inadvisable.

Dangers

The main local trouble spot is an underwater bridge, very shallow, called Saint Patrick's Bridge. It starts 500m E of Kilmore Quay pier, and reaches out, in a crescent shape, all the way to Little Saltee. It is particularly troublesome on the E going tide. Boats not travelling fast enough, or not laying off enough, will be pulled down onto the bridge, where rough and accelerated water is hard to escape. This happens almost immediately after leaving the harbour. If caught, it is best to ferry glide in behind Little Saltee. 3.5 knots is achieved in springs.

Saltee Sound, between the two islands, is another trouble spot. Sebber Bridge at X956-978 is a shallow reef, which extends northwards from the NE tip of Great Saltee. The tide sets more or less E/W through the Sound, over the shallows. On the W making tide, especially with a wind from the W, the water becomes very rough indeed N of Great Saltee.

SPA

Peregrine, Chough.

Tides

Trip planning requires care for the strong tidal streams, the timings of which do tend to catch out the unwary.

Tidal streams change about three to five hours behind local HW and LW. Local kayakers strongly disagree on the timings, giving times varying by up to 2 hours. It may well be that timings vary considerably with wind conditions, and whether there are springs or neaps occurring. One thing all local kayakers agree on is that on leaving the harbour area, you always look at one of the many lobster pot buoys to check that you have your calculations right.

Local HW is about the same as Cobh (actually Cobh +0019). The published information is that the E making flood tide in the two sounds flow for 6 hours, beginning at about Cobh HW −0030. This is the same as saying about an hour before local HW. The W making ebb tide flows for the other 6 hours from HW Cork +0530. This is the same as saying 5 hours after local HW, or an hour before local LW.

Local paddlers say this cycle begins an hour or even two ahead of that. If so, the E making flood tide begins at Cobh HW -0230 or so. They say that slacks occur when the tide is halfway up or down the harbour wall. If it is halfway up and rising, the E making flood is about to start. If it is half way down and falling, the W making ebb is imminent.

Avoid the crossing on the strongest of the E making tide, especially if there are any slow-boats in the party, for fear of Saint Patrick's Bridge. Avoid also the strongest of the W making tide to avoid the run off over Sebber Bridge. Cross the race as high as possible, as the water really kicks up downstream of the gap.

Little Saltee Island

X966-996   Sheet 77

This island is less frequented than its better-known and more interesting neighbour. Historically, 3 people or so lived on Little Saltee until the mid-19th Century, when rumour insists it was connected to the mainland. Little Saltee was farmed until World War 2. The farm speciality was early-season new potatoes, but corn and other vegetables were also grown. 12 people were needed at harvest time. A thresher was brought over, in parts, in small boats. The island was abandoned and overgrown until recently.

Since 1999, the owners now farm pedigree cows, sheep, and fallow deer. Soon there may be rare Soay sheep, from the Scottish island of same name, just S of Skye.

The main house and some of its outbuildings have been made habitable. The courtyard has been tidied. There is a fine ruin of a two-storey barn and interesting remains of corn stands in the yard immediately W of the main building. There are the remains of an old well within the courtyard but it did not hold water in April 2003 and appeared long disused.

Landing

A flagpole above the main landing on the NW side at X966-996 presumably indicates when the family is in residence. Landing is possible among boulders below the house, normally reasonably sheltered by offshore boulders and rocks. One may also land elsewhere less dependably. Try the SW side on any of three storm beaches facing the Great Saltee. These are very much easier on lower tide levels.

Camping

The most suitable level ground for camping is in the area just W of the main house. Bracken and bluebells dominate the island and there are few grassy areas along the flatter western side. The vegetation is broken, lumpy and heavily grazed. The most pleasant areas are on the southern edge overlooking the storm beaches and the sound to Great Saltee. Do ask permission if the owners are in residence.

Great Saltee Island

X952-974   Sheet 77

This is a beautiful island. Grazed and easily walked or camped on, this island is lovely and deservedly popular with Irish paddlers.

The island is a famed bird-watching spot, and is often inhabited by birding visitors in season, mainly spring and autumn. Once inhabited by 20 people, the island became uninhabited relatively early by Irish island standards. There are monuments and references to Prince Michael of Saltee on the island. He bought the island in 1943, crowned himself Prince in 1972, and died in 1998.

Renewed interest in the island by his extended family has resulted in some of the scrub being removed around the remains of the old rick yard and the corn stands are more clearly visible.

Landing

Land at X952-974 on the N side, E of the middle. The main landing area has recently been improved with a channel having been cleared through the boulder beach, which in June 2003 gave a welcome sandy strip even at the lower stages of the tide. There are steps above to a house in trees. This landing is sheltered in most conditions.

Camping

Camping is not permitted on Great Saltee when inhabited by the owners.

Predictably, members of the family are almost certainly in residence in August, long weekends, or periods of settled good weather. The tradition of flying the Prince of Saltee flag from the flagpole above the landing when the family are in residence has been renewed. There are sev-

Kayaks launching from Great Saltee, Co. Wexford - David Walsh

eral new signs at the landing point regarding the terms by which people will be tolerated at all on such occasions. No camping is permitted at these times and day-trippers must vacate the island by 1630 hrs.

If camping while an island is unoccupied, it is critical to behave responsibly. Do not upset or disturb stock and keep away from private places.

Having said all that, the camping is excellent. There is water in a well at the house, but like all wells, it thrives with use and goes off otherwise. It looked very good in June 2003. There is also a bothy to the rear of the house, which saves camping, and is freely available with the usual bothy rules. Again, it is only available when the family are not about the place.

Circumnavigation

Circumnavigation gives good fun in tidal races off the appropriate points, but beware that there is much eddying. There is excellent cliff scenery, and a particularly pretty channel just E of the S tip. Sea conditions at the southern tip become fearsome in strong winds or with wind against tide.

Keeragh Islands

S866-059   Sheet 77

These two islets lie in Ballyteige Bay, 12km W of the Saltees, relatively close inshore. They are small low-lying Birdwatch Ireland bird reserves. There are two distinct islands, but they are always regarded as the one.

Landing is awkwardly practical at the N tip of each island, on either side of a projecting spit. On the bigger, northern island, there is an easy beachlet in a cut at the SW, facing the smaller island. Approach from the beach at Cullenstown at S869-077, 2km to the NNE.

Stay away in spring and early summer, as nests are too numerous to avoid. The ruin on the larger island was built in 1800 for survivors of shipwrecks, but is now dilapidated. There is still a sealed box inside with what looks like electricity going into it, suggesting a phone?

SPA

Arctic Tern.

Ballycotton Island, Co. Cork - Séan Pierce

County Waterford
Helvick Head - *Ceann Heilbhic*

Helvick Head is a lovely spot, a noted holiday area. There is the 'new' pier at Helvick at X313-892 - *Cé Heilbhic*, just inside the head. This is a busy working trawler harbour. The 'old' pier is at Ballynagaul at X299-888- *Baile na Gall*, now quite silted. This is a noted small Gaelteacht area. The Clancy Brothers first made their musical name here. They emerged in the early 1960s to inject pride in English speaking Ireland. The area as a whole is called Ring or *An Rinn*. The name probably derives from the mighty machair system guarding the inner bay called locally the Cunnigar - *An Coinigéar*.

Rock climbing

Helvick is a noted rock climbing spot. The cliff is about 1.5km SW of the gap between Helvick Head and The Gainers. The crag is immediately underneath and is accessed from the noted viewpoint and car park at X307-882. The rock is an isolated pocket of purple mudstone with some sandstone. This is said to be much better than pure red sandstone. It is solid, and takes good gear. The rock nearer to the head looks good from below, but is awkward to access from above, and may not be as good, being sandstone. Enquiries to Gerry Moss germoss@eircom.net.

SPA

Peregrine, Chough.

The Gainers
X319-893   Sheet 82

Known locally as Goat Island, this unpretentious group of fragmented rocks is really an extension of Helvick Head itself. The grass-topped inner island is the largest and is reachable on foot at LW springs. The outer rocks are pleasant to explore for their gaps, passages and small cliffs. The inner gap is a welcome escape route on passage and is usually navigable.

Landing and Embarkation

Land in or about the gap itself onto sheltered rocks.

Embark from the 'new' pier at Helvick at X313-892 - *Cé Heilbhic* where there is easy parking and launching beside the RNLI station inside the harbour. Toilets and water are available.

Round of Mine Head

Helvick is also the popular launching or landing spot at the E end of the round of Mine Head - *Mionn Árd*. Launch at the W end of this trip at a sheltered beach, either at Ardmore itself or nearer at X205-798. The journey may be broken at any of the many sandy beaches and coves, subject to conditions on the day. Mine Head is the highest lighthouse in Ireland, but the kayak on passage will not see it from immediately below because it is set back from the cliff edge. The only escape on the 15km passage is at Ballymacart Cove at X253-810, perhaps too close to the Ardmore end to be practical. Too close maybe to the other end is a beautiful beach known locally as *Faill na Staicín* at X298-877.

County Cork

Tidal Overview - Cork SE

Tides are generally weak between Cork Harbour in the W and Knockadoon Head, 30km to the ENE. However, there are significant races off the headlands and in the sounds between the islands (Ballycotton Sound and Capel Sound), where 2 knots is achieved. Slack water is thought by local paddlers to be at much the same time as LW/HW Cork. In Youghal Bay, southerly winds raise a heavy sea, and the tidal streams are rotary and very complex, running strongly over the bar, which is in mid-bay directly S of the river entrance, so caution should be exercised.

Capel Island

X100-700   Sheet 81

This attractive, 37m high island is just off Knockadoon Head, which separates Ballycotton Bay from Youghal Bay. It is privately owned but became (mostly) a Birdwatch Ireland nature reserve in 1994. The stub of an unfinished lighthouse on its highest point dominates the island. Stone walls surround the building, and a small, square out-house is worth investigating to see the dramatic drop from the hole in its floor. The seaward side of the island is most attractive and there is a colony of breeding Cormorant (60

pairs in 1995) at the SW corner. Otter are also present. There is no water, and a possible deterrent to camping is a herd of goats. There were 30 or so in 1995, only 12 in 2002.

Embarkation

There is a pier and slipway at X092-703 for embarkation at Knockadoon Head where there are two well-sheltered beaches. The only water hereabouts is at houses and the local Dominican summer school camp, and the nearest shops and facilities are at Ballymacoda, 5km to the W.

Landing

A low headland projects NW from mid-NW side of the island. There are beaches at either side of the base of this headland. The beach to the SW side (on a direct line between Knockadoon Pier and the tower on the island) does not exist at HW and is more exposed, but access to the interior is easier. The beach to the NE side does not exist at HW and access to the interior is scramblier. At HW, a deep-water landing may be had onto rocks on the sheltered cove E of this headland.

Tides

Local HW/LW is as Cork. A fierce tide runs through Capel Island Sound, and while the timing of slack water is not known with any certainty, it is thought by local paddlers to be much as for LW/HW Cork. In Youghal Bay, southerly winds raise a heavy sea.

The coastline westward to the beach at Ballymakeagh at X050-688 is very pleasant, and there are great views eastwards to Ardmore and Helvick.

Knockadoon Head was the fastest developing rock climbing crag in Ireland in 2003.

Ballycotton Islands

There are two contrasting islands lying just off the coast from Ballycotton village in E Cork.

Embarkation

Embarkation is best from a small slipway at the village where there is a small field in which to park, and a very easy gradient yielding a short carry of 50-100m maximum. This is about 1km WNW of the harbour, opposite the Garda barracks. It is reached by a laneway beside a shop

Cobh, Great Island, Co. Cork - Séan Pierce

at W989-643. There is water available here and also at the harbour from public taps. Ballycotton has good facilities, B&Bs, pubs and restaurants. The harbour itself is slightly further E at W999-637. Launching is difficult, but is possible from either of two slipways reached by narrow, steep alleyways. Descent to the beach is also possible behind the toilets on the main pier. In addition, there are steep, narrow steps halfway down the outside (E) of the pier which gives awkward access to a small beach. The W pier of the harbour is little more than a breakwater.

Tides

In Ballycotton Sound and between the inner island and the coast, 2 knots is achieved,. Slack water is thought by local paddlers to be much as for LW/HW Cork.

Small Island

X004-637   Sheet 81

Known locally (quite logically) as the Inner Island, it is low and grassy, with extensive reefs and rocky shorelines at low water. It is just accessible on foot at LW, though not easily, and it involves getting your feet wet. Landing is best on the eastern side, facing the outer island, where there is a small beach, just where the island is waisted. There is no water. In 2002, three full-blooded male goats proved quite a deterrent to would-be landers or campers. Blowholes.

Ballycotton Island

X011-637   Sheet 81

Known locally as the Outer Island, and also as the Lighthouse Island, it is 50m high, steep and rocky. The lighthouse and associated buildings dominate the high part of the island. There are two landings, each difficult, each consisting of a flight of steps to a pier, located on the N and E flanks respectively. There is a small sea-arch on the SE tip. There are breeding Shag, Great Black-backed Gulls, and Herring Gulls.

Cork Harbour

SPA

(Parts only) Bewick & Whooper Swan, Golden Plover, Bar-tailed Godwit, Common Tern.

Great Island

W805-665   Sheet 87 / Sheet 81

This island is unique amongst Irish islands in having a large town, Cobh. The island is located in the centre of Cork Harbour and is dominated on its southern flank by the town of Cobh. It is joined to Fota Island in the NE by a short bridge at Belvelly at W791-708. Access has improved in recent years with the introduction of a passenger and vehicle ferry between Carrigaloe and Passage West at W772-675, thereby shortening road travel time to Cork City.

The island has a long history of human settlement dating back to the Phoenicians, but owes much of its development to its fine natural harbour. Its naval importance and its use as a port for transatlantic liners has left the town with a long nautical association. Much of the town's fine architecture dates from the early 1800's.

Historic attractions include a fine cathedral, Cobh Heritage Centre and Old Church Graveyard, where many of the victims of the Lusitania are buried. The town's long association with the White Star Line's Titanic and Mauritania has been re-kindled recently with the opening of the Titanic Rooms bar and restaurant in what was the old White Star Line Shipping Offices.

Great Island is 7km long by 4km wide. The geology is Old Red Sandstone overlaid with Limestone in the valleys. The northern shorelines are estuarine, and the island is separated from the mainland at its western and eastern flanks by two river gorges. A full circumnavigation is an interesting day's paddling, bringing the kayaker through urban, industrial, estuarine, agricultural and scenic landscapes.

Circumnavigation

Embarkation for a circumnavigation is recommended from White Point at W786-658 or alternatively at any of several slipways in Cobh, perhaps the best of which is under the town clock directly opposite Eddie English's Sail Training Centre at W805-665. It is recommended to follow a clockwise route around. The entire distance is about 27km, or 5 hours paddling, but allow for stops.

Tides

Tidal flows in the river gorges (W and E sides) run to 3 knots in springs but these can be utilised to advantage in the timing of one's passage. The critical factors in a circumnavigation are (a) to

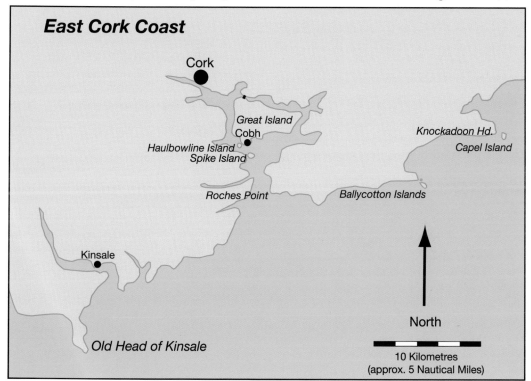

East Cork Coast

Cork

Great Island
Cobh

Knockadoon Hd.
Capel Island

Haulbowline Island
Spike Island

Roches Point

Ballycotton Islands

Kinsale

North

Old Head of Kinsale

10 Kilometres
(approx. 5 Nautical Miles)

pass close enough to HW where the tides meet, which is under Belvelly Bridge W791-707, and (b) to clear Rosslague Point at W800-703 just to its E before the ebb exposes the mudflats.

A trip in spring/autumn/winter is best from a natural history point of view as both Lough Mahon to the NW and the North Channel have large numbers of ducks and waders to provide interest.

The western river passage is a busy shipping lane to Ringaskiddy Port and Cork City. Care is required passing the old dockyard at Rushbrooke and IFI fertiliser jetties at Marino Point at W772-694. The Ro/Ro ferry service at Carrigaloe-Passage West also moves surprisingly quickly.

Camping

Camping is possible and quite pleasant from Ashgrove at W860-696 at the NE point, to East Ferry, to Morlogue Point at W852-672 at the SE point. Water is not available but the area is pleasantly wooded and there are several grassy fields that are quite remote.

The eastern river passage down to East Ferry is quite scenic and one has a choice of two hostelries for lunch. The Morlogue Inn at W853-683 is situated on the Great Island side about halfway down and Murphy's Bar is on the mainland opposite.

Once around Morlogue Point at W852-672, passage is westward towards Cobh. A Birdwatch Ireland nature reserve is located at Cuskinny Bay at W818-673. The Spit Bank Lighthouse at W812-658 marks the edge of the Spit Bank and is worth a detour. The tidal flow is weaker on the Spit Bank and gives better views of Cobh than the main channel, being that bit out and thereby gaining perspective. Spike Island at W805-645 and Haulbowline Island at W789-655 dominate the views to the S.

Haulbowline Island

W789-655   Sheet 87

A small island located just S of Cobh town in Cork Harbour. As the name suggests the island has naval associations and the island is totally dominated by buildings of the Naval Service on its western side. Many of these buildings date from the 1700-1800's when Cork Harbour was a significant port of the British Navy. The oldest buildings face Great Island and a Martello Tow-

er at W789-655 dominates the island's highest point. The eastern end is spoilt by the decaying remains of Irish Steel, a major steel manufacturing company which for many years ran its operation here, but became bankrupt a few years ago. The extreme eastern side is reclaimed polder on which the slag and spoil from this industrial site was dumped. The Naval Basin is also on the eastern side of the island and kayakers can enter to view the ships of the Irish Naval Service.

The island is joined to the mainland on its southern side by a road bridge from Paddy Blocks to Rocky Island near Ringaskiddy.

Landing

Landing is not encouraged but is possible at several slipways on the southern side and in the Naval Basin. Ferries run from Cobh to piers on the northern side for Naval personnel. Small boats should be wary of these when passing along the northern edge. The NW corner of the island juts out into the main shipping channel between Cork city docks and the ferry port at Ringaskiddy, so kayakers rounding this point should be careful at all times.

Tides

The main river channel from Cork City and the ferry port at Ringaskiddy flows through a narrow passage between Haulbowline and White Point on Great Island just NW. The tidal flow achieves 2 knots at this point. The main tidal flow splits at Haulbowline with the much lesser flow running along the southern side of the island.

Spike Island

W805-645   Sheet 87 / Sheet 81

This island is located very close to the centre of Cork Harbour and the distinctive flat-topped fort dominating the island is now a civilian prison. The island is a good rest/lunch area for kayakers touring the harbour area. Most of the rest of the island apart from the extensive fort is grassland with some copses of Scots Pine along the northern and western sides. The eastern and southern sides are steeper with scrub and furze dominating the vegetation. Landings are possible at most points of the island but probably best at the NE corner at W807-649 near a very large limestone warehouse. A ferry service for

Military and Prison staff runs from Cobh to the island pier at the NW corner at W800-648.

The island's history is largely military because of its strategic position and the importance of Cork Harbour in British Naval history. The island commands the approaches to the outer and inner harbour and formed a triangle of defence with the twin forts of Camden at W809-618 and Carlisle at W819-624, located on either side of the narrowest part of the entrance to the harbour. Spike Island has a distinctive flat-topped appearance due to the presence of its large sunken fort. The fort has witnessed various uses by both the British and Irish governments ranging from Internment Centres to Military Prisons and Military Training Areas. The island was also used occasionally as a Quarantine Zone for imported livestock.

Old Head of Kinsale, Co. Cork – Séan Pierce

On the northern side facing Cobh, there are many old military style houses and storage areas. Most of these buildings are now in an advanced state of disrepair. The foreshore is predominantly shingle and stony beaches and the area between Ringaskiddy Point at W794-647 and the western shore dries out to expose large areas of muddy estuary. However, the route is navigable by kayak at all stages of the tide.

Tides

The Spit Bank lies off the island's northern shore and is marked at its NE edge by the Spit Bank lighthouse at W812-658. Tidal flow on the bank is less than in the main harbour channels and may be useful to kayakers travelling up or down river against the flow.

Landing

Traditionally, landings have not been encouraged. The military had sentries posted at all points to deny access. However, this practice has been relaxed in recent years and kayakers remaining away from the main fort area have not been challenged.

Tidal Overview - Cork SW

Off the coast from Fastnet to Cork Harbour, the tidal streams achieve 1-1.5 knots in springs, and eddy strongly at the headlands. The flood makes for an E going stream starting at Cork -0420 and finishing at Cork +0150.

Sandy Cove Island

W640-472   Sheet 87

Sandy Cove Island is an unremarkable lump that shelters the entrance to Sandy Cove, a small deep inlet just W of the mouth of Kinsale Harbour. The island is grassy and almost lush. Surprisingly perhaps it is grazed only by goats. There are many large holiday homes opposite on the mainland. Therefore, camping would most likely be discouraged. No water was found.

Herring Gull breed here. There is a suspicion that rodents do too.

Landing and Embarkation

Embark from a slip at W637-473 to the NW of the island. The trip is about 200m. Good parking. Landing is directly opposite at the W end of the island onto sand or shingle. The sound will always be sheltered but may have nice clean surf waves as the swells from one side meet the tide from the other.

Old Head of Kinsale

W625-406   Sheet 87

This mighty headland extends 7km out to sea, W of Cork Harbour. Magnificent and rocky, it 'boasts' a golf course over the entirety of its outer parts, denying pedestrian public access over much of its amenity. This is said to be the finest, and certainly is among the most expensive golf courses in the world, to which the very rich, mainly American break-takers, fly in especially. A major battle has been conducted in the courts and on the ground between the competing interests of entrepreneurial private property on the one hand and the Keep Ireland Open spirit on the other. It is claimed that a traditional right of way existed historically, but this is denied. Both sides seem to accept that casual strollers cannot co-exist with golfers, and no compromise is thought possible by either camp. There was a rock-climbing crag at the head itself, now disused.

The grid reference given is for a narrow neck halfway out, to the E and W of which are Holeopen Bay, E and W respectively. Through this narrow section, S of which lies the golf course, run three caves. One (narrow but deep) is kayak friendly and should in most conditions allow passing kayaks to avoid the rounding of the headland itself. One (broad but bouldery) might also do so at HW. A third allowed researchers a glimpse of light and might require cool nerves. The caves are immediately inside a prominent sea stack on the W side, and under the golf course flagpoles on the E side.

Cliffy and gorgeous, do not readily pass by without a visit.

Embarkation

Put in at either the muddy beach just NW of a pier on the E side at W619-434 or at a sandy beach backed by an hotel on the W side at W610-430. Either way the shuttle is only about 2km, easily walkable.

Tides

Expect clapotis on the windward/uptide side. When the flow is at full strength, major eddies set up on the downstream side of the head. Thus, the flow is always southwards on both sides close in. These collide with the mainstream at the head, so expect a race off the tip of the head itself and a little downstream. It is reported that when winds are calm enough or from other than the southern quadrant, the mainstream race stays off the tip itself, somewhat out to sea, so that kayaks may scrape through inside. The flood is eastwards from HW Cobh -0420 to +0205 and reaches 2.5 knots in springs.

SPA

Peregrine, Chough.

Glandore Harbour

Tides are very weak inside this S Cork inlet. There are two islands inside the harbour itself.

Adam's Island

W237-326   Sheet 89

This 28m high island lies in the mouth of Glandore Harbour. The high profiled island has very steep cliffs on the SW and E sides. Landing is possible with difficulty on the N extending reef on the rocky N side, where it is possible to paddle through the reef. The island does not appear to have ever been inhabited. No water. Craft entering Glandore Harbour obey the saying "Avoid Adam, hug Eve" in deference to the shallows hereabouts.

Eve's Island

W230-335   Sheet 89

An 8m high, waterless, grassy rock inside Glandore Harbour, with landing easiest on the N side.

Rabbit Island

W223-315   Sheet 89

Just off the headland between Glandore Harbour and Castle Haven, and E of a beach marked Squince Harbour, this pleasant, formerly inhabited island is worthy of any camping stopover. The best landing place is halfway along the N coast, on a sheltered pebble beach under a ruined house. There is sheltered camping beside the house, but no water was found.

The island is waisted N/S at this point, and camping may also be had on the other, S side of the waist, also from a pebble beach, for that 'oceanic feel'. Land also at any number of other pebble beaches on this much-fragmented, attractive island, which is well worth pottering around, on foot or afloat.

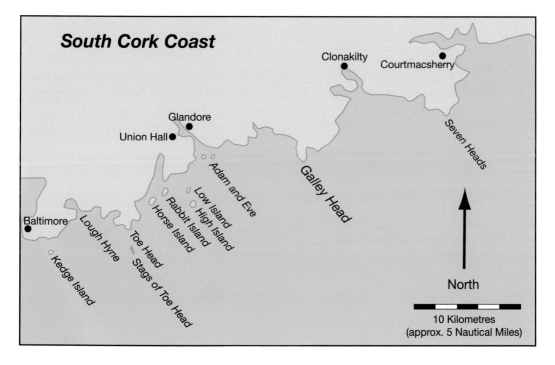

59

High Island from Low Island, Co. Cork - Séan Pierce

This island is privately owned (1997) by an owner who would prefer exclusive use of the S facing beach referred to above at W222-314 for picnics and boat, but otherwise would allow well behaved visitors to use the rest of the island in passing.

There are wild horses, burrows, Chough and Linnet on the island. Otter were seen on the W side and at the Stack of Beans on the E side.

High Island

W220-297   Sheet 89

2km out from the headland between Glandore Harbour and Castle Haven, this splendid steep, craggy, rugged, grass topped island is not for the faint-hearted. Any landing is from deep water onto rock, but there are two very sheltered coves on the N side, one facing E and the other W towards Low Island. The easier scramble to the summit is from the E cove, in proof of which I point to the blood on the rocks at the foot of the W cove, which is mine. The main nesting birds are Lesser Black-backed Gulls, and Shag. The main interest for the kayaker is the varied host of creeks and rocky passages on the Low Island side, and the sporting, surfing reefs and bumpy water generally on the outside, especially with a tide running.

Low Island

W217-298   Sheet 89

Low Island lies close by to the NW of, and is dominated by, High Island, its impressive neighbour. Landings may be had on the SE side facing High Island, or also on the NW side. In each case, land easily onto a sheltered pebble beach. The big goat reported in earlier editions seems to be gone and no longer makes camping insecure. However, camping is insecure in that the ground is very sandy, reluctant to hold tent pegs, and this type of topsoil is thought to be rodent friendly, and there are lots of them! The island is not dramatic.

Horse Island

W178-290   Sheet 89

Located S of Castlehaven and Castletownshend and tucked in against the shore, the island is grazed to the summit. It has a tower, splendid views, and while no animals were seen, it appears to be grazed by sheep. The landing is in Flea Sound on the N side of the island.

The Stags of Toe Head

W150-246   Sheet 89

These rocks are 1.5km or so directly off Toe Head. They present one amorphous blob from the N, but from the E or W side they present their true character, which is three tall parallel reefs separated by creeks. The centre creek dries at low tides, giving the better chance of a landing as there are baylets on either side, to be chosen according to wind direction. There is no water; this is just a very exposed waystop. Nesting auks and gulls. Note especially the flag marker SW of the rocks, marking the 'other end' of the wreck of the 'Kowloon Bridge', reputedly the largest shipwreck in the world. Marvel at its size as the distance to the flag is considerable.

Tides

Tides run strongly in Stag Sound, between the Stags and Toe Head, achieving 2-2.5 knots in springs, when a sustained W wind will extend the flood and weaken the ebb. Generally, the flood runs from HW Cork -0435 to +0150. Local HW/LW are about half an hour ahead of Cork.

Lough Hyne

Lough Hyne, an inland salt-water lake, is Ireland's only officially designated 'Marine Reserve'. On the island in the middle stands the ruins of O'Driscoll's Castle, from which it gets the name, Castle Island. The Lough fills for 4 hours, from local HW -0200 to local HW +0200, and empties for the remaining eight hours. Local HW is about 20 minutes before Cobh. At the narrow entrance, known as The Rapids, the water changes direction, depending on the state of the tide. Standing waves worthy of the interest of surfers form on outgoing spring tides near low water. The ingoing stream also makes for a good rush of water, worthy of play. The lough is famous for its night paddles, as there is excellent phosphorescence in the sheltered water.

The lough is a pretty place, surrounded by hills covered by deciduous forests. The easiest launch,

and most convenient car parking, is at a slipway on the N shore. There is camping at the pier on the W shore for the waterborne passer-by.

The interest of the lough to scientists lies in its deep, tidal, salt water in a controlled environment. Academics from universities all over Europe come to research the marine life to be found in the lough and its rapids. For instance, the lough boasts the biggest scallops found anywhere.

It is much loved by divers, as depths of 45m can be had with good visibility close to the shore in a sheltered environment, although any disturbance of the silty bottom soon puts an end to the visibility. The necessary authorisation/permit may be had locally.

Typically of such a formation, the outgoing stream continues long after the tide outside has started to rise; the same happens in reverse although it is less pronounced. HW/LW outside the lough are about half an hour ahead of Cork.

Castle Island

W097-284   Sheet 89

Castle Island is in the middle of the lough. On the island stand the ruins of O'Driscoll's Castle, from which the name comes.

Bullock Island

W103-276   Sheet 89

Just downstream and E of the rapids of the famous Lough Hyne, this steep wooded island is joined to the mainland to the N by a spit, which is only covered at the highest tides, and on either side of which one may land. There is no camping and a steep track leads up into the dense woods where marine scientists have a shack for their observations of the special marine world locally. There are caves in the SW of the island.

Kedge Island

W066-243   Sheet 88

A rocky islet lying about 3km E of the southern entrance to Baltimore Harbour, there is no easy landing, but there is a sheltered (from westerlies) inlet in the NW with reported rich flora and fauna (seals).

West Cork
Roaringwater Bay to the Beara Peninsula
County Cork

Roaringwater Bay

Roaringwater Bay, in the extreme SW of Ireland, is excessively named. In fact, its many islands guarantee sheltered water in almost all conditions. Its user-friendly aspect makes it a most popular area for watersports and boating. The area generally tends to be very popular in summer, because there is always somewhere to hide in Roaringwater Bay.

From Sherkin and Cape Clear Islands in the S to Mizen Head in the W, it is more accurately called Long Island Bay. Roaringwater Bay proper is tucked into the sheltered NE corner.

A feature of virtually all the islands, caused by their sandstone geology, is 'waisting'. Waists are narrow points where the islands are almost cut in two, and sometimes three, by the sea. Indeed, they may soon be. These waists are heavily relied on in the text for locational descriptions. Beaches or landing points, and other places, are often located by reference to the waist. This waisting is not always obvious from a casual glance at the half-inch OS map, but the modern OS 1:50,000, sheet 88 does much better.

Embarkation

The many islands of the bay are reached from the pretty towns of Baltimore to the SE or Schull to the NW. Each town boasts every possible convenience to the holidaymaker. Here, as elsewhere in the region, the standard of pub and restaurant food is superb. Hostels and accommodation of all kind abound. Vehicles may conveniently be left in either location. Both towns are famous for their sailing schools, Baltimore having the edge perhaps. Baltimore has a regular year-round ferry to Sherkin and Cape Clear Islands. There is a ferry to Cape Clear Island in summer from Schull.

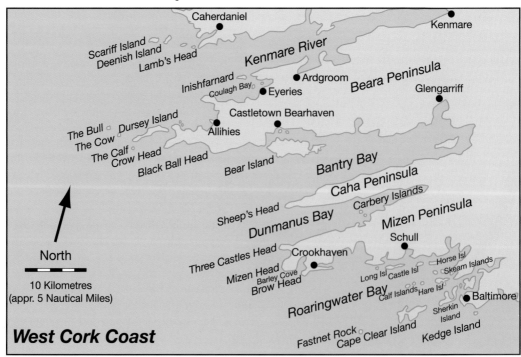

West Cork Coast

Tides

The big picture is that the flood flows E from Mizen Head through the islands of the bay, and outside Cape Clear Island. Among the islands of the bay, the flood generally turns S and then E where circumstances suggest. In this way, the flood runs E along both the N and S sides of the islands, and generally S through sounds that run N/S. The reverse is also true, the ebb flowing generally W and N through the sounds.

This is particularly true of Gascanane Sound, between Sherkin and Cape Clear.

Important and predictable exceptions occur. The flood streams N through the sound between Long Island and Castle Island and ebbs S. This allows the large enclosed water area of Schull Harbour to the N to be filled and emptied. In the same way, the large enclosed water area of Baltimore Harbour fills from both sides, N and S. In the sound between Sherkin and the mainland, the flood is N and the ebb is S.

Sherkin Island

W028-257   Sheet 88

Population 90.

Embarkation and Landing

The pier in Baltimore Harbour is the embarkation place for the island. The main pier on Sherkin is on the E side of the island just below the abbey, all clearly visible from Baltimore. There is a water tap on the pier. The strand on the S side of the pier is a very sheltered, stony beach.

Camping

Prominent, ivy-clad O'Driscoll Castle stands 300m N of the pier. Below the castle is a very steep slipway, and above the castle is the hotel. The best camping is above the slipway. It is best to ask in the hotel. There is another water tap just outside the hotel and below 'The Jolly Roger' pub.

Circumnavigation

The Globe Rocks, awash at LW, are just N of the pier. The sound at the NW of the island between it and Spanish Island is called 'The Sound'.

Dock Pier is just W of the N entrance to The Sound, in a safe, well-sheltered ENE-facing cove at W023-273. Along the whole N side of the island, beware of the Cape Clear Island ferry, as the depth is shallow and the boats are very frequent in summer. Many yachts will also be encountered, many of which are being driven by beginners, and further care is needed in that regard.

The very sheltered Kinish Harbour on the NW side, which mostly dries, has a mighty current, perhaps 2kn, at the entrance at W017-259. Beware of Carrogoona Rocks just E of the entrance. It is only a 150m carry to Cow Strand at W014-253 from the quay at the SW side of the harbour.

W of the entrance to Kinish Harbour is the Sherkin Island Marine Station. The landing point at W010-259 involves a lot of weaving in between offshore rocks but the landing itself is quite sheltered. The Marine Station, in addition to its research activities, privately publishes works on bird life and natural sciences, particularly aquatic flora and fauna. Especially recommended is their 'Ireland's Marine Life, A World of Beauty', a stunning collection of underwater pictures taken locally in Roaringwater Bay. The price at time of writing was €20.00, plus postage. Contact them on 028 20187 or by e-mail at SherkinMarine@eircom.net.

Cow Strand is the more southerly and smaller of two strands in the large curved bay on the W part of the N side of the island. It is a bit public in summer but a great spot nonetheless. Silver Strand at W012-255 is just to the N of Cow Strand. It is probably the best beach on the island and camping is to be had in the cliffs at the S end. Above both beaches, an islander collects modest camping fees. Both beaches slope gently and attract big swells, getting dangerous when the wind is SW to NW.

3-400m S of Cow Strand is Priest's Bay at W012-247, which is very secluded. SW of Priest's Bay is the nice, crescent-shaped, sheltered Trabaun Strand at W010-245.

On an anticlockwise trip around, the coast from here to the well-named Horseshoe Harbour at W027-254 is more or less inaccessible all the way. An exception may be Tracrua at W003-240, a narrow inlet just S of Sherkin Point. Horseshoe Harbour lies just W of the sound to the E of the island, very near everything and very secluded. The rocky landing is in at the back.

Tides

The stretch of water around Cape Clear and Sherkin Islands is regarded by locals as serious, and not to be underestimated.

The tidal stream floods E on both the N and S sides of Sherkin Island. Baltimore Harbour fills from both the NW (between Sherkin and Spanish/Ringarogy Islands) and from the S between the mainland and Sherkin. These flood streams meet in the middle of the harbour at Lousy Rocks. After that, the combined stream heads E and then NE into Church Strand Bay, NE of the town. The ebb is the reverse. These flood tides begin at HW Cobh +0545, and the ebb at HW Cobh -0025.

Gascanane Sound is between Sherkin and Cape Clear Island. The SE flood and the NW

ebb each start about half an hour earlier, at Cobh +0520 and -0055.

In many places, especially Gascanane Sound, the tide runs fiercely, at up to 3kn, causing dangerous eddies and overfalls, especially near the rocks in the middle of Gascanane Sound, known as Carrigmore Rocks and Gascanane Rocks. The steep-to rock on the Sherkin side of the sound is Illaunbrock.

Cape Clear Island - *Oileán Cléire*
V954-218   Sheet 88

This Gaelteacht island is truly the Land's End of SW Ireland. Cape Clear is actually the most SW point of Cape Clear Island, called Pointabullaun at V943-197. Mountainous, steep, and imposing, the island is home in winter to about 135 people or 110 voters and many more in summer. A ferry runs all year from Baltimore - twice daily in winter, more often in summer. In summer, there is also a ferry from Schull. The island has pubs, B&Bs, restaurants, two hostels, a well-appointed campsite at V954-212, windmills, very basic shops and provisions, and the most famous bird observatory in the country at V954-219.

The island is extremely waisted, the waist being known as 'The Waist', with the North Harbour to landward, and South Harbour on the seaward side. The waist itself is high and narrow, and the roads in the vicinity of the waist are extremely steep, that giving access to the E end of the island being called the A1 and having a gradient of about 1:4.

The co-operative club serves excellent meals and drink on the harbour, and Cotter's Bar is also located here. There is a third wee pub up at the waist. A fourth, modern pub, Danny Mike's, has been built just S of the waist, and excellent food may be had from breakfast to dinner time.

There is the ruin of a lighthouse on the middle summit, which was the main landfall light for ships arriving from America during most of the 19th Century. Its light was too high up, and therefore too often obscured by fog. It was decided, after 100 lives were lost in a shipwreck in 1847, to build a lighthouse on the Fastnet Rock.

The island would repay a fortnight's visit, and the walking repays fitness.

South Harbour, Cape Clear Island, Co. Cork - S. Pierce

Off North Habour, Cape Clear Island, Co. Cork - Séan Pierce

Landing

The main landing is at the beach in the well-sheltered pier in North Harbour, where the ferry comes in. For a fleeting visit, land on the sandy beach, dead ahead of the harbour entrance. For longer visits, consider the remoter mud/shingle beach under the bird observatory in the inner harbour, hard right just inside the harbour entrance.

Should conditions allow, landing is also very sheltered in South Harbour. Land here easiest at the stony beach on the E side, inside the lovely old quay and under the youth hostel at V958-213.

Circumnavigation

A circumnavigation is a committing 15km and requires good conditions and planning. Note particularly that the tidal timings vary at each end of the island. The crux of the trip will always be off Cape Clear itself, W of South Harbour, but Gascanane Sound may provide technical interest also.

Begin and end at North or South Harbour. Landings, as waystops only, may be had on the N side, where roads are shown going down to the sea, near the little rocky island Illauneana (V970-235). Both are stony landings, that to the E being steep also. The landing apparent on the map at V984-230 on the E side is very difficult. It is an exposed, steep slipway, impossible without good conditions and best avoided. There are no landings on the SE side, nor W of South Harbour round to North Harbour.

There is a mighty sea arch at Pointanbullig on the E side of the South Harbour entrance.

Camping

The main camping is a well-appointed campsite at V954-212. For kayakers, this is inconvenient to the North Harbour, involving a long carry past the waist. Better by far is to land in South Harbour, on the W side, under the campsite.

The only possible camping 'sauvage' may be had inconveniently, on the N side where roads are shown going down to the sea, near the little rocky island Illauneana (V970-235). Nothing is known as to availability of water.

Hostels

B&B and a hostel may be had at Cotter's Bar, just above the main pier.

There is an 'An Oige' youth hostel at the South Harbour at V958-213. Those landing here will be well rewarded for their extra effort in terms of the welcome, as an outdoor pursuits centre runs from the hostel called 'Cleire Lasmuigh' or in the English, 'Cape Clear Island Outdoors Activity'. Calm conditions are needed to paddle around to this spot.

Birding

At the pier in North Harbour is the Bird Observatory building, like a youth hostel. This (in season) is strictly for birders. The birding season locally is the autumn months of August through to November, so paddlers may be welcome at other times. Even in season, especially for those possessing binoculars and who know a covert from a supercilium, it may be worth asking.

Because of its extreme SW position, Cape Clear Island is directly in the path of long distance birds and cetaceans gaining and regaining the North Atlantic from all points E and S. Accordingly, Cape Clear is internationally famous for its migrants and vagrants, and virtually nowhere else in the country has as many rarities, and mega-rarities.

Most bird observation is done near the waist and on the W end of the island. Dawn and dusk sea-watching of both birds and cetaceans is done mostly from Blananarragaun at V947-197, which juts out at the extreme S tip of the island. Get there by following a path along the top of the cliffs on the W side of South Harbour. When approaching, it appears inaccessible, but keep your nerve, it is easy enough to scramble out. Morning or evening, this is one spot you will never have to yourself.

The area just behind the Youth Hostel is also a renowned birding spot, especially for the smaller passerines, and much ringing and counting takes place hereabouts. Good birds are seen further E on the island as well, especially on the N side, among the sheltered wooded spots.

Climbing

There is excellent rock climbing on the Bill of Clear, thin, well-protected slabs, and some steeper work, with plenty of scope remaining. These are reported in the 'New Climbs' bulletins of the late '80s.

Tides

The flood tide arrives at the W end of Cape Clear and runs along the N and S coasts from HW Cobh -0420 to +0150, reaching 2 to 2.5kn. The situation is more complex on the E and W sides.

In the E, the SE flood and the NW ebb each start (much earlier than above) at HW Cobh +0520 and -0055.

In the W, the flood separates at the Bill of Clear (V937-204), which juts out from the N tip of the W side. The N branch is uncomplicated. The S branch sets up heavy confused seas as it continues to Blananarragaun, the point 1.5km to the SE, which juts out from the southern tip. After Blananarragaun, it makes a *big* eddy anticlockwise around the outer part of South Harbour.

On the ebb, there is a *big* eddy set up by Blananarragaun, clockwise to the Bill of Clear and back along the cliffs under Cape Clear. Thus, there is always a race off Blananarragaun when the tide is running, and usually a heavy, confused sea state between Blananarragaun and the Bill of Clear. A local paddler is known to have said that he would be concerned that the S/W end of Cape Clear is 'rather exposed', that 'tidal streams can vary' and 'generally seem to be going the wrong direction'. This is apparently 'not a place to be in very bad weather conditions'.

In many places, especially Gascanane Sound, the tide runs fiercely, at up to 3kn, causing dangerous eddies and overfalls, especially near Carrigmore Rocks and Gascanane Rocks in the middle of Gascanane Sound.

Offshore to the mighty Fastnet, the tides run E/W.

Fastnet Rock - *Carraig Aonair*
V886-163   Sheet 88

Fastnet is remote. It lies about 20km from Baltimore or Schull. It is easiest reached from Cape Clear Island at about half that distance. The rock itself is 24m high and the lighthouse projects way beyond. It is a bleak, desolate place, its buildings all shuttered, its paths narrow, its stairs steep.

Fastnet Rock, Co. Cork - Séan Pierce

A first attempt to build the lighthouse was in cast iron, completed in 1853. It wasn't a success. In 1899, they began a granite replacement. This was first constructed in Cornwall of numbered blocks, 2,074 of them, weighing 3 - 5 tons each. These were then dismantled, taken to Rock Island, off Crookhaven, and reassembled. Then they were dismantled again, and reassembled again on the Fastnet. This was achieved without fatality, unusually in the Irish experience. The whole task was completed in 1904.

Landing

This is one of the more exposed lighthouse island landings, always subject to surge and scend. Certainly, few enough kayakers get here, because it is remote, but far fewer still go ashore, because to do so is so difficult. Fastnet is on a shallow shelf, always kicking up in the 200m or so around the rock. The landing platform is at the SE corner. Consider sending half the party ashore at a time, for safety. It is said that the steps for landing are proud of the water at LW. This has not been absolutely verified, but if so, it would complicate a slingshot approach to trip

planning, where one would leave Cape Clear on the ebb, arrive at the Fastnet at LW and return on the start of the flood.

Tides

In prevailing westerlies, local kayakers agree it is perhaps best to do the whole thing on the flood. This allows one to arrive in plenty of time to land, take photos, and rest before coming 'home' on the last of the flood. The flood runs E from HW Cobh -0420 to +0200 over most of the gap between Fastnet and Clear. However, near the rock itself, it swerves towards the S.

Spanish Island

W031-274   Sheet 88

The island is overgrown with difficult vegetation. The main landing spot is on the E side, under the ruined house. This island was obviously once a valued asset, but has now gone to ruin.

On the E side, there is a mangrove swamp type of environment, Aghillaun Pool. It dries out at springs, is isolated, and possesses a primitive feeling. It might be a campsite for refuge in bad westerly weather. There is a sheltered landing in a shallow bay on the E side of the N entrance to Baltimore Harbour.

Aghillaun

W036-283   Sheet 88

A small, interesting satellite of Spanish Island to its NE. Its 3 tors make interesting scrambling. No water or camping.

Sandy Island

W024-276   Sheet 88

Off the N side of Sherkin Island, this 5ha island has no sand. There is an old effort at a slipway on the E side near the old 1960's style holiday home. The house collects its own rainwater, but has mains electricity. Goat, heather, gorse. Would benefit from more grazing.

The Catalogues

W018-275   Sheet 88

Smaller offshoot of Sandy Island, to its W. Heather and gorse mainly. Many goats.

Land on a small sandy beach on the E side.

Hare Island

W007-277   Sheet 88

This inhabited low-lying island is the biggest in central Roaringwater Bay. It is 'T' shaped, with waists both W and S of the junction. The main residential area and fishing port, noted for its quaint bridge, is on the N side of the W waist. The ferry comes in at the extreme E point from Cunnamore Pier at W012-288 on the mainland opposite. Note the steps cut into the solid rock long before the modern pier was constructed.

There is a famous restaurant on the island, the waiting list for which is legendary. Noted for its food being obtained on the island, the restaurant is known as 'Island Cottage', phone 028 38102.

Landing

There are landing points at either side of each waist, the best being on either side of the S waist. Of these, the E side probably just wins out, as the island is generally more attractive at its E end. Generally, the W end is more rugged where landings to camp may perhaps be forced for privacy.

The W side of the S waist is a good waystop, as there is fine shelter for picnicking behind a stone wall.

There are two islets on the N side, but the sounds are narrow, and the more easterly dries at springs.

Tides

Tides run strongly around both sides of the island, flooding SE and ebbing NW, achieving 2kn in springs off the W side, downstream of Anima Rock, halfway across to Calf Island.

Skeam East

V996-290   Sheet 88

A most attractive, tall, conifer-topped island. Goats and cows graze, and there are ruined stone farmhouses. The island is interesting, varied, and attractive. There is a sea-arch in the SW. Generally a lovely island.

Landing and camping

There are landing places either side of the central E-W waist, on sheltered beaches, (sandy W and pebbly E). There are idyllic campsites just above both. There is a small, remote pebble beach on the SW with good camping. No water found, anywhere.

Tides flood generally E and S around the island, the ebb reversing the process.

Skeam West

V985-287   Sheet 88

This E-W lying island, NW of Hare, is also waisted E-W. Coming from the NW (Schull) direction, there is a prominent wall, a slab, and some deep cuts, seen along the N side. The W end of the waist is not at all obvious, but is to be found at about the position of the wall. Here a sheltered pebble beach leads onto a rough long-grass campsite.

A landing may be had also at the slab, in a deep cut, typical of this island.

On the E side of the waist, opposite Skeam East, is another sheltered pebble beach, below refurbished, stone holiday houses. Here water perhaps may be had in summer.

The island is ungrazed and so is unattractive to most passing campers.

Middle Calf Island, Co. Cork - David Walsh

Tides flood generally E and S around the island, the ebb reversing the process. There is the ruin of a church.

Calf Island (East)

V970-269   Sheet 88

The low-lying Calf Islands occupy the most central position in the whole bay. Hares are said to roam free on all three islands. Calf Island East is the most attractive of the three Calf islands.

There is a holiday house by the deep cut into the S side. Residents may therefore appear, but unlikely perhaps. Behind the cut is a brackish lake, where grazing cows congregate. Camp at the cut.

Camp elsewhere, particularly on the E side where there are many attractive little beaches backed by machair. The most attractive of these is in the N. There is also a splendid, similar campsite on the W end of the N side.

Lesser Black-backed Gull.

Calf Island (Middle)

V954-258   Sheet 88

The central Calf Island is grazed by cows, and is a most attractive island with abandoned houses in the middle. There are pebble beaches for landing in the middle/W sound. A noted feature of the island is the wall building between the fields, very toothy, very dramatic. Lesser Black-backed Gull.

Calf Island (West)

V949-256   Sheet 88

The W island is overgrown. It has no real beach, and perhaps there is a connection with Calf Island Middle. There are abandoned houses in the middle. Landing is in the sheltered part of the sound. Local paddlers prefer this of the three Calf islands for single overnight trips.

Carthy's Islands

V954-280   Sheet 88

A scattered group of little islands. Only the largest, westerly island has easy, all-weather landing, onto stony beaches in cuts on the E

Castle Island, Co. Cork - Séan Pierce

side. These should be chosen according to tide height. These islands make a pretty group. They also make a strategically placed waystop for any tour of Roaringwater Bay, particularly one based out of Schull.

Both Common and Grey Seal are present. Lesser Black-backed Gull.

Horse Island

V976-303   Sheet 88

This E-W lying island, just E of Castle Island, is waisted N/S near its W end. A landing may be had N (by a pier) or S (on a beach) of the waist. The island is not grazed by domestic animals of any description. Accordingly, the grass is universally long and unsuitable for camping. Experimental forestation is being conducted, with both deciduous and coniferous trees, even on the highest ground. There are magnificent refurbished stone-built houses, one very substantial. They have generated electricity, and their own water supply.

Castle Island

V959-297   Sheet 88

A most attractive island, reached easily from Schull. Sheep graze so the camping and walking is easy. The island is very attractive to explore, being formerly sparsely populated. The boreens are nicely laid out, and the views are excellent. Good value all round. Chough nest, and Peregrine hunt.

The E going flood tide commences at HW Cobh -0605 and the W ebb at HW Cobh +0005, reaching 1.5 kn in Castle Island Channel (on the N side).

Landing and Camping

The obvious landing point is at the beach at the pier under the castle at V959-297. In settled weather, more private and attractive camping may be had at a landing place on the S side of the waist on a beach at V959-296. Best camping of all perhaps, sheltered and with short grass, is by a group of abandoned houses at the extreme NE tip at V965-300. Here a landing may be had either side of a pebble spit. This site may be best

Long Island, Co. Cork – David Walsh

for a stay of any duration, being remote from the normal access at the pier. No water found anywhere.

Long Island

V920-285   Sheet 88

Landing and camping

The main landing to this inhabited island is midway along its N (sheltered, landward) side opposite the mainland, on a beach inside the pier.

The main habitation is in this area. There is more habitation further W. Further W again, the island is waisted N/S. On both sides of the waist, there are beaches and attractive camping sites. That on the S is less obvious as it is in a hidden and sheltered cove. Just further W of the waist, on the sheltered N side, is the wildest camping site. It is in a cove near the western tip of the island. Water is in the houses, and may be elsewhere.

The island is best known for its lighthouse (white tower) at its eastern end, with landing steps, marking the entrance to Schull Harbour.

A significant interest on this island is how they get livestock to and from the mainland. They tow them. One boat tows another, and the towed boat has the cow attached to its stern, held fast. In more leisurely days, the cows swam the channel.

Coney Island

V908-288   Sheet 88

On the E side of the mouth of Croagh Bay, a small, ungrazed, privately owned island with a refurbished holiday home. Beaches on NE and SE tips and on the W side.

Goat Island (Beg)

V888-269   Sheet 88

The smaller Goat Island is extremely difficult to land on. It has a white conical marker on its seaward, southerly tip. A deep-water landing may be had in the channel with a most exposed scramble up a ramp on a slab of rock. Alternatively, perhaps on a very good day, landing may be made elsewhere.

Goat Island (Mór)

V893-274   Sheet 88

The main Goat Island is 'L' shaped and has a ruined cottage and lazy beds on the eastern leg. Fences suggest recent grazing. Certainly, despite the lack of obvious grazing, in the summer of 95 the island was not overgrown. It was really quite inviting, a most attractive island. A deep-water landing may be had onto a natural but steep-sloping ramp at the E tip, just S of a prominent sea arch. At the join of the 'L', there is a sea arch where, except at the highest tides, there is a sand bank in the middle, but no reasonable access to the interior.

Dunmanus Bay

Carbery Island

V845-357   Sheet 88

The largest of the group of islands nestling in against the S shore of the bay, about halfway down. This island is the only one of the group with a dwelling. It was privately owned by an Englishman in 2001, who reputedly used it for a fortnight or so in August each year. The house is beautiful, built to a very high specification, in local stone and aged pitch pine. It has its own generator, deep well, and septic tank. The island suffers for being ungrazed and is thus given over universally to long grass, gorse, and heather.

Landing

Land at a beach below the house midway on the E side. Here a pontoon has been thoughtfully provided. No water is available to casual passers-by. Camping is not easy because of long grass. Respect the privacy of the owner at all times.

Cold Island

V852-359   Sheet 88

The remotest and smallest of the group, to the ENE of Carbery, an ungrazed lump of remote grass and rock. Known locally for its seal population, there is also a strong roosting colony of Sandwich Tern. No water. No camping. Land at a sandy beachlet at the E end of a cut, which almost severs the island from an area of rock to its N.

Furze Island

V853-354   Sheet 88

An inappropriately named island in the middle of the group, this pleasant grassy island benefits enormously from the grazing of just a couple of cows. Almost as large as Carbery, one may camp almost anywhere. Land at the NE tip onto shingle and boulder. Cows need water so water there must be, but none has been found, yet. Many seals off the NE.

Horse Island

V856-352   Sheet 88

A small member of the group closest to the mainland on the Mizen side, it boasts a large Sally tree *(Salix Caprea)*, most unexpectedly, in the NE corner. Land just below the tree onto a gravel spit that, at LW, separates the island from an off-lying rock. Alternatively, land at the head of a deep inlet at the same point. Ungrazed. No water. No camping.

Glengarriff Harbour

A pleasant, sheltered spot for an excursion on a short or windy day. It is interesting to dodge in and out among the smaller rocks and islands of the bay, trying not to disturb seals and other wildlife, admiring the posh houses and boats, goats, and generally luxuriant landscape. Some of the islets are individually mentioned. Note the warnings on visiting Garinish. Do not disturb the seals. Local boats bring tourists to view the seals so any messing about is less than appreciated. The local boats can phut-phut up to within a few feet of the seals and be ignored. Familiarity breeds contempt. Kayaks, being unfamiliar, are held in high esteem by the seals, who panic on sight. Otter are reported, and terns. Camping is neither appropriate nor welcomed, nor was it found.

Embarkation

Probably easiest from a sheltered pier and slip about 1km S of Glengarriff where the Castletown Bearhaven road meets the sea at a spot called locally 'Ellen's Rock' at V925-552. Smaller ferries than those from Glengarriff ply from here, and the landing spot on Garinish can be seen 1km to the E.

Garinish Island - *Ilnacullin*

V934-550   Sheet 85

The island is State owned and much visited for its Italian gardens. The gardens are open in summer from about 11.00 to 5.30. There is a Martello Tower on the summit almost obscured by the trees of the plantation. Unusually, its sides are vertical. It boasts of being the first such tower on the Irish coast, which, if so, was by a whisker. Superb to visit by kayak or ferry. Expect a race at the SW tip, where the sea is shallow.

Landing

To avoid serious upset, land only at the official landing point, midway on the N side, in a shallow cove. There is a stony beach at LW, and otherwise a slip. There is also a pier, a cafe, and a turnstile through which pay to enter. There is a boathouse in a cut in the NE side and a slip nearby at V936-550, servicing the restricted (private residence) part of the island. There are shingle beaches either side of the Yellow Rocks off the S side.

Bark Island

V937-560   Sheet 85

Rhododendron and fern saturated, a small, humpy island, ESE of Glengarriff town. Land either side of prominent waist. The island has nothing to recommend it to kayakers though it is a significant navigational marker for visiting yachts.

Murphy's Island - Garranboy Island

V943-557   Sheet 85

Fern and Scots Pine covered rocky lump, hard in by the NE shore, inside a prominent mussel farm. Otherwise inconspicuous up against the shore. Of little interest other than it is owned by Maureen O'Hara. Land by the S tip onto rocks.

Garvillaun

V940-551   Sheet 85

Prominent if small island, off the NE side of Garinish, fern and pine covered. It is best not to land at the cut halfway along NW side, as seals inhabit the island. Even more are on its sister rock, Ship Island, just SE. They are a tourist attraction, so please, *do not disturb*.

Bear Island - *An tOileán Mór*

V686-446   Sheet 84

Bear Haven, a natural harbour of naval importance for centuries, separates this massive island from the mainland. The permanent population is about 200. The distinctly mountainous W end of the island, opposite Castletown Bearhaven, is the most convenient to reach. There are many 'Private' signs about the W end, but the Beara Way gives access to the interior. Walking on the high ground is lovely, along little-used waymarked trails and the scenery is wonderful. Ardnakinna Lighthouse at V672-423, marking the W entrance to Bear Haven, is very recent, lit in 1965. The only village is towards the E end at Rerrin, where the island is narrowest.

The many guns and fortifications on the island were mostly built as recently as 1910, and some held IRA prisoners during the War of Independence. There are two Martello Towers where there were once four, two having being knocked down for later military building works. The island and its fortifications were held by the British, even after Irish independence, until 1938. They were handed over to the Irish , with other so called 'Treaty Ports', after a trade war. This was soon much regretted, when Britain went to immediate and terrible war with Germany. Two 6 inch guns can still be seen at Lonehort Fort, the biggest fort on the island.

Two ferries ply between the mainland and the island. The western ferry is from downtown Castletown Bearhaven. The eastern ferry is from Beal Lough at V717-463, 3km E of the town.

Embarkation and Landing

The harbour of the major fishing town of Castletown Bearhaven is the logical embarkation place. Launch at the slipway at V680-461. The western ferry sets out from here. The slip is just opposite the SuperValu supermarket, which is seriously well stocked. Good parking. The grid reference marks the nearest ferry landing point in a small sheltered bay inside the W end, where kayaks may also land.

Tides

Bear Haven is a natural harbour/sound varying from narrow and mountainous at its western

Ardnakinna Point, Co. Cork - David Walsh

entrance, to low and shallow at its eastern end. Tides flow in and out at both ends simultaneously, meeting in the middle. The stronger tides flow through the W entrance, at 2kn, and turbulence may be expected. Tides are not strong otherwise in the sound. At the eastern entrance, they reach 0.5kn. Tides enter and leave much as with local HW/LW, to and from about HW Cobh -0045.

Circumnavigation

There are many interesting spots in the 21km around the island, some of which are listed here, clockwise from the W end.

V674-433   Just inside the narrowest point of the western entrance to Bear Haven, it is reachable by backpacking or paddling. The landing is onto sheltered steps, easily identified inside a large yellow buoy and below a zigzag track. A seriously idyllic camping spot, midge free. Shore fishing. Water nearby.

V677-440   Gun forts (private) at Fort Point, and also just S at V677-435.

V696-447   There are a number of choices for more private camping away from ferries, but for those constrained to use the inside channel, perhaps the nicest would be about 1km E of the western ferry arrival point. Keep away from either ferry as the water is churned up and the swimming unattractive.

V741-443   There is a handy stony beach at a slip just inside Rerrin Bay, on the E side. Rerrin is in the E and the only village on the island. Hereabouts the island is waisted which is most convenient to inspect the conditions outside. The village has restaurants, pubs and other facilities. The eastern ferry leaves from Beal Lough at V717-463 about 3km E of Castletown Bearhaven. The eastern end of the island is by far the prettier, welcoming, and more civilised.

V748-447   E of the eastern ferry is low lying, but there is a super campsite in the shallow bay near two houses, and also elsewhere E of there towards Lonehort Point.

V755-443   Lonehort Harbour lies SW of Lonehort Point. Though storm beaches separate the two, the harbour is the more dependable resting point on a circumnavigation. A bump may be expected at several points along the outside, including Leahern's Point.

V755-435   Leahern's Point, sheltering Lonehort harbour.

V739-434   Storm beach at Coosavaud (means 'Boat Harbour'), E facing, by a slipway.

V721-427   Splendid little cove with a very narrow, S facing entrance, just NE of prominent Greenane Rock, gives great respite. It is better than the nearby and more obvious SW facing cove below houses at V724-428.

V672-423   There is no respite from the above cove until the lighthouse at Ardnakinna Point, but watch for the waterfall at about V712-424, and there are others.

V671-424   Illaundoonagaul, almost an island, has sea arches of the finest variety, which, being inside the entrance, are very inspectable.

Dinish Island

V688-457   Sheet 84

In Bear Haven, sheltering the town, this island is now connected to the mainland by a bridge, and consists entirely of an industrial park, mainly of the heavy marine variety. It is worth the walk around to see the big boats and big machinery. Land anywhere except in the NW sector (facing Castletown Bearhaven) where the main quay is. Sea kayakers might want to camp by the boathouse in the NE corner so as to walk into town, but otherwise of zero interest to small boats.

Minane Island

V695-457   Sheet 84

In Bear Haven, 1km E of Dinish. Small, rough, unmeritorious, flat little island with coniferous plantation hiding old ruins. Land most anywhere that is sheltered.

Dursey Island

V506-414   Sheet 84

Huge but sparsely populated island (permanent population of 9) of Great Blasket proportions. It is connected to the mainland by cable car (the only such in Ireland) at Dursey Sound. The Beara Way runs the length of the island - along the main roadway outwards and over the hilltops back. It goes past the signal tower on the summit, and makes for a splendid day's walk. The main area of habitation is about one third along the island but there is no village as such. There is no beach.

Embarkation

In calm conditions, launching is practical (if a bit awkward) at Dursey Sound, from the pier at V507-418. Certainly, no exploration of the outer parts of the island or the off-lying rocks would be sensible if conditions made launching impossible here. More dependably, there is a magnificent, sheltered strand at the pier and slip at White Strand Quay, in the extreme SW of Allihies Bay, at V523-428.

Passage at Crow Head, Co. Cork - Séan Pierce

Dursey Island, Co. Cork - David Walsh

Landing and Camping

The pier and steep slip at V506-414 are well sheltered, just outside the S entrance to the sound. No water was found nearby but there must be. Camping is possible just SW of the slipway towards an old churchyard. There is no easy landing other than at the slipway. Rock pools just S of the slipway, which form and un-form with the tide, may provide a landing.

Tides

The 14km circumnavigation is a challenging experience, and races may be expected off the twin outermost points, and elsewhere as tides and wind dictate. Tides flow up to 4kn in Dursey Sound and constantly boil, especially over a rock in mid-channel, under the cable-car wires. There is usually clapotis at the NE corner of the sound, which kayakers have found to extend 1.5km to Garinish Point to the NE. Beware flukey winds at the N entrance. The flood eddies on both sides of the southern entrance.

Off the outer tip of Dursey lie the Calf, the Cow and the Bull, mighty, remote and challeng-ing rocks. Until recently, no kayaks had landed. Off these, the main tidal streams around Ireland split. One stream heads S through Dursey Sound and on to Cork, Wexford and Dublin. The other heads N to Kerry, Mayo, Donegal and Antrim. The two streams meet again at the Isle of Man. The Bull has a huge lighthouse complex built on it. The Cow has nothing. The Calf has an aban-doned stump of a lighthouse.

Tides flood E along both sides of Dursey Is-land and S through Dursey Sound, from HW Cobh -0500 to +0130. On the flood though, there is extensive eddying in the bay between the S entrance to Dursey Sound and Crow Head to the S.

Illanebeg

V504-410   Sheet 84

A small, sheep-grazed island just SSW of the slipway on Dursey, attached to Dursey except at higher waters and deeply cut from the E, W and S. Despite casual appearances, there are no easy landings possible at any stage of the tide.

The Bull Rock, Co. Cork – David Walsh

The Bull Rock

V406-402   Sheet 84

The Bull lies 4km WNW of Dursey Head, the headland at the outer tip of Dursey Island, itself 6km in length. This remote rock appears from Dursey direction as a mighty pyramid with a lighthouse complex on top. A landing on it by kayak is one of the top dozen or so obvious Irish challenges.

A huge tunnel running E/W splits the Bull. The sides of the tunnel are even and smooth as glass. Navigation of the tunnel is undemanding, and in fact, a landing may be forced on the S side of the W entrance, though it leads nowhere.

The Bull boasts wonderful scenery all round, and is a significant breeding Gannetry.

Landing

Landing is difficult. There is the standard platform with steps on the S side, at the foot of prominent steps leading vertically up to the lighthouse. However, at LW, the bottom step is a bit high, and rock ledges on either side are subject to much movement of surge and scend. Worst of all though, the spot is vulnerable to a strong sideways current, being entirely exposed. Any mistake will be severely punished. The SE corner of the rock is but a few seconds away, after which a swimmer will be in a full-blooded tide race.

There is a severe looking landing spot on the S side of the E entrance to the tunnel, just tucked inside the SE corner. This is a gloomy spot, and there is nowhere easy to park a boat once off the water. It seems even more subject to water movement. A vertical band of iron rungs up the sheer wall looks very off-putting, but in fact, there are steps too. Access to the top is possible from here, if conditions on the day demand this landing be used.

Tides

Tides flow strongly past Dursey Head. On the ebb, a distinct line of smooth/rough water stretches unbroken all the way to the Calf, with the run off extending well out towards the Cow. Lea Rock lies just a cable or so off Dursey Head,

77

and considerable turbulence may be expected here, so keep away, between the Rock and the Head. The ebb seems to run from the Head towards the Cow, or a bit N. The flood is the reverse. The flows are very strong off the corners of the outer islands.

Tides flood E along both sides of Dursey Island and S through Dursey Sound, from HW Cobh -0500 to +0130. On the flood though, there is extensive eddying in the bay between the S entrance to Dursey Sound and Crow Head to the S. The flood and ebb at Dursey Head and outside start a little later.

Embarkation

Launch from Dursey Sound or White Strand Quay, as described previously in the Dursey Island section.

SPA

Storm Petrel.

The Cow

V425-397	Sheet 84

Halfway between Dursey Head and the Bull lies the Cow at V425-397. Landing by kayak on the Cow seems impossible for all practical purposes and has never been achieved that is known. The Cow is an inhospitable place. Sheer walls surround it. A mighty sea arch lies off its SE side, and the passage out is challenging. Along the S side of the island lies a thin, offshore rock called Gull Rock, which provides shelter for a rest on passage. Lesser Black-backed Gull.

The Calf

V442-377	Sheet 84

The Calf, 21m high, lies 1.5km SW of Dursey Head, with its off-lying rock, the Heifer, about half its size and height. There is a red iron pillar on the Calf, the stub of a lighthouse destroyed in 1881. Nothing is known of its landability.

Allihies Bay

A truly beautiful place. Stony mountains of remote and rugged appearance back the bay. The village has little more than basic facilities. The main strand and pier at V573-443 below the town is backed by machair, and has a paying campsite. There is a magnificent, sheltered strand at the pier and slip at White Strand Quay in the extreme SW of the bay, at V523-428, where campervans are discouraged.

Long Island

V524-429	Sheet 84

Small grassy sheep-grazed island immediately opposite the popular quay at White Strand Quay in Garinish Bay, in the SW of Allihies Bay. There is a quay opposite the mainland quay and matching sheltered strands. Shore angling is popular off its outer rocks. No water. Nice camping. Obvious put in point for Dursey Island.

Garinish Island

V523-432	Sheet 84

Almost split in two at HW, this island is separated from the mainland except at LW and lies just NW of Long Island, which together form absolute shelter for White Strand Quay. Grazed by sheep. Cliffy on its N side. Possible rock climbing here and on the mainland on Garinish Point at V520-430 to the W.

Coulagh (Eyeries) Bay

A beautiful bay of superb scenery that is all the better for being somewhat off the tourism track. Sheltered from all but strong NW winds. There are only basics available in Eyeries village. There is a choice of embarkation points but perhaps the most central and convenient might be the pier below the village. Launch at its sheltered storm beach at V642-514. The pier is 1km NW of the village.

Illaunnameanla

V646-528	Sheet 84

Small, ungrazed island, hard in against the N shore of the bay. Many seals. Interestingly, it seems to be a maritime horticultural experimental area. There are many different types of young trees planted. Land on the E side. Nice.

Eyeries Island

V635-519	Sheet 84

Small, flat, sheep-grazed island with spots of sand on the SE side for landing. Camping maybe, water no. Unattractive.

Black Ball Harbour, Co. Cork - Séan Pierce

Inishfarnard

V600-527   Sheet 84

Splendid big lump of a formerly inhabited island, with a fish farm off its SE side. The whole island is attractive to visit, with a distinct ridge, sheep, and abandoned houses and fields. No water was found, though there must have been at one time. The population was once 24. There are many nice cliffs and arches on the N side.

Landing and Camping

The main landing for boats is not so convenient for kayaks, as it is a deep-water landing. It is in a cove inside the fish farm on the SE side, at V609-529. Better altogether for kayaks is onto a choice of storm beaches, the best of which is at V600-527, in a WSW facing cut on the N side, looking onto Bridaun. There is splendid camping 100m from the beach. Good fishing hereabouts also. Landing is possible at various tide levels on the ENE facing side of the waist at V602-526.

This is however less convenient, as large blocks make life awkward, though not at HW.

Another recommended spot for landing is near the E end of the N side in a NW facing cut, onto a storm beach at V607-531, where excellent camping is available after a small scramble.

Bridaun

V595-524   Sheet 84

Bridaun is the outer and larger of two islets off the W tip of Inishfarnard. Between Bridaun and Inishfarnard lies Bridaun Beg, which is separated from both by narrow cuts on each side. Grass covered but ungrazed. Bridaun and Bridaun Beg are of interest for their rock scenery, narrow channels and slots.

Kerry
Kenmare to the Dingle Peninsula
County Kerry

Sneem Harbour Islands

V693-638   Sheet 84

For this cluster of islands, launch from a slip at the mouth of the Sneem River. The entire bay between the Iveragh and Beara Peninsulas is called the Kenmare River. The slip is accessed down a 1.5km cul-de-sac off the main Ring of Kerry road. The turn off is about halfway between Sneem and the Parknasilla Hotel. The islands are described in an anticlockwise tour from the slipway.

Einaun Island

V690-636   Sheet 84

Wooded, coniferous, rhododendrons, mussels, uninhabited, wild, impassable either side at LW.

Garinish Island

V693633   Sheet 84

Lovely wooded, coniferous island with rhododendrons, huge ferns, seals and mussels. It is inhabited, somewhat tamed, and private. The channel to the N is impassable at LW. Many boats anchor in its quiet NE harbour. There are paths

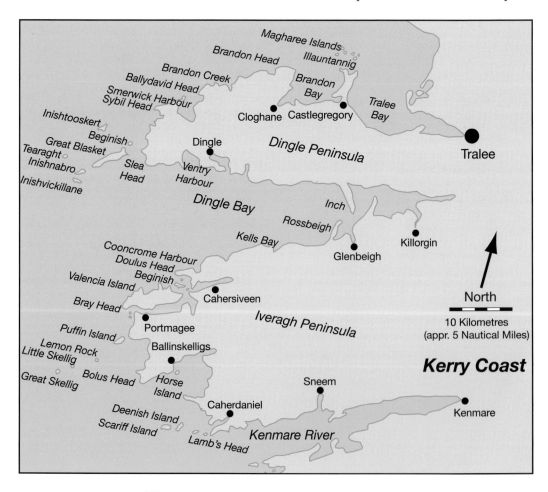

winding all over the island, ending at lovely little seating spots, where perhaps to sit and read? The only remote place to land is at an E-facing stone beach on the SE side, midway along the island.

Inishkeelaghmore

V685-623   Sheet 84

Grass-covered rock, but nice. Deep-water landing onto rocks in a vaguely defined cove towards the W end of the N side. There is an oceanic feel to the island, more than with any of the others in the group. There is a miniature rock climber's cliff on the S side.

Inishkeelaghbeg at V687-624 is really just a grass-covered rock off its N side.

Illaunleagh

V662-622   Sheet 84

About 500m off the shore. Land onto boulders in the NE-facing cove on the N side. Long grass and even longer ferns mar this once-grazed island. Camping just about possible, but no water. Panoramic. The most westerly of the group. Nice enough.

Carrigavunig at V676-625 is a useful waymark en route to the island. Just a rock.

Sherky Island

V690-616   Sheet 84

This is the largest of all this group, and specifically is the largest of the group of the three outermost islands, Sherky, Illaunanadan and Inishkeragh. Some decrepit houses are being over-run by sheep. No roads. Land at the NE under a prominent house inside the remains of a pier, which was clearly built by Ozymandias, and not by Nimmo.

"I am Ozymandias, king of kings.
Look on my works, ye mighty, and despair."
Percy Bysshe Shelley

(Nimmo was the great West of Ireland pier-builder and engineer of the 19th Century. Unlike those of Ozymandias, his works are a lasting testimony of what is achievable.)

There are also storm beaches midway along the NE side and at the NE end of the SE side. Unattractive.

Illaunanadan

V694-619   Sheet 84

Middle and least attractive of the three outer islands. Land on NE side. There are places for small tents.

Inishkeragh

V696-623   Sheet 84

Most attractive of the three outer islands. Storm beaches, almost joined up, run most of the SE side. There are multiple single tent places. A group could camp on the W side very nicely, which would mean a 100m walk.

Illaunslea

V700-637   Sheet 84

Illaunslea dominates the view immediately to the SE of the slipway. A wooded, coniferous, inhabited, somewhat tamed and private island with rhododendrons and seals. Of no apparent interest to the passer-by.

Lamb's Head Group

V525-566   Sheet 84

This group of islands on the SW tip of the Iveragh Peninsula extends over a wide area. It ranges from sheltered islands close inshore in the SE, to Ballinskelligs Bay to the NW. Lamb's Head itself is central, and is usually visible. The islands may be accessed from a range of points.

The central islands include the biggest and remotest of the whole area, and perhaps may be most easily reached from a working harbour at the end of the road to Lamb's Head. For campers, this spot is the business - panoramic, sheltered, calm water for swimming, fishing, and a noted rock climbing spot.

Islets off Castle Cove

This group of islets off the E side of Castle Cove Bay is reached most easily from the beautiful White Strand at V606-597, 50m off the main Ring of Kerry road.

Illaunacummig

V609-594   Sheet 83 / Sheet 84

This is the largest of the group. Land at a small beachlet at the NE corner, closest to the

Early morning off the Kerry coast, Co. Kerry - Séan Pierce

mainland. Long grass and gorse. No water. No camping. Few redeeming features. To the E is Illaunakeesha at V611-594, to the SE is Daniels Island V611-592 and to the SW, Illaunnanoon at V606-593, all requiring deep-water landings. Most of the fragmented Cammarna group of islets at V605-596, near the launching place at White Strand, may be accessed on foot at most stages of the tide. Paradoxically, these are the nicest of the lot hereabouts, for a few hours quiet sunbathing, if nothing else.

No water, no camping.

Illaunsillagh

V620-599   Sheet 83 / Sheet 84

Almost a double island, being more or less cut in the middle. The cut provides a shingle beach on its landward-facing, N side. Long grass and gorse, ungrazed, uninhabited. Very close in by the Iveragh shore, the channel is very narrow and seals and mullet play tag in the shallow lagoon. Its merit is in its privacy so close to so much.

No water, no camping.

Illaunnaweelaun

V550-571   Sheet 84

An unexpected wee jewel of a grass and heather covered, ungrazed hump. It is separated from Lamb's Head to its N by a 50m wide sound, and then by Burned Island at V549-570. Burned Island is barely detached from the land, and is meritless. There will always be a sheltered landing point somewhere along the length of the sound, almost regardless of conditions, onto sloping rocks.

The rock architecture along the S side will, some day, provide magnificent rock climbing. This will be of high calibre on good red sandstone, 'clean as a whistle', and of all grades. The hardest and best route would be under the summit itself at 27m. This is the best 'secret crag' this writer has seen in many years.

Launch from Rath Strand to its N at V549-578, or more dependably from the huge Wavecrest Caravan Park at V554-581.

Lamb's Island

V533-561   Sheet 84

This very steep, conical islet is detached from Lamb's Head to its N by a 50m wide sound. A deep-water landing is possible on the E side of the sound. Here it is just possible, with great care, to scramble to the summit. Perhaps only a frustrated ex-climber would bother. There are lovely views from the top.

Two Headed Island

V514-561   Sheet 84

Grass-covered lump of rock, almost cut in half at a midway waist. On the NW-facing side of the waist is a deep sheltered pool, where a deep-water landing is possible. Beware - the entrance to the pool is narrow and beset by turbulence during big sets. Get your timing right entering and leaving. No water, and no camping. Marvel at the raised storm beach in the middle.

Moylaun Island

V500-563   Sheet 84

Grass covered lump of rock. Sheep were reportedly landed on the eastern side of the NE point, at a ramp inside an almost broken away rock. All of this is uninviting to kayakers. Much commitment would be required. Kayakers might prefer a deep-water landing in the cove on the W side. No water and no camping.

Deenish Island

V469-561   Sheet 84

Lovely 144m high island, well out to sea. There is a fish farm in the bay on the NE side. 17 Chough were counted in one flock on 28th August 1995. Overall, superb.

Landing

There is an easy landing in a cove in the S extremity of the E-facing Deenish Harbour. This is under the prominent house onto a sandy beach. At HW however, the beach is stony. The strand can be hard to see behind boulders at LW.

Tides

Tides run in the sound inside Deenish, reaching 1kn in springs. The flood reunites off the N tip of Deenish causing turbulence locally. They run N with the flood and S with the ebb, to and from HW Cobh -0100.

Camping

Good camping abounds. Water was found in a good well up behind the house.

Scariff Island

V454-560   Sheet 84

This is a huge, 252m high, exposed, mountainous lump of a truly offshore island; it was once inhabited by monks. There is an old oratory, very high up, roughly in the middle. There are the remains of a more recent inhabitation lower down, all on the SE side. Local lore says that the children of the settlement got measles and died, ending the human colonisation of the island.

The undergrowth is mostly quite long, and despite there being no obvious grazing, gorse has not conquered all. Wellingtons are suitable for general exploration of the long grass and ferns of the island, even on the finest days. Reports of good spring water could not be confirmed even though old wells were found.

There is the appearance of a path down along sloping ground to a cove midway along the S side of the island, called Lamb's Cove. There is a wall down to the head of the cove. This may perhaps have been to facilitate fishing. The Farbregagh (literally - imitation man) at the N tip is a huge sea arch.

Landing

Access is by a relatively sheltered, deep-water landing in a small cove in the NE corner, called Coosaneeve. Here, the monks cut a stairs of splendid steps in the solid rock (as monks did). These are wondrous to behold. They go all the way down to LW, and are hard to see until very close in, so perseverance is recommended. Local information suggests that the water in the cove is calmer on a dropping tide, but the logic for this is obscure.

Tides

Tides run more strongly in the sound between Scariff and Deenish than they do inside Deenish, reaching 1.5kn in springs. On the flood, the tides reunite off the N tip of Deenish causing turbulence locally. They run N with the flood and S with the ebb, to and from HW Cobh -0100.

Abbey Island

V522-583   Sheet 83 / Sheet 84

Abbey Island is named for the early Christian abbey at V522-583, in the NE corner. This overgrown island is attached to the mainland to the NE by a spit of sand, except at the highest of spring tides or the wickedest of storms. The graveyard attached to the abbey is still in use. Where the island abuts the mainland, there are sandy beaches on each side. To the NW lies the sheltered Derrynane Harbour. To the NE lies Derrynane Bay, with its famous surf beach reaching towards the beautiful Lamb's Head peninsula. ENE lies the popular holidaymaking village of Caherdaniel. The S and W coasts of Abbey Island are cliffy and give a good bounce most of the time. The W side is indented and interesting.

No water and no camping.

Lamb's Island

V516-585   Sheet 83 / Sheet 84

Lamb's Island lies NNW of Abbey Island and is separated from it by the narrowest of deep channels. The channel may dry at the lowest of spring tides. This island combines with Abbey Island to shelter Derrynane Harbour at V517-287. The harbour is used equally by working and pleasure boats, including in summer, a windsurfing and canoeing school. Camping is possible at the outside end of the narrow channel at V516-585, with some privacy despite so many holidaymakers. The beaches are gravel and therefore uninteresting to most tourists. There is a decrepit fish-holding tank at the N end. The SW side is indented and interesting.

Horse Island

V437-644   Sheet 83

A most attractive, formerly-inhabited island just E of Ballinskelligs Pier at V433-644. There are two former dwellings, the lower of which is being restored. The island is high to its SW. The W and S sides of the island are cliffy and give a bouncy circumnavigation under most circumstances. The E side has some intertidal beaches in coves. At least one of these is so obscured as to give a smuggler or piratical feeling. Sea urchins.

Landing and Camping

Land at a mud beach on N side. Behind the upper dwelling, there is a well with good water beside a wall. Camping at beach.

Valencia (or Valentia) Group

V373-730   Sheet 83

Portmagee Bridge is the epicentre of this varied group of islands, ranging from the Skelligs in the SW, to Beginish in the NE and including the mother of the group, Valencia Island itself. Also included is a guide to the coastline from Puffin Island in the SW to Rossbeigh in the NE.

Embarkation

The embarkation place for the south-westerly islands of the group is at Portmagee. Launching is difficult enough, being over weedy flats. This is achieved from the car park at the bridge, from the pier, or further down Portmagee village. The village is a cul-de-sac, which incorporates pubs, restaurants, and a simple grocery shop. The 'Skellig Experience Interpretive Centre' (reputedly well worth the visit) is on the island side of the bridge.

Ferries go from Portmagee to Skellig.

Great Skellig

V250-608   Sheet 83

Nothing that the visitor has read or been told about this island, nor even the sight of it from near or far, at dawn or dusk, will prepare one for the reality when one lands.

Monks

Monks inhabited the island from at least the 6th Century. A monastic settlement thrived here through Europe's Dark Ages. Inhabitation may be much older, as monks were most practical individuals, well capable of adopting, adapting and improving on the practices of those who went before them. The settlement consists of beehive-type huts, built on the very summit. Actually, they are built on the secondary of two such summits, but only a pedant would say so.

Keep clear of the actual summit of the island, which requires climbing. Many have ascended and been unable to descend.

Beehive cells, Great Skellig, Co. Kerry - David Walsh

The visitor will be left incredulous at the system of roads and pathways accessing the different parts of the island. Those who conceived and built what is to be seen here wouldn't remove their caps in the presence of those who built the pyramids.

Marvel at the pathways and walls, the stone staircases, the dwellings, the churches, the sheer drops everywhere. Some parts of the Skellig are very dangerous, and for the avoidance of doubt, there are no shops, facilities of any kind, or toilets. There is definitely no drinking water, despite some literature saying otherwise. The many wells are disused and unclean.

Embarkation

For the kayaker, the Skelligs are a major challenge. They are further out from a landing than any other island dealt with in this guide. Further, there is a serious risk that on arrival, conditions will not be suitable to land. Therefore, the trip should only be undertaken in settled weather. Ideally, choose dead calm conditions. In any event, do *not* choose wind from the E/NE. Alternatively, those fit enough to turn round and

go home again without breaking their journey could try. The journey out is about 20km from Portmagee, or about 3 hours for an average, competent group. Therefore, the level of fitness required across the party should not be underestimated. The Skelligs are thought to be, from certain perspectives, the single most committing paddle in Ireland.

Three launching options present themselves:

1. Portmagee is the normal departure point. The journey is a bit longer, but the put-in or take-out is always dependable. Launching is a bit awkward, being over weedy flats, but manageable.

2. A return journey in only 5 hours is possible from a small beach called Keel in Saint Finan's Bay at V390-685. This though, is less dependable, as it surfs. It saves half an hour's paddle, each way, not inconsiderable if the journey has to be done both ways.

3. Also in Saint Finan's Bay, and 2km closer again, is Boat Cove at V376-686, reached from the road by a 500m track down to a

pier and slipway in a small harbour, known locally as Glen Pier. Ferries go from Glen Pier to Skellig.

The problem with launching from anywhere but Portmagee is that, in anything but calm conditions, Saint Finan's Bay is an inherently hazardous place. There are cliffs for many kilometres either side of the beach and harbour, and the beach is liable to surf. Portmagee offers a calm put-in or take-out at all times, on a main road. Saint Finan's Bay must therefore be of interest only to those on passage, on holiday in the immediate area, or in exceptionally calm weather. The difference in the journey for those fit enough for the task does not outweigh the logistics involved in finding the right conditions. This applies to going and, particularly, coming back hours later.

Breaking the journey

There is the possibility of reducing the overall commitment level in terms of non-stop kilometres to be travelled. At V345-679, Puffin Island may be landed on, leaving a 13km journey 'only'. Puffin may be reached from Portmagee at about 7/8km to the NE, or at 4.5km from Keel to the E. Routing via Puffin has the further advantage that it, then Lemon Rocks, then Little Skellig, then Great Skellig, all form one long straight line. Beware, the line is not dead straight, but is very usable. Also, this route crosses the tidal flow at right angles making navigation simpler.

Tides

Between the Skelligs and the coast the tides flood N and ebb S to and from about HW Cobh -0100. They achieve a spring rate mid-channel of 1.5kn. Local HW is HW Cobh -0100.

Landing

The landing is on the NE tip of the island, looking across to the Little Skellig. It is a small pier with narrow, steep steps, up which the kayak must awkwardly be carried. These steps have no handrail. Rope work and teamwork may be necessary, especially at LW. Arriving while the tour boats are present (1100 to 1700 hrs. approximately) may greatly increase these problems.

Two other landings may be possible should conditions dictate. There is a sheltered bay in the SW, where a landing may be forced under the new lighthouse at V246-604, onto a steeply shelving ramp, but which goes nowhere. There is a much better landing onto disused steps at V247-607 in a deep bay, called Blue Cove, on the NW side. It seems these steps are usable only at HW, so some planning is required. There are carved steps and a disused pathway up onto the main parts of the island. The present condition of the path is unknown. It is reported that Dúchas intend to improve this path to provide some flexibility. In any event, a waystop is fairly dependable here at HW (HW Cobh -0100).

Camping

Parties day-tripping should leave the mainland early to maximise their day, but parties overnighting might leave in late afternoon. The island is under the joint control of Dúchas and the Commissioners of Irish Lights, from whom permission may be sought to overnight. Apply well in advance. Dúchas are refurbishing the Skellig environment generally, as well as excavating archaeologically.

There is nowhere for a tent, and no question of a bivouac anywhere but on the NE pier itself. The whole question of access policy with regard to the island is very fluid, and nothing should be taken for granted. Arrive well equipped and well victualled, just in case. The reaction of the authorities to your arrival may be influenced by how you, your gear, your attitude and your competence come across.

Lighthouse

The lighthouse was commissioned in 1826 and automated in 1987. The light character is 3 white flashes every 10 seconds.

SPA

Peregrine, Chough, Storm Petrel, Leach's Petrel.

Birds

In the darkest hours of night, the Kittiwake finally go quiet in time for the Manx Shearwater to set up their incomparable cacophony, their hysterical shrieking, their blood curdling

Aag-<u>aah</u>-mem-non

Aag-<u>aah</u>-mem-non

Aag-aah-<u>mem</u>-non

Aag-aah-<u>mem</u>-non

Off Great Skellig, Co. Kerry - Fred Cooney

The birds come ashore only for a couple of hours each night during the breeding season. They even spend their winter out in mid-ocean. They call (to use the most neutral term possible) so that their young can identify them and answer back. Where they breed, they breed in huge colonies.

To say there are Puffin on the Great Skellig is an understatement. Nowhere else may the tourist see these crazy birds in Halloween masks in such numbers. They can be seen at close quarters and are easily photographed. Much film is wasted until the visitor slowly realises how really close one may get to these wee creatures. There are also large numbers of Kittiwake and many Storm Petrel.

Little Skellig

V270-618   Sheet 83

Very much the support act for its famous neighbour, Little Skellig nevertheless has a character all its own. It is home to seriously vast numbers of Gannet, which inhabit every non-vertical inch of its mighty whitewashed cliffs. Best wear a wide brimmed hat and don't look up! The island has its own awe-inspiring shape that may have inspired Disney. It is possible, though difficult, and certainly pointless, to effect a landing there. Nobody is going anywhere in this vertical world. There are sea arches also, most of which go nowhere.

Lemon Rocks

V309-637   Sheet 83

Truly an excellent waystop when going to or from the Skelligs, if conditions are really calm. Tides run strongly in the shallows so otherwise keep away.

Puffin Island

V345-679   Sheet 83

A big, high, chunky island at the NW tip of Saint Finan's Bay, about 5km S of the entrance to Portmagee Channel. The cliffs on all sides are huge, except on the E, where it is difficult to find a flat grassy bit to camp on. The island is split N/S midway along. Puffin, rabbits and sea-pink abound. This is a lovely, wild, pleasant, 'must' of an island.

Little Skellig, Co. Kerry - Séan Pierce

Landing

Deep-water landings may be had in a number of places but nowhere better than in a sheltered, SE-facing, bouldery cove just S of the narrowest part of Puffin Sound. Tether to ropes left there by local scuba divers and fishermen for lunch stops. There is good clear water at all times in a well-filtered pool to one side, under a waterfall. An easy ramp gives access to the interior.

SPA

Peregrine, Chough, Storm Petrel.

Coastal Section - Saint Finan's Bay to Portmagee

V376-686 to V373-730, Sheet 83

This 9km coastal paddle can be twice that if pottering, especially if one includes a circuit of Puffin Island. Not to do so is to miss out on 'a magnificent piece of savage marine architecture, with dizzy cliffs carved and eroded by the Atlantic breakers and set at crazy angles by the mighty forces of past geological movements' – 'In the Kingdom of Kerry' by R.Hayward, 1945. Ideally,

calm conditions should prevail, to allow paddlers inside the many rocks and islands dotting this stretch. Vertical cliffs in excess of 100m contribute to the sense of exposure and commitment.

Embark at the pier 3km inside Puffin Sound, known locally as Glen Pier at V376-686, where there are some fishing boats and scuba-diver traffic. This has two slipways and lots of parking space, but is exposed to the W. It is also the nearest access point for a paddle to the Skelligs. Before landing, look for a long narrow inlet almost opposite the slipway, which leads to a long low arch with a few openings to the sky - though this wee adventure needs HW.

From Puffin northwards, there is only the 'savage grandeur of the rock-bound, storm besculptured coast'. The islands - Horse, Long, Short and Black Rocks, guard the entrance to the main Portmagee Channel. Opposite them are a number of deep inlets where landings can be made onto gravel or stones. Much easier landings are to be had onto gravel beaches just inside the headland delimiting the channel proper. Approaching the Portmagee Channel, avoid the fishing boats, and in summer, the numerous Skellig ferries. Land at Portmagee at V373-730.

Long Island

V347-725   Sheet 83

This much-fragmented island lies to the SE (mainland) of the western entrance to Portmagee Channel. The highest part of the island is rocky, and this is the only one of the group which is grazed. No water is evident. An earthen, circular mound is apparent, showing an early Christian site, and an associated killeen, or children's graveyard. Prominent Bull Rock stands off the W tip. Long channels separate the various parts of the island.

Short Island is separated from Long Island by a cliff-lined, long, narrow channel, and Black Rock is the substantial rock just off Short Island.

Landing

Deep-water landings are easy. One is onto sheltered rocks facing the mainland. If there is no swell, another is possible onto a slab about one third the way down the adjoining narrow channel. This has the more difficult access to the top.

Horse Island

V347-727   Sheet 83

Grazed by sheep, this small grassy island lies just NE of Long Island. The easiest landings face the mainland and Long Island. For the passer-by, this island marks a convenient landing and camping beach on the mainland directly inside it.

Approaching the mainland, look for an obvious cave, which dries, with a small blowhole. After landing, note the warning signs, which restrict access to a major blowhole. The old maps show a tunnel linking the cave to the major blowhole, but which is no longer evident. Deaf Rocks are a string of substantial rocks running alongside and separated from Horse Island.

Valencia (or Valentia) Island
Oileán Dairbhre

V370-730   Sheet 83

Population 700. A large and varied island lying ENE to WSW on the north-western tip of the Iveragh Peninsula. Valencia marks the southern tip of the entrance to Dingle Bay. Inside the island is the flat and sheltered Portmagee Channel, joining Knightstown in the NE to Portmagee in the SW.

Knightstown is the only town on the island. A ferry runs from here to the mainland opposite at Reenard. Portmagee is a town on the mainland to which the island is connected by a bridge. The bridge opens to allow larger vessels through. The outer parts of the island are 9km or so of committing cliffs, by far the most dramatic of which are at the W end at Bray Head at V327-725. There is only one waystop on the outside section, about halfway along.

A circumnavigation is an obvious challenge, being logistics free, but is quite long at 25km or so. Many interesting stops might be made, and there are committing stretches on the outside.

Tides

The tide flooding NE past the island to fill Dingle Bay enters Portmagee Channel from both ends simultaneously, meeting a couple of kilometres E of Portmagee. The flood rises from HW Cobh +0450 to –0135, about half an hour before local HW and LW. Streams reach 2kn at Portmagee itself, and 1.5kn at Knightstown and Fort Point Lighthouse.

Circumnavigation

To save effort, these tides should be carefully planned. A suggestion perhaps, presuming ever-present SW winds, is to embark from Portmagee on the last of the ebb. Utilise the slack/early flood up the exposed part of the coast. Then enjoy the full-blooded flood in, to, and past Knightstown, almost home.

Bray Head has a watchtower and huge overhanging cliffs, with fragmented rocks lying off the base with channels between them. NNE from here, reflected waves and strong tides, especially at the protruding points, make for an interesting passage.

The only waystop on the outside part of the island is onto a storm beach at V358-762, tucked inside Shrone Point in an E-facing cove. This is about halfway between Bray Head and Reenadrolaun Point, at the lowest part of this section of the island. It is reachable by boreen if neces-

Puffin - Séan Pierce

sary. There is good camping and water may be had in the nearby river. If the journey is broken on Horse or Long Island, just 8km of paddling will reach this point. Nevertheless, the steepest cliffs and strongest tides are in this section so expect to be challenged to some degree.

The cliffs on the E part of the outside are higher, but not as steep, and get a little shelter. Expect a bounce again at Reenadrolaun Point at V384-786, after which the going should ease considerably.

Overhead at this point is Valentia Radio, one of the main coastal radio stations of Ireland. The first transatlantic cable was laid from here to Trinity Bay in Newfoundland, a process that began in 1855. In 1857, the 'Agamemnon' was nearly lost in a great storm when the cable snapped, at the edge of the continental shelf, 560km out to sea. Later, in 1859, the 'Great Eastern' completed the whole of the task solo. Adjacent to the radio station is an abandoned slate quarry.

There is a good, sheltered beach just inside Fort Point lighthouse at V404-783, with camp-

ing in the grounds, for use in distress only. There is also a less convenient slip outside and W of the point, with better camping but a more awkward landing. Really, those looking to camp in isolation hereabouts would be better to go to nearby Beginish.

Knightstown is a pretty spot, worth visiting. All the island's facilities are here - pubs, restaurants, dive schools, lifeboat, ferry, harbour, sailing. The channel back to Portmagee has fine views, but should be avoided at LW or with contrary tides.

Illaunloughan

V366-731   Sheet 83

Illaunloughan is a small, low-lying island, about 400m from Portmagee. One may walk out to it from the mainland in low spring tides. This is an early church site, and the burial place of 'children and adult strangers'. There are ongoing 'digs' and some re-building by overseas research groups. There is a stone-lined, spring-fed, holy well on the S side. A few steps lead down to it, and it has a large stone lintel for a roof. Water quality is questionable, due to lack of use.

Beginish

V424-786   Sheet 83

Inappropriately named, (*Beginish* translates as 'Small Island'), this quite large and lovely inhabited island sits in the middle of the ENE entrance to Portmagee Channel. There is a prominent watchtower on top. The residential section is entirely on the western side of the island. The views are idyllic, but are perhaps just a tad too near civilisation.

Archaeological excavations have revealed early field systems. Also revealed is a reasonably preserved semi-submerged dwelling. This has a ramp leading down to the doorway. The ramp is now sand covered. This construction is unique for its time and is accepted as a Viking settlement. It was probably used as a stopping place during sea voyages between Cork and Limerick. Further digs are planned to reveal an expected burial ground. It is thought-provoking to note that, at the end of the 19th Century, there was sand to a depth of seven feet on this side of the island. Erosion, and especially the introduction of rabbits, led to huge loss of sand in about 50 years. This led to the exposure of the Viking settlement. On the southern side, W of the waist, are the remains of an early Church site. Also nearby is a killeen, and a small standing stone with crosses inscribed on both sides.

Camping

The best camping is on the southern side of the E end. Here the island is waisted and the land is machair, backed by little hillocks. These have pleasant beaches both sides, sandy on the N and pebbled on the S.

Church Island

V430-786   Sheet 83

Church Island lies just E of Beginish. One may walk to it from Beginish at very LW. Otherwise, land at sheltered rocks on S side. Named for its rectangular church, of which two walls are in ruins. There is also a good circular dwelling. The two buildings are quite obvious. Dúchas attempts at preservation were not very successful. Look for the wall system around the island, which marked all ground inside as consecrated. Only 'Holy Men' could sleep inside. A small gap,

still visible, on the E side, allowed 'lay' people day visits to the Church. There are the remains of a 'special' grave on the S side. There is also a water collection hole at the back of the circular building, of suspect quality.

Embark from the N end of a beautiful, sheltered, beach, White Strand at V435-794. Good car park at northern end.

Lambs Island

V420-791   Sheet 83

An ungrazed, small, dull lump of an island, NE of Beginish. No water was found. No camping. Land at a spit in the SE, facing the N beach on Beginish.

Launch from White Strand.

Coastal Section
Reenard Point to Rossbeigh

V434-776 to V645-910, Sheets 83 / 70 / 78

This trip describes the S side of Dingle Bay, from Reenard Point at V434-776, outside Cahersiveen, to Rossbeigh Beach at V645-910, a distance of about 32km. It is a trip of two distinct sections. The first is more remote, with a mountain ridge separating road from sea, with the mountain dropping to the sea in sheer cliff faces. There are two deep inlets on this part, both with sheltered piers.

The second section has numerous stopoff places, and where steep earth and rock banks rise to the main road which parallels the shore, high overhead.

Reenard Point at V433-776 is the easiest embarkation place for car access, being close to the main road. A summer ferry runs from here to Valencia. There is a superb seafood pub on the pier. Alternatively, the beach at White Strand (NE of Church Island at V436-793) can be used. Admire in passing, the extensive beach on NE Beginish.

Rounding Doulus Head at V404-804, next along are Cooncrome (pronounced Coosecrown) Harbour at V444-816 and Coonanna Harbour at V480-842. Both are wide, deep harbours with pier and beach but no other facilities.

The onward trip is just as committing with the next landing about 10km away at Kells Bay at

V555-880. Kells Bay is a wide, deep inlet, with a sheltered pier - a noted beach and holiday spot. On the way, look for a stream falling clear to the water, where the cliffs form a bottleneck into which you must go to get under the waterfall. Also on the way, you come to Gull Rocks at V520-873, which are really little islands - sheer, high and close to the cliff-lined land. There is a sense of isolation around them.

Finish at Rossbeigh (or Rossbehy) beach and sand dunes. This is a noted family beach, a typical machair, with hotel and holiday village. There is even a small sweet shop and chip shop, open during summer. The council maintain public toilets, water, and rubbish collection. They charged €7 per tent per night in 2002. Pitch where you like, except in the football field or tennis courts. Rossbeigh can have decent surf, and the dunes have been mapped for orienteering events. This area has been and remains *the* meeting ground for all Irish paddlers and surfers for the Christmas/New Year break.

The Dingle Peninsula
Corca Dhuibhne

Coastal Section
Dingle Town to Slea Head

Baile an Daingin go Ceann Sléibhe

Q445-010 to V317-967 Sheet 70

Dingle is a major fishing and tourist town, at the head of a sheltered bay. Embark at the harbour or from a small car park at V453-997, halfway out the harbour on the E side. Paddlers and dolphin watchers have been known to camp near the old tower. There is a path into town from here along the shoreline. If you are a small group, you will have the luxury of being greeted by 'Fungie', the local friendly dolphin, an experience not to be missed. However, you must also work your way around the many tour boats trying to spot him.

Only the mouth of Dingle Harbour is narrow, and once inside the bay opens wide. Buoys guide the fishing and yachting craft to the extensive harbour facilities.

The trip to Slea Head is 16km without landings, unless a detour is made into Ventry Har-bour - *Cuan Fionntrá*, halfway along. Hug the cliff line, and in calm water explore the many arches, caves, coves, and stacks.

If visiting Ventry, land at a pier on the south-western side, 1.5km in, at the S end of a sandy beach. In the harbour, there are some fish-farming cages and sometimes basking shark.

Blasket Islands - *Na Blascaodaí*

Sheet 70

This group of islands, the most westerly, not only in Ireland but in continental Europe, is surely the finest in the country. There is a regular ferry to the Great Blasket only. There is little in the way of anchorages for bigger boats at the outliers, which are also rugged and exposed. Therefore, sea kayakers are privileged to have the finest way to explore the group as a whole. The Blaskets are a showpiece of Irish sea kayaking. That said, among the outliers, only Beginish and Inishvickillane have landings that are in any way dependable. Good conditions are needed elsewhere to avoid having to swim ashore, or worse. Expect to have to work for any landing. The commitment of the group should be consistent.

The islands are uninhabited. Great Blasket was abandoned in 1954. Earlier in the century, 215 people lived there. There was also a single house on Inishvickillane. The Great Blasket now only has summer homes and there is one on Inish-vickillane. There is an interpretive centre for the islands on the mainland at Dún Chaoin.

Embarkation

There are several places from which to embark, none of which are easy.

Q314-002   Dún Chaoin Pier, from which the ferry operates, is the logical embarkation place, being sheltered. It has good parking, less than private camping, no water, but the pier is reached by a most unpleasant, steep carry. Launching is off a very steep slipway, or to one side in calm conditions. Group co-operation is often necessary.

Q312-005   There is a small bouldery beach at the end of the laneway past the interpretive centre, which may be suitable for small groups in settled conditions.

Q316-033   Clogher beach has a car park above but can surf with any swell from the W.

An Trá Bán, Great Blasket, Co. Kerry - Séan Pierce

V313-981   Coumeenoole or Slea Head beach lies almost 1.5km N of Slea Head itself, tucked inside Dunmore Head (V302-980). It gives a shorter trip. It often surfs, yet has merit for embarkation. With N winds, or when calm, it is very much the preferred option. The carry is better than the pier at Dún Chaoin, and the parking is excellent.

Tides

Tides in the Blasket Sound - *An Bealach*, and elsewhere through the islands, flood N and ebb S, twisting with the channels. An exception is the channel between Inishnabro - *Inis na Bró* and Inishvickillane - *Inis Mhicileáin*, in which the flow is always W. The tide races in the sounds, including Blasket Sound, have a fierce reputation. The N-going flood starts at about Cobh HW +0430 and the S-going ebb at -0130. Local HW and LW are about Cobh -0110, so the streams turn about half an hour ahead of the local HW and LW. The stream timings are affected by strong winds. In particular, sustained southerlies make the flood run for longer and stronger.

The speed of the tidal streams in the main channels varies, but is generally 1 - 3kn. In the narrower channels, in springs, the stream can reach up to 4kn, except between Inishnabro and Inishvickillane, where it is always weak.

In Blasket Sound, the N-making flood rushes past Dunmore Head - *An Dún Mór*, at V302-980, and eddies clockwise around Dún Chaoin Bay. Small boats could do worse than follow the example of the ferry, which follows the coast SW almost to Dunmore Head before crossing the sound. In wind, this may also get your boat above the bumpier parts of the tidal race, for a much smoother passage. On the S-making ebb tide, try a more northern route, taking shelter from Beginish.

Beware of reported local magnetic anomalies.

Bibliography

Recommended reading must start with 'Twenty Years A-Growing' by Maurice O'Sullivan, translated from the Irish (*Fiche Blíain ag Fás*),

For a more complete list, add the following:

Great Blasket, Co. Kerry - David Walsh

'The Islandman' (*An tOileánach*) by Tomás O'Criomhtháin

'Peig' by Peig Sayers

'An Old Woman's Reflections' by Peig Sayers

'The Western Island – The Great Blasket' by Robin Flower

' The Blaskets, People and Literature' by Muiris Mac Conghail

'Méini - The Blasket Nurse' by Leslie Matson

'Letters from the Great Blasket' by Eibhlís ní Shúilleabháin

'Island Cross Talk' by Tomás Ó'Crohán

'A Pity Youth does not Last' by Micheál O'Guiheen

'The Blasket Islands – Next Parish America' by Joan Stagles

'Island Home - The Blasket Heritage' by George Thomson

'Blasket Memories' edited by Pádraig Tyers

'Hungry for Home' by Cole Morton

SPA

Peregrine, Chough, Storm Petrel, Leach's Petrel, Barnacle Goose, Greenland White-fronted Goose, Common & Arctic Tern.

The 'outer four' Blaskets, Tearaght, Inishtooskert, Inishnabro and Inishvickillane, boast internationally important numbers of breeding Storm Petrel and Manx Shearwater.

The Great Blasket - *An Blascaod Mór*
V280-977   Sheet 70
Landing and Camping

If camping, choose between isolation and convenience. For isolation, land on White Strand –*An Trá Bán* at V277-980, near the ramp and camp just above. More conveniently, land at the unsatisfactory slipway at the pier at V280-977, SE of White Strand. The slip/pier is difficult to make out until close. The pier is somewhat sheltered, but some surge is always present. Even though the landing is slightly more awkward, the carry is shorter from boat to campsite. The camping hereabouts is most convenient among

Inishnabro Pinnacles, Co. Kerry - Mike McClure

the ruins of the village just above the pier. Water is from a tap high up at the south-eastern end of the village, convenient to the pier, but a longer walk from the beach.

Be aware that in 2003, a proposal went before Kerry County Council to ban all camping on the island. This was being fought by all right-thinking people. Should that battle be lost, there will undoubtedly be B&B available.

On a day trip, the *An Trá Bán* at V277-980 beach is easier.

There is a splendid cafe for daytime snacking. Rock climbing has been opened up on the island, with a cliff just SW of Gurraun Point at V283-977 (the most E point of the island). Splendid walking tracks run high along both sides of the ridge of the island, like a necklace, giving an excellent circuit. On circumnavigation, tides run strongly at the three corners. The lee side of the island is often subject to fierce downblasts of wind. Tides run strongly in Black Sound between Inishnabro and Great Blasket, where the wind can be funnelled and strengthened.

The narrow gap off the northern tip is subject to sudden unexpected surges or boomers as big sets pass. Through this gap go circumnavigators or venturers to the outlying islands. The passage is between a rock off the main island and a small islet at V272-985, being the innermost in a string of such rocks. In an autumn gale in 1588, one of the largest ships of the escaping Spanish Armada entered Blasket Sound and ran safety through this gap. Thus they performed one of history's most remarkable pieces of seamanship. Two other Armada ships were wrecked locally.

Inishnabro - *Inis na Bró*

V212-925   Sheet 70

Landing

Landing is midway on the south-eastern side, in a tiny cove. The entrance to the cove is under a tall narrow arch, into a sheltered pool, open to the sky. The landing is onto boulders, and very much subject to surge and scend, especially in SW winds. The cove runs SW/NE and is unmissable when travelling from the SW, but is hard to see going the other way. The cove is distinctly the tallest along this side, opposite Inishvickillane - *Inis Mhicileáin*. It is situated just E of the only shallow bay along. Here there are the remains of a stone wall overhead, just visible when close. Scramble up the gully behind. The tall arched entrance is narrow but the pool is wider.

Kayakers with laden boats have found this landing very difficult with any swell running. Inishvickillane - *Inis Mhicileáin*, is more reliable altogether for those in the outer regions of the Blaskets.

The island looks like it is covered with heather, but this is actually solid Sea Pink on the S side. There are magnificent cliffs on the N. The island is distinctly saddled when seen from N or S. There is a fantastic array of buttresses on the E end. The cliffs of the N side are huge and impressive.

Landing place, Inishnabro, Co. Kerry - David Walsh

Tides

A tide race ebbs SE at the NE corner. Tides run strongly in the sound between Inishnabro and Great Blasket, and the wind can be funnelled. The flow in the sound between Inishnabro and Inishvickillane always flows weakly westwards, being an eddy of the main flow N/S in either direction. Therefore, there is often a lump in the narrow W end of the sound where tides collide.

Inishvickillane - *Inis Mhicileáin*
V207-916   Sheet 70

The most southerly of the group, this is a very attractive island. On a high plateau is a holiday home, outhouses, a deer herd, a helipad, and White Tailed Eagle (hopefully). The island is owned by a sometimes resident, colourful, cultured, popular yet controversial Dublin character. He merits police protection as a retired public figure and values his privacy. The house is designed to fit discreetly into the hillside, and is built of local stone and timber. The whole is an example of how these things might be done right. It is said the owner is present mostly in August, when kayakers should keep below the HW mark.

Below the house lies a cove at the NE corner of the island. Once there was a teleferique system here for uploading material. It is no longer operational, and has been left as an unsightly mess.

Landing

The landing is on the western end of the N side, opposite Inishnabro, just inside the narrows, onto a sheltered semicircular stony beach. This is the most dependable of all outlying landings. The always W-making current in the channel is weak, so the landing is only out of bounds in the severest of relatively rare easterlies. There is a retractable pontoon-landing device at steps on the point just N of the landing beach. The now disused path up from the beach is getting overgrown since the pontoon was installed at the nearby point, but is still manageable.

The island is much talked of in 'Twenty Years A-Growing' as a place inhabited by fairies. The outhouse is where O'Sullivan had his rabbits stolen in the dead of night by passing sailors, who left a tin of tobacco in payment. Paddlers

Inishvickillane, Blaskets, Co. Kerry - David Walsh

may find 'Mickey the Pillar' at the western end of the S side at V207-908, and Mickey can also be seen below the 'Hollow of the Eagles', the flat stretch of the plateau to the SW. Mickey is a pillar of rock, the top of which looks like a man sitting wearing a wide brimmed hat. Moon Cave is nearby. Circumnavigation is recommended for the spectacular rock scenery.

Tearaght - *An Tiaracht*

V177-947   Sheet 70

Tearaght is the most westerly and remote of all the Blasket islands. Up to its prominent lighthouse are steps and a funicular railway that appears as a vertical band. From any distance, this looks like an escalator up the face of the conical rock. The island appears as a single pinnacle from E and W, but from N or S it seems to be almost divided into two. A mighty tunnel pierces the col between the two parts.

Landing

There are standard landing platforms, with steps up, in the coves N and S of the arch, both on the E-facing side. There is no current flowing at either steps because the arch is shallow and non-navigable, certainly at LW. Though the swell is continuous, be prepared for a quite manageable, if very wet landing.

The western side, with the lighthouse, is 116m high and the eastern end is 200m high. The eastern side consists of jumbled blocks, which mean that a trip to the summit might be very difficult. Rock fall has damaged some of the paths and great care should be exercised exploring. There are breeding Puffin and Manx Shearwater.

The Tearaght is among the most committing paddles in Ireland.

Foze Rock - *An Feo*

V152-892   Sheet 70

Even more committing is the Foze Rock, 6km SSE of the Tearaght, and 5km SE of the gap between Inishvickillane and Inishnabro. It is anecdotally accepted that Kerry paddlers have been out there, but it is not known whether they landed. This is probably the most committing

Inishtooskert Pinnacles, Co. Kerry - Séan Pierce

paddle in Ireland. It is the most westerly landfall in Europe.

Beginish - *Beiginis*

V282-988   Sheet 70

Beginish means 'Small Island'. It is indeed a small island, NE of the Great Blasket, with a ruined house.

The landing place is onto a relatively sheltered, stony beach on the NW side, but also in shelter in bays on the NE and SE.

Significant numbers of tern - Common, Arctic and a few Roseate.

Inishtooskert - *Inis Tuaisceart*

Q236-002   Sheet 70

Inishtooskert means 'Northern Island'. It is a dramatic island with major cliffs on the NW side and a distinct cockscomb shape at NE end.

Landing

Landing is not easy, being onto a severely sloping slab, with little shelter, on the SE side. A handrail up from the top of the slab is visible when close in. There is a sheep pen on the grass above. From further out there is a large obvious dorsal-fin shaped slab, and the landing is just SW of this. Landings may be forced elsewhere in the lee of the island, but beware of steep scrambles. Unloaded, borrowed, plastic boats are an advantage.

The island features a minor monastic ruin at Q234-004, marked St. Brendan's Oratory, on the only flat section of the island in the SW. In more recent times, it was used as a domestic dwelling. There are fields around it. It is a low-lying, drystone hovel with a smoke hole on top, and a very narrow, low entrance. There is a local story of how the widow of a recently departed, corpulent husband got him out through this awkward entrance. She took him out in pieces. The island well repays the effort of landing.

St. Brendan's Oratory, Inishtooskert, Co. Kerry - David Walsh

Coastal Section -
Sybil Point to Brandon Point
Ceann Sibéal go Ceann Bhréanain

Q309-060 to Q528-173 Sheet 70

28km of stunning cliffs, broken only by the 2km width of Smerwick Harbour, the way-stop at Brandon Creek, and the 1km width of Sauce Creek. It is impossible and pointless to try to land elsewhere. Paddle close to the cliff line to appreciate the waterfalls, caves, arches, and many 'islands' of cliff, which merge with the background. The cliffs of the Three Sisters (*Triúr Deirfiúir*) and Sybil Point at the SW part of the section is a must.

Smerwick Harbour
Cuan Árd na Caithne

Q378-102   Sheet 70

Smerwick has a 2km wide mouth with Dunacapple Island at Q378-102 on the E side. The harbour holds this width for almost 4 southerly km, and is open to the N. Shelter, depending on the wind, can be had by tucking inside either

of the 'arms'. This is very much a tourist area with villages and sandy beaches.

A landing can be forced onto boulders immediately at the W end of the Sisters (about 4km NE of Sybil Point), but cliffs bar any ideas of making it a land escape route.

Brandon Creek - *Cuas Bhréanain*

Q422-120   Sheet 70

Locally known as *Cuas*, Brandon Creek is the more westerly of two similar inlets when viewed from the sea. There is safe landing in all weather onto a double slipway. It is the anchorage for the small, local fishing boats. Camping on the pier, or on the small, green area nearby. A river runs alongside but is litter strewn. Limited car parking - be tidy as this is a working pier, and the fishermen load and unload. The pub is 1.5km to the S with phone, food, and shower.

Walking NE to the cliff edge brings spectacular views and eventually joins a recognised track to Brandon Mountain. This creek was the launching point for the leather boat 'Brendan',

99

whose epic voyage was led by Tim Severin. They set out to show that, as with the legend, early Irish monks could have sailed to America via Scotland, the Faeroes, and Iceland. Their trip is detailed in the book 'The Brendan Voyage' by Tim Severin, an excellent read.

Sauce Creek

Q488-157   Sheet 70

Land onto gravel, or boulder at HW, and sometimes through dumping surf, the SW corner being best. No landward escape route, as there is a very steep scramble through loose, shale gullies onto the mountainside.

Magharee Islands
Oileáin an Mhachaire

Q623-215   Sheet 71

Also known in English as the Seven Hogs - *Na Seacht gCeanna*, this is a scattered group of (actually eight) small low islands. Nearby Lough Gill is well known as the stronghold of the Natterjack Toad. They lie on the northern side of the Dingle Peninsula, off Rough Point at the end of the isthmus, which divides Brandon Bay from Tralee Bay. Basking Shark and Blue Shark are reputed to be common in these waters in the summer months. The area teems with bird and other wildlife.

In Irish, the islands are called *Oileáin an Mhachaire*. Machair is a coastal feature consisting of a raised dune system immediately inside an exposed sandy beach, behind which there is often a flat grassy area. Machair is much loved by birds, (who call it a 'roost'), by sheep (who call it a 'meal'), by golfers (who call it a 'links'), and by tourists (who call it a 'campsite'). Certainly, its well-drained, short grass is excellent for camping.

Embarkation

Embarkation is from Scraggane Pier at Q613-196 just inside the W point of Scraggane Bay. There is a wide, gradually sloping slipway, ample paying campsites and toilets. A pub and shops can be found at Fahamore, 1km to the SW.

Tides

The sound is not deep, and can cut up rough, usually when a westerly wind or big swells are against the ebb tide. The E-going flood tide starts at HW Galway +0505 and the W-going ebb starts at HW Galway -0120. It flows at 2 or 3kn in springs. The tide also sweeps strongly through and to the N of the islands.

SPA

Common, Little & Arctic Tern, Chough, Barnacle Goose, and Great Northern Diver (Loon).

Illauntannig

Q623-215   Sheet 71

Illauntannig is the largest and most hospitable of all these islands. It boasts a summer home with outhouses, just in from the beach. It has plastic windows, double glazing, and its own private water collection system. Landing is easy at the steep, sandy beach on the E side, or elsewhere for those who like to scratch and scrape. Camping is most convenient at the landing beach, where shelter can be had behind walls. It is possible to camp almost anywhere else that a landing is made. The W side is the most exposed.

The monastic site just S of the beach has stone huts and oratories surrounded by a protective stone wall. The complex includes a well-preserved *souterrain* about 40m in length, leading from the central hut to beyond the outside wall.

The island is generally quite flat. Numerous Oyster Catcher and Tern (mostly Arctic) nest.

Reenafardarrig

Q625-217   Sheet 71

Nice grassy islet, just NE of Illauntannig, with landing possible on the sandy S shore opposite Illauntannig. The other sides are rocky. The island is separated from Illauntannig by a bar/reef, so that there are breakers coming through the gap, particularly at LW when underwater obstructions are a real danger. No water. There is a 3-sided, 1m high sheep shelter on top.

Illaunboe

Q619-218   Sheet 71

Illaunboe is almost joined to Illauntannig by a reef at LW. Landing is possible on the E side of this flattish island. The other sides have rocky foreshore. A stony, grassy islet, uninviting.

Monastery, Illauntannig, Co. Kerry – David Walsh

Mucklaghbeg

Q637-214   Sheet 71

A rocky knoll, 1.5km E of Illauntannig, with plenty of guano and birds. The technical difficulties would make landing 'interesting', even in calm weather.

Doonagaun Island

Q615-201   Sheet 71

A grassy knoll with a sandy SE side where a landing is possible. Landing elsewhere is rocky. Doonagaun is passed on the way out to Illauntannig. No water.

Illaunnanoon

Q605-198   Sheet 71

Just off the mainland coast, W of Scraggane Pier, this is a rocky outcrop with grass growing on top. A reef extends SW which is exposed at LW, and landing is possible on the S and SE sides. There is no water and this is not a place to go camping. There is interesting life in the exposed rock pools. Birds, grass, and rock.

Illaunimmil

Q605-221   Sheet 71

A larger member of the group, 2km WNW of Illauntannig. Landing is just possible, in calm weather, by a difficult deep-water landing, onto large boulders. This is a storm beach at a cave just on the sheltered (E-facing) side of the NE tip. There are cliffs all around the island. There is a second cave, midway along the E side, which is really a huge collapsed blowhole. Many Rock Dove nest in the arch overhead.

Inishtooskert

Q601-225   Sheet 71

Just NW off Illaunimmil, the island is surrounded by cliffs and shallow water. The swell builds all round on even the calmest days, breaking on the exposed reefs. Landing would always be very challenging.

The Mid-West
Shannon Estuary to Galway City
including the Aran Islands

County Kerry

Carrig Island

Q977-486   Sheet 63

The S/SW of the island is joined to the mainland by a small bridge and a spit of marshy, grassy land, covered only by high spring tides. Carrig also has an inhabited farm and a Napoleonic battery at Q977-486 on the NW. The population is 13.

The major attraction is the well-preserved Carrigafoyle Castle on the SE. The castle is more accessible from the water. Land at HW to avoid mud flats. The castle is a most interesting waystop, not to be missed by the passer-by. Thought to have been impregnable by 16th Century standards, Cromwell wasn't convinced, and he was proved right.

County Clare

Islands off Kilrush

The two low-lying islands off Kilrush make for an interesting day out. The area is particularly good for people teaching maritime skills, the tides being strong and even turbulent, yet enclosed and with a 'safe' feeling. The best embarkation place is at Cappagh Pier at Q985-540.

Tides

The ebb race between Hog Island and Cappagh Pier extends over 500m, extending NE from the eastern point of Hog to just off the pier itself. This is a splendid play area, fast and steep, yet enclosed and therefore safe enough. It is easy to escape, having distinct eddy lines. A swim, even a long one, deposits the swimmer close to a friendly shore, outside the gates of Kilrush Creek. Certainly comparable in power to the race at New Quay in the N of the county, the extra 'enclosed feeling' is a safety factor that makes it preferable.

Scattery Island

Q976-526   Sheet 63

The island seems to have been named for a dragon (*Cathach* in Irish, giving *Inis Cathach*). It has a long and varied history and its origins are mostly associated with St. Senan - born in 488 A.D. He founded the Christian settlement there in the 6th Century. It was a holy island until the Vikings took over for a century or so before being recaptured by Brian Boru in 975. The Vikings must have been pleasantly surprised when they first arrived, to find the access door to the round tower at ground level. This makes it the most easily accessible round tower in Ireland.

There is an abandoned village on the northern end of the E side. Many of the cottages are intact. The island was inhabited until 1978. No artificial fertiliser was ever used on these fields so the island is of ecological interest as a semi-wild grassland.

The lighthouse and battery are at the southern point. The battery is in good condition but access to the roof through the hole in the ceiling is now impossible. Metal grids prevent entry to the inside of the battery.

The lighthouse was first established in 1872.

There is what looks like a peat marina cut into the sod at the southern end of the E side. This is just N of the lighthouse. It could hardly have been a commercial success.

The island has plentiful rabbit and in 1999, Golden Plover and a Short-eared Owl.

Tides

The tidal streams between the mainland and the islands tend to be stronger than between the islands. In each case they flow SE with the flood and NW with the ebb.

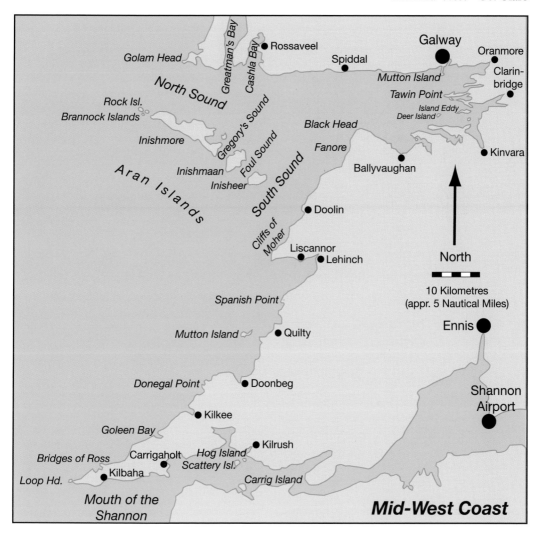

Mid-West Coast

Landing and Camping

Land on Scattery at a muddy-sandy beach at a pier towards the northern end of the E side. Also, less conveniently further over S towards the battery/lighthouse. Fresh water is unavailable, but there is a holy well behind the round tower. It looks good, and certainly might be drinkable if boiled. Camping is possible anywhere, but permission is needed from Dúchas.

Hog Island

Q986-533　Sheet 63

Little neighbour of Scattery Island and less interesting. A drumlinesque few acres, there are horses, Shelduck and goats. The island is privately owned and camping is not permitted.

The West Coast - a tidal overview

Local HW is generally:

From	To	HW Galway
Mizen Head	Loop Head	-0100
Loop Head	Slyne Head	0000
Slyne Head	Erris Head	+0015
Erris Head	Tory Island	+0040
Tory Island	Malin Head	+0100

Offshore tidal streams

Tidal information inshore along the W coast of Ireland is only occasionally reliable or available. There just aren't enough boaters about sending in information. It is known that offshore, the mainstream flood makes N from HW Galway -0320 to +0305, and ebbs in reverse. This is consistent between Loop Head in the S and Aran Island in Donegal. It is also very little different - half an hour earlier - the rest of the way N and E around the corner to at least as far as Malin Head.

The offshore mainstream makes itself felt where the land projects to meet it.

For example:

- Along the coast from Loop Head to Kilkee
- Out the back of the Aran Islands
- At Slyne Head
- Out the back of Inishshark, Inishbofin and Inishturk
- At Achill Head
- Outside the Inishkeas
- At Erris Head
- Along the coast from Rathlin O'Birne to Aranmore
- In Tory Sound
- From Downies to Melmore Head.

Inshore tides

Inshore, where paddlers operate, it is a little more complicated. It is widely accepted that tidal streams inshore turn before tidal streams offshore. The islands and the much-fragmented coastline set up eddies. The bays and inshore channels, from the Shannon Estuary in the SW to Lough Swilly in the far NE, fill and empty almost simultaneously. The variation between them is twenty minutes or less.

This inshore cycle of bay filling and emptying is associated with the offshore main stream. As soon as the offshore stream begins to slacken off, the inshore tide starts to flow in the opposite direction. Here is how it works.

The offshore mainstream floods N until HW Galway +0305, but inshore, the bays start to empty that bit earlier, at HW Galway +0100. The inshore bays start to empty as soon as the offshore flood starts to slacken.

The offshore mainstream ebbs S until HW Galway -0320, but inshore, the bays start to fill that bit earlier, at HW Galway -0500. The inshore bays start to fill as soon as the offshore ebb starts to slacken.

To summarise, the bays mostly fill on the offshore flood, and they mostly empty on the offshore ebb. It is just that the inshore cycle starts an hour and a half earlier than offshore. As soon as the offshore flood or ebb slackens to about half pace, the process is exhausted, and the inshore cycle the other way is triggered.

Thus, all the bays and channels on the West Coast fill from about HW Galway -0500 and empty from about +0100.

Water movement in bays

It has to be stressed that these timings relate to the entrances to bays. Up near the head of a bay, or even halfway up, the timing tends to be that bit later. Further, in bays where a large expanse of water is filled through a narrow or constricted entrance, it can be very much later. Bays with restricted entrances, into which large rivers flow, operate to different rules again.

The information that is commercially available about W coast tides relates to entrances of bays. The people who draw charts and write Pilot books concentrate their efforts here. The reason is that mariners are always anxious to come and go with a favourable tide. Given that the W coast of Ireland consists almost entirely of such bays, this is very useful. The conscientious route planner is remarkably well informed for large sections of the coast.

Care should be exercised in using information from the table on the facing page.

- Rates of flow are spring rates, mostly if not exclusively.
- They are not necessarily consistent throughout the bay.
- The value given may not be for the mouth of the bay itself, but for some other spot inside the bay which has been deemed more important. The reasons for this may not be readily apparent.
- Similar arguments apply for start and finish times, though less vigorously so.

Common sense should be used, or better again, consult the Irish Coast Pilot for more detailed information.

All times are given relative to HW Galway

Bay and place	Max. Rate	Starts to fill	Starts to empty
Shannon Estuary (off Carrigaholt)	Strong	-0520	+0050
Galway Bay - South Sound	1.00	-0520	+0105
- Foul Sound	1.50	-0520	+0105
- Gregory Sound	1.50	-0520	+0105
- North Sound	0.50	-0520	+0105
Kilkieran Bay	1.50	-0520	+0105
Bertraghboy Bay	1.75	-0520	+0105
Clifden	1.50	-0500	+0100
Streamstown	Very strong	-0500	+0100
Cleggan Bay	Weak	-0500	+0100
Ballynakill Harbour	Weak	-0500	+0100
Killary	0.50	-0500	+0100
Westport Bay	2.00	-0505	+0040
Clew Bay (Weaker flow)	0.50	-0530	+0040
Clew Bay (Stronger flow)	1.50	-0530	+0040
Achill Sound South (off Achillbeg)	2.50	-0450	+0135
Achill Sound South Inner	5.00	-0450	+0135
Achill Sound North (Bull's Mouth)	9.00	-0450	+0120
Blacksod Bay Outer (Achill/Duvillauns)	1.25	-0515	+0050
Blacksod Bay Inner (N+E of Blacksod Pt)		-0450	+0120
Frenchport		-0515	+0050
Broadhaven	2.50	-0450	+0100
Broadhaven Bay	1.00	-0515	+0050
Killala Bay	Weak	-0450	+0115
Ballysadare Bay	1.00	-0450	+0115
Sligo Bay Outer	1.00	-0450	+0115
Sligo Harbour	3.00	-0505	+0115
Ballyshannon (Bar to Town)	2.00	-0415	-0015
Donegal Harbour		-0530	+0045
Killybegs Harbour	0.25	-0450	+0015
Gweebarra Hbr.	9.50	-0500	+0015
Rosses Bay Inner		-0520	+0050
Aran Sound N+S		-0520	+0050
Rutland Channels N+S		-0520	+0050
Cruit Bay Inner		-0520	+0050
Sheephaven (+ Ards Bay entrance)	Strong	-0500	+0105
Mulroy Bay (entrance)	1.50	-0520	+0105
Lough Swilly (at Buncrana)	1.50	-0505	+0055

All of these carry a warning. No one in a small boat should ever pass a lobster pot without checking which direction the tide is flowing. It's like going out in the rain without a coat because the weather forecast is good.

Lighthouse, Scattery Island, Co. Clare - Séan Pierce

The Coast of West Clare

This varied coastline changes greatly in character. The SW Clare coastline is synonymous with vertical slate cliffs. These begin at Kilbaha in the Shannon Estuary, just E of Loop Head and run NE for 60km or so, uninterrupted except for the occasional small boulder beach or long sweep of sand. The cliffs go all the way to the limestone Burren hills in the N of the county. There are few enough landings among the limestone escarpments between Doolin and Ballyvaughan. Steep cliffs then give way to the deeply indented bays in low-lying farmland on the NE edge of the Burren.

Those who have set themselves to paddle all the way around Ireland, a mighty crew, properly fear the southern section of this county, from Loop Head to Doolin. It is one of the significantly exposed parts of the entire trip.

West Clare is here divided into small day excursions, which allow one to intensively explore.

Kilrush area to Carrigaholt
Q985-540 to Q849-511 Sheet 63

14km of stony shore with strong tides.

Embarkation is at Cappagh Pier at Q985-540 which is also the embarkation for Scattery Island. The rocky shoreline E of here goes all the way to Aylevarroo Point at Q997-529, the low-lying point on the horizon to the E. To the W lies the entrance to Kilrush Creek Marina. Access through the lock-gates at Q984-544 is easy in season when the gates are normally manned. Call on VHF Channel 80 to be certain.

From the Creek, a stony shoreline extends to Querrin, past the mouth of Poulnasherry (Oyster-Hole) Bay. Poulnasherry is a tidal inlet, so don't explore on an ebbing tide. Querrin Spit encloses an interesting, marshy area, accessible only above LW, 3km W of the mouth of the Poulnasherry marsh. At Querrin, there is a handy embarkation point with good road access at the pier and slipway in front of the handball alley at Querrin Quay at Q925-541. Best avoid the lower tides for fear of slime.

Round Tower, Scattery Island, Co. Clare – David Walsh

Corlis Point is at Q915-530, followed by rocky reefs. Next is stony Doonaha Beach at Q883-527, where a caravan park and gun battery can be seen. Just E of Carrigaholt is Haughs Bay, secluded in that access is easier from the sea than from the land. Beware of LW at Carrigaholt, which leaves a mudflat inside the old quay. Better to land at the stony beach outside the pier.

Carrigaholt to Kilbaha

Q849-511 to Q738-480 Sheet 63

15km of varied coastline.

The bay S of Carrigaholt is Kilcredaun and has an isolated stone beach below the Irish College visible above. The well-preserved Carrigaholt Castle is prominent on the point SE of Carrigaholt.

There is a battery on top of Kilcredaun Point at Q850-494. Six such batteries were built towards the end of the Napoleonic Wars to guard the estuary against a French invasion. They were built in matching pairs. This one is matched by a similar construction on the Kerry side at the Cliffs of Dooneen at Q885-478. Upstream, the next two are at Scattery Island and Carrig Is-

land. The last two are at Kilkerin Point and Tarbert Island, where the estuary is at its narrowest and most tortuous.

Batteries were a more formidable proposition than Martello Towers. Martello Towers are a common feature on the E coast, but there are only two on the W coast. Both of these are in N Clare. Batteries were D-shaped or semicircular, and had much bigger armaments. These normally included 2 howitzers on the roof of the blockhouse and 6 guns along the outer perimeter.

Typically, a battery also had a dry moat and a drawbridge. Scattery Island battery is in good condition although access to the roof is no longer possible. Kilkerin Point has been renovated in recent years.

A school of porpoise and Bottlenose Dolphin are resident between this point and the Kerry coast for a number of years. They make full use of the sweeping tides to feed and frolic.

Rinevella Bay has a pebble beach with a sunken bog and forest at its western extremity at Q817-493. Next, Rehy Hill at Q801-484 slopes gently

View North from Loop Head, Co. Clare - Séan Pierce

into the water. Kilcloher Head at Q773-474 has a cave and marks the end of an impressive section of cliffs, including some long narrow caves and 'The Opera House' - undercut layers of rock sloping into the water.

Tides

Tidal streams are strong at Kilcredaun Head at Q851-493 where the estuary suddenly narrows and turns SW after its long westerly progression to the Atlantic. Locals say the ebbing spring tide reaches 4kn. The tide fills NE from HW Galway -0520 and empties SW from HW Galway +0050.

Kilbaha to Loop Head

Q738-480 to Q686-471   Sheet 63

6km of unremitting cliffs.

Kilbaha is a wild place, pretty, and remote. Best to approach by road from the N, the Bridges of Ross side. The coastal road along the estuary from Carrigaholt is often blocked at Rinevella Bay (Q823-497) by storm damage. Note how Kilbaha Pier is constructed without any mortar at all. There are two pubs and basic facilities. The

Lighthouse pub does excellent bar food. A paddle to Ross Bay or the Bridges means a short road walk back, allowing a mighty paddle with no logistics or shuttle. Kilbaha has slipway access with shelter from off-lying reefs sloping into the bay. A little hut with caves underneath marks the SW extent of Kilbaha Bay.

The outermost 6km of the Shannon Estuary has the character of the coast outside it. Tides now play a significant role as wind from the S can cause unpleasant sea states. Along the striking cliffs towards the head are many narrow caves, including one cavern whose narrow entrance causes light to refract upwards through the water. Halfway between Loop Head and Kilbaha is Dunmore Head at Q718-466 where a sheltered break may be had inside. Dunmore Head is almost cut off, and is locally called Horse Island. There is a wonderful cave running N/S through the headland. There is a very steep storm beach just E of Loop Head where landing is possible in good conditions.

SPA

Peregrine, Chough.

Loop Head to Bridges of Ross

Q686-471 to Q735-504 Sheet 63

7km of cliffs lie between Loop Head and the Bridges of Ross.

Tides

Tides hereabouts, even in close, are the main W coast offshore mainstream. They run along the coast from Loop Head to Kilkee at up to 1kn in springs, with the flood running from HW Galway -0320 to +0305.

Loop Head

Loop Head is a big square-cut, jutting headland. It consists of vertical black cliffs over 30m high. There is a detached section right at the head itself. This is called Diarmuid and Gráinne's Rock. It is a vertical tower 100m by 20m, separated from the mainland by a deep, narrow gorge. In very calm conditions, it is possible to paddle through this gap.

Diarmuid and Gráinne fled from Fionn and the Fianna, a long time ago. Their near capture is recorded widely all over Ireland in places named after them, such as this. From the mainland, marvel at the cairn on top of the rock and wonder how it got there. It wasn't Diarmuid or Gráinne. Mick Fowler and Steve Sustad, two English climbers, put it there in 1990. They have specialised in climbs such as this. They abseiled down, swam out, climbed up, and then tyroleaned back (shinnied along a rope suspended between rock and mainland) to the mainland, leaving their mark behind. The feat has not been repeated.

Around the Head, there is always a swell, which booms on the off-lying reefs. There is a huge lighthouse which is rarely visible from below, except from way out.

The cliffs relent after Black Rock at Q703-490. The view southwards from here looks bleak as rising black cliffs stretch out to sea. The detached rock, 2km NE of the head, is Gull Island at Q701-482. The prominent point by it is Bullaunaleama, with its significant arch, with hundreds of birds occupying its ledges. 3km ENE of the Head lie two shallow bays with storm beaches where landing is possible, Fodry Bay and Ross Bay at Q733-500, handy to the road.

The Bridges of Ross is a N facing, natural harbour. Once there were two bridges, but one fell into the sea. The remaining one is on the western side of the mouth of the inlet, just E of the Point of Ross. There are two inlets within the harbour. Access is normally easier from the wider one, being the more E of the two. There is a track down to a boulder beach. The bay is not completely cut off in rough conditions, as the mouth is wide enough. Care should be exercised though.

Bridges of Ross to Goleen Bay

Q735-504 to Q825-560 Sheet 63

This is 11km of beautiful committed paddling with no real landings between the two points. Worse, the mouth of Goleen Bay is closed out in swell. Goleen Bay is otherwise an excellent waystop and possible embarkation point. It has though, an awkward, mucky carry in. If heading N, and if Goleen is closed, then Kilkee is next stop. This makes for a trip of over 18km in total.

Between Ross and Toorkeal at Q762-513 are continuous cliffs with one sea stack. The N-facing, V-shaped baylet at Toorkeal has, in the cliff to its W, a remarkable T-shaped cave. This leads in over boulders to a sheltered steep-sided cove.

Gowleen at Q785-535 (no road access) is rarely accessible due to rocks at the mouth of the bay. Croan Rock marks its northern edge.

Gowleen Bay is a further 5km to the NE. The hill with radio masts, SW of Goleen Bay, is Knocknagarhoon at Q814-551. There are impressive caves and inlets along this section.

Tides

Tides in this section are as mentioned previously - the main W coast offshore stream runs along the coast from Loop Head to Kilkee at up to 1kn in springs, with the flood running from HW Galway -0320 to +0305.

Goleen Bay to Kilkee

Q825-560 - Q886-604   Sheet 63

About 8km of vertical cliffs and steeps slabs.

Goleen Bay is an excellent waystop and possible embarkation point, well sheltered, but beware of rough seas closing out its narrow entrance during big sets.

The castle at Castle Point (Q835-577) cannot now be seen. The deeply undercut cliff here is popular with mackerel fishermen. From Goleen Bay to here are steeply sloped rock layers dipping straight into the sea. Offshore lies the distinctively shaped Illaunonearaun at Q827-570. There is no landing but it boasts fine arches and caves at its NE tip.

SPA

Storm Petrel, Barnacle Goose.

There is a lovely arch at Foohagh Point at Q853-590, but watch for the submerged rock on its northern side. There is a most beautiful stack to its S called Green Pillar Rock, also called 'The Candle' by divers. A large hole has eroded through the centre, and there is a splendid jump off the landward side of the hole.

The bay just N of Bishop's Island at Q856-595 has the remains of some huts. There is a straight, 200m long cave in the SW corner. The island itself is visible only from the land opposite, and no landing is possible to kayaks. There are caves in the cliff wall opposite Bishop's Island and a mighty sea stack on the corner. Clapotis often occurs in the sound, especially in the shallower, inside part.

Approaching Kilkee Bay, just outside Duggerna Rocks, are a couple of nice caves, with the innermost having two entrances. The second is almost hidden by the big rock sticking up in the corner, or at HW. Waves tend to rear up between here and Knockroe Point to the S. The bay just to its S is Intrinsic Bay, where Goat Island is the tiny sloping rocklet heavily populated with birds. Avoid the tiny inlet behind the island.

On Duggerna Rocks, at the southern side of the bay, are the famous Pollock Holes. These are famous for their natural swimming and snorkelling pools of all sizes. Covered at HW, they are refreshed twice daily. The Pollock Holes are deservedly a most popular attraction. The offshore rocks at this point are busy dive-sites.

The inner bay has a beautiful, horseshoe strand, which is very well sheltered. As the town is right behind, the best landing is at the pier at the northern end of the beach. Scuba divers, both CFT and PADI (Comhairle Fo-Thuinn (Irish Underwater Council), Professional Association of Diving Instructors), organise themselves from this pier. Kilkee is a serious player as a tourist town.

At the northern end of Kilkee Bay, a number of underwater reefs run S from George's Head. These are known by frightened kayakers to boom on even the calmest days. The sheltered Byrne's Cove at Q883-614 on the N side of the bay is popular with male naturists. The prevailing south-westerly swells, coupled with reflection off the cliffs, makes for turbulent water in this corner of the bay.

Kilkee to Doonbeg
Q886-604 to Q962-663 Sheet 63

This section is around 14km.

Kilkee to Farrihy Bay is about 5km and is a pleasant trip with rock layers, sloping steeply into the sea.

George's Head protects Kilkee Bay. The head has a cave opening to the S. The bay just to the N is Chimney Bay. Offshore are two rocky outcrops. That nearer Kilkee is known as Biraghty More at Q883-633, which is a popular scuba dive-site. It boasts a good jump into the sea on the landward side. Facing Biraghty More on Corbally Point is a small cave. Further N is Biraghty Beg.

Farrihy Bay has a reef at the mouth. On the southern side of the bay is Corbally village where landing is possible, but there is a long carry to the road. Corbally village is mostly holiday cottages now, but the native villagers were noted Irish speakers up to 1950 or so. Clerical and lay 'Gaelgeoiri' were common visitors in summer months. There is a rocky beach at the NE corner of the bay with good road access, but sharp reefs force a long carry at LW. This is not a rough weather landing spot by any means.

Donegal Point at Q896-654 is turbulent at most times. It separates Farrihy Bay from a small, sheltered inlet to its N, called Bealnalicka. There is a rock beach here with steep access above the inlet to an in-fill quarry, which has road access. There are splendid caves at the inner, southern side of the inlet. One cave is a gem. It goes all the way S, through the headland into Farrihy Bay. The roof of the cave has collapsed halfway along, and being open to the sky, there are curious lighting effects even in poor ambient light conditions. Expect rough conditions at the southern entrance to the cave, and in the middle. Two reefs run outwards from the N entrance to the caves.

Ballard Bay is noted for its sheer spectacular cliffs. Visit the caves inside a distinctive notch called the Horse Shoe at Q905-658. The caves are in the southern side of the bay, just W of the Napoleonic signal tower at Q910-656. A rocky shoreline leads around the headland to Carrickfadda known locally as the Blue Pool, a rock ledge at the outer NW end of the headland. Carrickfadda is popular with fishermen, despite some being tragically swept out to sea by boomers over the years.

On the W side of Doonbeg Bay, there is the remains of a castle at Killard Point. There is good road access to a sheltered slipway at Q953-673. Access is also possible at HW, right up into Doonbeg itself, at a slipway N of the bridge, at Doonbeg Castle. The Doonbeg area is also shown on Sheet 57.

Doonbeg to Spanish Point

Q962-663 to R034-777 Sheet 57

The character of the coast all the way from Loop Head to Spanish Point is mostly steep, rugged, slate cliffs interspersed with sheltered bays, large and small. S of Doonbeg, the terrain is mostly suited to those who like to potter and explore in detail. This now gives way to exposed surf beaches.

The coast 9km N of Doonbeg is mostly surf beach, including the famous Doughmore (White Strand on the OS 1:50,000 map). Doughmore is famous with surfers for its reliable surf and mean rip-tides. Do not lightly decide to land hereabouts.

Doughmore is famous with others for the golf played in the machair system behind the beach. Doonbeg Golf Course was developed controversially in the last few years. Golfers won out against conservationists. More recently, the golfers have applied to Clare County Council for permission to deposit 80,000 tons of rock and boulders at various points on Doughmore beach, to halt coastal erosion. Did they not realise that dunes are by definition impermanent? Was this not on the cards from the outset? This is one of the most beautiful remote and natural beaches in Ireland. While the land belongs to the golf course, the beach belongs to everyone. It is not the public's fault if some of the greens were badly situated.

Lurga Point, 2km WSW of the village of Quilty, has a NE facing slipway at Q996-742, sheltered by a reef, and is a most convenient embarkation point for off-lying Mutton Island.

There is a somewhat sheltered storm beach just 1km S of Caherrush Point at R020-768. Here are farms and generally a welcoming environment, with water and camping on request.

The curved beach immediately S of Spanish Point is a famed surf spot, absolutely to be avoided except in calm conditions.

Mattle Island

Q972-721 Sheet 57

Mattle is 2km S of Mutton Island and will always play a secondary role to the larger and more attractive Mutton. Cormorant and Shag roost on the grass top. Cormorant colonise the summit while Shag have their home perched over a deep cut that penetrates the NE point.

Landing

Land in a cut at the southern point, or in various points along the SE side, depending on tide and conditions. A reef runs well out to the ENE, and landing may often be had in its shelter.

Mutton Island

Q983-747 Sheet 57

Mutton Island lies 1.5km off Lurga Point. There are three modest houses, nicely sheltered under a low hill, at the narrow, eastern end on the SE facing side. The middle one is still roofed. The houses are just NE of a lake which is just E of the narrow middle of the island. There is a significant signal tower midway along the exposed western side. The northern and western sides are high and craggy.

Landing and Embarkation

The landing place is onto a stony beach at a projecting spit at the narrow, north-eastern point. There are also landing points nearer the houses. If circumstances dictate, there is also a useful landing in a W-facing cut at Q982-747. Camping is equally convenient to all these landings. Embark from a sheltered and conveniently reached beach and slipway at Q996-743 at Seafield Harbour, tucked inside Lurga Point just 3km WSW of the village of Quilty.

With tide running, a most fearsome sea state is said to kick up S of Mutton Island. Beware also the reefs off the W of the island, beloved of wilder surfers.

SPA

Barnacle Goose, Great Northern Diver.

Gadwall, Shoveler, Wigeon, Teal and Mallard were seen on the lake in March 2004. Also seen were Barnacle Goose, Snow Bunting, Twite, Snipe and a herd of goats.

Carrickaneelwar

A great slab of rock with minimal grass lies at Q984-758, 1km N of Mutton Island. Various slabs on the S side usually provide an easy landing. This rock has a fine feel to it. Seal, Barnacle Goose, Mallard and Teal were seen in March 2004.

Spanish Point to Liscannor

R034-777 to R068-884 Sheet 57

No organised information is to hand about this committing stretch of coast, consisting of low cliffs and surf beaches.

The bay to the S of Liscannor is Lehinch and a famed surf spot, absolutely to be avoided by sea kayaks.

Liscannor to Doolin
The Cliffs of Moher

R068-884 to R058-971 Sheet 51/Sheet 57

To the N of Liscannor are the famous Cliffs of Moher, running NNE for 16km or more from Hag's Head at R011-897. Hag's Head lies 3km W of Furreera (R042-880 Sheet 57) in Liscannor Bay, or about 6km W of Liscannor Harbour. Small parties will start or finish this classic excursion at Furreera. Larger parties may prefer Liscannor, as it has the better parking, easy access at the harbour, and in the village itself, facilities including restaurants, pubs, hotel and hostel. The Cliffs of Moher are the highest vertical cliffs in Ireland. Except for one stack off O'Brien's Tower, and a few storm beaches, landings are few. Even then, these are only accessible in very settled conditions. These cliffs provide the most dramatic and committing day paddle in Ireland. If doing the Cliffs of Moher, choose light winds, or south-easterlies, which will wash over the top.

Doolin claims, with some validity, to be the secret capital of Irish music. It is Mecca to every hitch-hiker and cycling tourist under the age of sixty to visit Ireland. Doolin boasts excellent music, hostels, camping (in a paying site conveniently at the harbour), seafood restaurants, chippers, as well as everything touristy. Doolin Pier at R057-970, Sheet 51 is the obvious embarkation place for the Aran Islands. Inisheer lies 8km to the WNW, or 10km to the main beach.

The slipway at Doolin pier is steep, less than well sheltered, and busy. Parking in summer is easier just 100m N, in front of the campsite. The launching is no more difficult off the rocky beach, despite a small, awkward carry. There is no other embarkation for many a cliff-bound mainland mile on either side.

Day excursions either side of Doolin are committing and amongst the best in the country.

Doolin has a coast and cliff rescue service. Contact Mattie Shanahan at 065 – 7074415, the leader of the local Coastguard (Doolin) Unit. Local information may be had from any of the local ferrymen, there being a number of busy, small ferry routes to the islands.

SPA

Peregrine, Chough.

Branaunmore - *An Branán Mór*

R037-924   Sheet 51

Branaunmore is the sea stack prominently visible below O'Brien's Tower at the main public viewing point on the Cliffs of Moher. For this reason, it is more often referred to among kayakers as O'Brien's Stack. Its importance lies in its strategic position, mid-trip along the Cliffs. Very occasionally, a trip along the Cliffs may here be broken, lunch taken, and legs stretched. Tall and thin at 61m high, this is a mighty stack, and although unreliable, do not discount the possibility of a landing. A shelf of rock extends out from the base of the stack on the seaward side, the Doolin side of which is peculiarly sheltered. Even when the gap with the mainland is closed out by booming surf, the N outer side is often quite free of surge and scend. Manageable groups will find it worth a look.

Branaunmore, Cliffs of Moher, Co. Clare - Séan Pierce

Crab Island, Co. Clare – Séan Pierce

Crab Island

R053-971   Sheet 51

Crab Island is a small, rocky islet just off the pier at Doolin. It is best known for the reliable right-hand reef break off its south-western side. Surfers ignore the nearby break on the mainland off Ballaghaline Point at R057-969, because it dumps. There is a stone building of indeterminate purpose on top of Crab, which looks like it might have been a wine cellar. Land onto a sheltered inlet on the NE side, which can be difficult, particularly in swell or at HW.

County Galway

It is more convenient to deal with the Aran Islands here rather than in the main Galway section, hence the diversion.

Aran Islands

Sheet 51

As Doolin is the first logical embarkation for the Aran Islands, they will be looked at now and the trip up the west coast of Clare will be continued later.

Embarkation - Clare side

Doolin in County Clare is the obvious embarkation place on the Clare side. Keep N of Crab Island at the harbour mouth. Inisheer is 8km WNW. There is no other embarkation point hereabouts, with cliffs for many kilometres either side.

Embarkation - Galway side

There is no one obvious embarkation point on the Galway side for Inishmore. Set out from anywhere convenient on the Connemara coast, probably around Lettermullan. Departure from the island N to the mainland requires care in identifying the landing spot, as the mainland coast is low-lying and rocky. The islands off the Connemara coast tend to merge with the mainland background. The best navigational markers are the signal tower on Golam Head and the small, automated lighthouse on Croaghnakeela.

Tides

Local HW/LW is the same as Galway. The flooding tide fills Galway Bay through the four sounds around the Aran Islands. The flood begins at HW Galway -0520 and the ebb at HW Galway +0105, or, say, one hour after local HW/LW. The direction of the flood is NE through the sounds either side of Inishmaan, NNE on the Clare side, and E on the Galway side. Ebb tide timings and directions are the reverse in all cases.

The flood under the cliffs on the long and forbidding SSW (seaward) side of Inishmore is NW, from HW Galway -0320 to +0305.

Tidal streams NW and SE of the group, off the Galway and Clare coasts, are weak. South Sound between Inisheer and the County Clare mainland achieves only 1kn in springs, and North Sound between Inishmore and the mainland even less, 0.5kn. Streams in the middle two sounds E and W of Inishmaan are much stronger. Be careful of both central sounds with wind against tide, which occurs mostly on the ebb as prevailing winds are from the SW. The stream between Inishmaan and Inishmore, called Gregory's Sound, reaches 1.5kn in springs. Also, being surrounded by cliffs, quite a sea state rises in Gregory's Sound. In westerly winds, a sea state occurs when the swell claps against the cliffs on the SW of Inishmaan. The stream between Inishmaan and Inisheer, called Foul Sound, also reaches 1.5kn in springs, but lacks the reputation of Gregory's Sound, there being no cliffs.

Inisheer - *Inis Oírr*

L982-028   Sheet 51

Population 270. On Inisheer there are provisions, pubs, music, hostel, airport, ferry, B&Bs, castles, ring forts, pretty scenery, nice walks, Saint Caban's Church now practically engulfed in sand, and has antiquities by the score. Altogether a most attractive island. Irish (and English) speaking.

Landings

The main landing place is at a NNE facing beach, midway on the NNE side, which may dump. Otherwise, try at the pier at the W end of the beach, where the ferry comes in. There is a paying campsite, with facilities, near the village.

L992-016   Trá Caorach, just W of the eastern point of the island, is a sandy beach. Nearby is the landmark wreck, the Plassey, rusting away above the HW mark since 1960.

L978-007   There is a quay, just NW of the lighthouse, by a slipway.

Inishmaan - *Inis Meáin*

L946-046   Sheet 51

Population 190. The island has an airport, ferry, provisions, B&B, pub, chipper and general facilities. An attractive island, almost exclusively Irish speaking. Note Dun Connor (*Dún Chonchúir*), which is one of the finest, complete ring forts in existence. Rock climbing on Inishmaan has developed since about 2001.

Landings and Camping

L946-046   The main landing spot is at Cora (*An Córa*), at the pier, or the beach nearby just NE for camping.

L954-060   At the NE corner, along the beautiful beach called Sandhead (*Ceann Gainimh*), but which dumps. Be careful not to disturb nesting Terns in spring and early summer. No water.

L943-067   Pier at E end of bay on N called *An Caladh Mór*, but there is a long carry at LW. No water.

L934-067   Better for the NW end of the island, there is a small pier and slipway, called *Port na Cora*. The carry is manageable at LW, there is convenient camping, and there is good water in a well nearby, up the boreen. This is also the best jumping off point for Inishmore.

Inishmore - *Inis Mór*

L883-088   Sheet 51

Population 850. Inishmore is the largest and most westerly of the three main islands. It has several small off-liers, dealt with here as a group. With its airport and all-weather ferry from Galway City, Inishmore, especially around the town Kilronan, has a very 'mainland' feel to it.

Landings

L883-088   Kilronan pier (*Cill Rónáin*), for all mainland type facilities.

L828-105   Kilmurvey (*Cill Mhuirbhigh*), W of centre on the northern side, has a sheltered sandy beach. The best campsite is on a grassy area on the western side of the bay, just N of the beach. This is just the other side of a pier, where

Curraghs on beach, Inisheer, Co. Galway - Séan Pierce

there is an easy rocky landing, and good water in a well. This is the obvious departure point on passage NW.

L777-116 Bungowla (*Bun Gabhla*), a sheltered pier and slip, facing across the sound to the Brannock Islands at the W end of the island. Sheltered slipway, manageable camping, water. This is the jumping off point for the navigation of the Dun Aengus cliffs, the unbroken 16km line of cliffs of the SSW side of Inishmore. This passage is a major challenge for kayakers. Note that there are no reports available of the beach at the other end of these cliffs at Portdeha at L904-067 in Gregory's Sound.

L831-092 In exceptionally calm conditions, in someone else's empty plastic boat, or in extreme distress, there is the possibility of a landing at about mid-point on the SSW coast. This is under Gortnagapple (*Gort na gCapall*), 1km E of Dun Aengus. A sloping natural slipway lies at *Port Bhéal an Dúin* on the right hand side of the easterly of two bays, where the cliffs are lowest of all. Rumour has it that this place is very occasionally used by curraghs. This is the slipway made famous in the classic film 'Man of Aran'. Otherwise, these cliffs are 14km of lee shore, best attacked from *Bun Gabhla* on the ebb tide in total calm.

Rock Island/Eeragh Island
An t-Oileán Iatharach

L759-122 Sheet 51

The more westerly of the two Brannock Islands. Landing is very difficult at the quay at the SE as it is subject to western and south-western swell. Indeed it is marked on Tim Robinson's map as hardly deserving of the name of 'quay'. Robinson hopped off a curragh here, but landing a kayak would be ambitious. In calm seas, landing is possible on some rocky ledges further up the eastern side of the island. At the northern end of the E side, there is a very small rocky beach, with some boulders, where there is another landing at LW to mid-tide. Camping is OK; there is no soil, but there is plenty of flat rock on the path to the lighthouse.

The lighthouse sequence is FL 15s, 35m, 23M (one flash every 15 seconds, the light is 35 metres high and is visible for 23 miles). It was first established in December 1857 and was automated 1978. No water was found but a herd of goats survive, so there must be somewhere. In an emergency the Irish Lights tanks might be accessible. Lots of limestone, but very little else aside from the lighthouse and a wreck.

Brannock Island
Oileán Dá Bhranóg
L769-118   Sheet 51

The more easterly of the Brannock Islands. Note that the following information is received second-hand, and may not be relied upon as fully as elsewhere. It was researched from Tim Robinson's 'Stones of Aran'. There is a bay on the S side (*An Caladh*) where a curragh can be nosed onto a very sheltered little sandy beach. No knowledge of water, but 20 acres of poor pasture for donkeys might provide camping possibilities. The 'most magnificent piece of Aran's cliff-architecture' - a sea cave with pillars and holes in the roof - is on the E side.

Straw Island - *Oileán na Tuí*
L909-085   Sheet 51

Straw Island, at the mouth of Killeany Bay (*Cuan Cill Éinne*), is a good resting stop. Good easy landing onto shingle beaches in the N and E. No great merit. Major lighthouse (11 m. high) which flashes twice every 5 seconds.

The Coast of West Clare continued

Doolin to Ballyvaughan
R057-970 to M228-083 Sheet 51

The famous Burren area is a geological phenomenon, being 1,000km² of 'karst'. This comprises exposed limestone rock pavements, crags, escarpments, sea cliffs, caves, and above all, flowers.

Flora - the Burren is profuse with rare wild flowers. Some of these are not otherwise found N of southern latitudes, while others are not found S of northern latitudes – here, they are side by side. The Burren shelves or drops vertically into the sea from Doolin to Ballyvaughan, with landings few and far between.

Climbing cliffs - halfway between Doolin and Fanore is the famous climbing sea-cliff of Ailladie at R092-034, developed since 1972. It is probably second only in popularity in Ireland to Dalkey Quarry in Dublin. The tallest smooth section is Mirror Wall, with the only apparent weakness being The Ramp [E1-5b] winding up from bottom left to top right, pioneered by Dermot Somers. The cleanest of the series of square-cut corners just S of Mirror Wall is *Pis Fliuch* [HVS-4C], a committing layback. It is very much amongst the best of Jimmy McKenzie's many fine legacies to Irish climbing. Further S by about 100m or more, look for the prominent Great Balls of Fire [E1-5b], said to be Brian Walker's best. It is the obvious fist-sized crack rising to two-thirds height from a ledge just above sea level; the escape is left and up.

There are other cliffs, large and small, between Doolin and Ailladie, and there has been some climbing development on the more prominent sections. All other Clare climbing will always be second rate to Ailladie.

Landings - there is a possible landing at a storm beach just a km N of Doolin, but it is of little logistical interest as there is no road access.

There is a shallow bay with a steep slip about 4km S of Fanore beach, just where the road is closest to the high tide mark, but landing even here is troublesome under the best of conditions. A dolphin, *Fáinne*, arrived here in 1997 or so and has remained ever since.

13.5km NE of Doolin and 4km or so S of Black Head, is the splendidly picturesque, dune-backed machair beach of Fanore at M137-085. The beach may dump even on a good day, but it is the nearest to a dependable landing on this stretch, so do not pass by without thought. Fanore has a public car park at the southern end of the beach with water and excellent camping in a paying site at the northern end of the beach. There is a lifeguard on duty most of the summer.

The coast for kilometres on either side of Black Head is scenic, and of special interest to shore anglers. Lines of them grace the low but sheer black cliffs all summer long. At the head, with its huge automated lighthouse, there will always be swell, especially when the tide ebbs into the regular westerlies. Under normal summer conditions, full-blooded Atlantic conditions suddenly yield to the protected waters of Galway Bay. Travelling northwards, the views of the hills of North Clare from hereabouts are at their most stunning.

3km around Black Head, the tiny pier (marked Coolsiva Quay at M181-108) at Gleninagh, gives a landing onto a small sandy beach. This is a pleasant spot for swimming, and is usually a reliable landing. There is camping and water in nearby houses. Car access is awkward, especially for larger groups. Many of the 'Wild Geese' are said to have left from this pier in Sarsfield's time, after the Treaty of Limerick in the 17th Century.

4km WNW of Ballyvaughan is Gleninagh Castle. Landing is difficult hereabouts, but it is worth the trouble as the castle is well preserved and home to breeding Chough.

The sea outside Ballyvaughan harbour is very shallow and care is needed not to ground at LW, even in kayaks. In particular, a spit of land known locally as 'The Rinn' juts out NE from the shore W of the village. It is a famed birding spot, and with its offshore shallows, it needs a wide berth.

Camping at the village is very public, on grass in front of the Rent-an-Irish-Cottages, or just W of the harbour. It may be possible elsewhere with permission. A better choice by far, is Bishop's Quarter beach at M245-095.

Ballyvaughan is a very pretty village, with all supplies. It is probably best known with tourists for the seafood in Monks Bar at the W pier, and cakes and delicacies in the Tea Rooms nearby. There is also the commercial Aillwee Cave, 3km to the S inland.

Illaunloo

M222-118   Sheet 51

Shown on the OS half-inch Sheet 14, but missing from the 1:50,000 Sheet 51. A rocky islet which makes a good waystop on a day paddle in S Galway Bay. Land on the downwind side, mostly easily. Neither water nor camping.

Poulnaclogh Bay

M271-114   Sheet 51

Poulnaclogh Bay itself is a most useful training area for beginners, being totally enclosed.

It is shallow and therefore most suitable on the top half of the tide. The tidal cycle is later than outside, at least HW Galway +0100, and at least +0130 in springs. The bay is much used by the outdoor pursuits centre at Turlough, near Bell Harbour at the head of the bay, for beginner windsurfing, canoeing, and sailing.

Entry is easiest at M271-114 at a small pier beside a hexagonal monument on the roadside. The south-western side of the bay has a large seal colony, and some otters.

Scanlan's Island

M253-104   Sheet 51

Scanlan's Island is a low, cultivated, agricultural island set out in large fields, lying 3.5km NE of Ballyvaughan. It is barely an island, being cut off only at HW, and being circumnavigable only on the very highest tides. The rest of the time it is accessible by land from the N at M258-115, near Finavarra village.

Scanlan's is noted here for the tidal race that sets up on the ebb at the narrows at its southern tip at M253-104. This is between the island and the mainland where Poulnaclogh Bay flows into Ballyvaughan Bay. The race runs due W. A significant height difference is discernible over as little as 50m, and the run-off in springs, with wind over, can go for over 500m.

Tide Race

Paddlers prefer playing in this race to the more powerful Aughinish Point race nearby, because of its ease of access and relative safety of escape. This race flows into the enclosed Ballyvaughan Bay, whereas Aughinish flows into the more open water of Galway Bay. It is shallow and bumpy with even a hint of westerlies - good fun to be in. Access is from Bishop's Quarter beach at M245-095, 1km SW and 2km NE of Ballyvaughan. The beach is easily accessible to vehicles, with a good car park and camping. Ballyvaughan has all facilities.

Tides

Slack water immediately outside the narrows is as Galway HW and LW. The stream at the narrows and inside Poulnaclogh Bay can be up to an hour and a half later. As some fresh water fills Poulnaclogh Bay, the most powerful flow

Martello Tower, Finavarra Point, Co. Clare - David Walsh

can be the first part of the ebb. This is normal for such configurations, especially after rain, and the surface water downstream of the narrows can taste quite fresh. However, the situation is very variable.

The whole area teems with bird life in winter. On land is found Snow Bunting, on Loch Murree Whooper Swan, Widgeon, Pochard and Teal. On the sea there are Brent Goose, many Merganser, Long-tailed Duck, and especially Divers. More than 130 Great Northern Diver have been counted in recent times. The area is particularly noted for the rarer Black Throated Diver. Clive Hutchinson's 'Birds in Ireland' records a flock of 18 in 1985. Singles and small groups are regular visitors. Grey Phalarope were seen here in significant numbers in October 2001.

Aughinish Island

M274-132   Sheet 51

Apparently, Aughinish was only completely cut off from the mainland for about 50 years. Once upon a time, it was joined to County Clare at New Quay to the S. Then a destructive tidal wave, caused by an earthquake off Portugal in 1755, swept into the area with such force it broke that connection. This explains the puzzling position of an ancient ruined church on the SW, opposite the Clare coast. For a time Aughinish remained an unattached island. But then the military needed to construct the Martello Tower (1804 - 1810) in fear of Napoleonic invasion. For access, they built a road across a causeway at M295-133 from the E, in County Galway.

In that way, Aughinish Island is part of, but divorced from, the rest of County Clare. Uniquely in Ireland, this island is separated from its own county by sea, but is joined to another county by road.

Circumnavigation

This provides kayakers with an opportunity for a short but interesting circumnavigation without logistical problems. Aughinish Point at M274-132 is at the W tip of the island. For best conditions, the circuit is best done clockwise if launching on the ebb, or anticlockwise on the flood.

Tides

The strong tides start and finish up to an hour behind Galway HW and LW. The streams are E (ingoing) from HW Galway -0500 and W (outgoing) from +0100. Do not push (if in a hurry) against the tide on the southern side of the island. Above all, avoid the S side for the main part of the ebb, especially in a westerly. A truly awesome tide race is set up here in such conditions. It extends over the entire mouth of the bay, and stretches from New Quay Pier to Aughinish Point and beyond. On the N side of the island, the tides are not generally strong. However, a shallow bar extends from Deer Island ESE to a point NE of Aughinish Island Martello Tower, where some rough water may be encountered.

Until 1992, there was an old cannon, with emplacements, on top of the Martello Tower, but these are now gone. The top used to be reached with difficulty by climbing, but the tower is now a private residence. This is one of only two such towers built on the W coast. The other at M241-117 is at Finavarra Point a few kilometres to the WSW, commanding the entrance to Ballyvaughan Bay, and still sports its gun.

The S side of the island was the scene of a tragic drowning on 29th June 1969, when 9 children, all from New Quay (except one from Kinvara), died when a boat overturned on its maiden sea trials.

County Galway

The coast of S Galway consists of low-lying, deeply indented farmland on the N edge of the Burren area.

Deer Island

M283-153   Sheet 51

This is a small but lovely and worthwhile islet in open water, 2km N of Aughinish in County Clare. It is 5km W of Eddy Island, and 4km SSW of Tawin. Several dozen seals will typically be lounging about in summer. Multitudinous Cormorants. Absolutely no water.

Land on a beautiful, sheltered, curved, sandy beach on the SE side.

A shallow bar extends from Deer Island ESE to a point NE of Aughinish Island Martello Tower (M287-136). Although the tides are not generally strong except between New Quay and Aughinish Point, the shallow water at this bar, as well as that off Aughinish Point, can be rough in wind.

Embarkation

Embark from around New Quay, County Clare. The easiest launch is from Church Point Beach at M274-124, or from the back of New Quay itself at M281-123. The quay was built in 1837, and is a working quay, so please respect it. At the quay is Linnane's Bar where there is pub-grub, with the best seafood in Ireland. It also has a phone and a shop. The nearest launch for Deer Island is from the causeway joining Aughinish Island to mainland County Galway at M295-133. Also, the island can be taken in as part of a circuit of Aughinish, as launching or landing can be easily had either side of the causeway.

Mulroney's Island

M367-119   Sheet 52

A tidal island in Kinvara Bay, on the western shore. Worth a visit, if only to view a huge oyster shell midden which occupies almost the entire north-western end of the island. Landing is at its most practical at HW, when one may land at the NE side. No water. Good secluded camping spot if attending *Crinniú na mBád*, the authentic festival of traditional Irish W coast boats. These are principally the Hooker (*Bád Mór*), and the smaller *Gleoiteóg* and *Néamhóg*. The *Crinniú* is held annually on the middle weekend in August.

Tides in parts of the bay reach 1.5kn in springs.

Fiddaun Island

M355-159   Sheet 52

An undistinguished small low-lying islet N of the entrance to Kinvara bay. Essentially a grassy raised gravel bank beloved only of nesting gulls in spring. Best landing in SE onto stony beach.

The tidal stream emptying Kinvara Bay turns W just S of Fiddaun.

Island Eddy

M351-164   Sheet 52

Eddy is a large and pretty island, low-lying, 2km NW of the mouth of Kinvara Bay. Formerly inhabited by seven families, Eddy was abandoned in 1947. The islanders settled on the

Island Eddy, Co. Galway - David Walsh

mainland nearby, mostly at Doorus and Clarinbridge. The village, now in ruins and overgrown, is in a line set back from the beach at the northern side of the E end. Deciduous trees behind the village gave good shelter. The island is grazed in summer.

The bigger part of the island lies W of the village and is reached by a narrow causeway. There are enormous lagoons on the northern and south-western sides.

A coral sandbank projects from the eastern end of the island. This dries out all the way to the mainland at the bottom of very low spring tides, when Razorfish can be dug on the lowest parts.

Embarkation

Put in at Kinvara, or a choice of nearer launchings. The nearest embarkation point is from a quay 2km NE of the island at M360-181, 6km WSW of Clarinbridge. Killeenaran at M372-167, 2km E, is more popular. Most conveniently accessed is the beach (locally called Trácht) at M341-138, 2km S and 5km NW of Kinvara, where there is plenty of parking, and toilets.

Landing

Land at the beach on the E end of N side, at the abandoned village.

Camping

Good camping can be had almost anywhere. No water was found.

Tawin Island

M300-193   Sheet 51

Kilcolgan Point at M300-193 at the western tip of the island is a useful waystop for a tour in inner Galway Bay. Land onto boulders and slabs, on whichever side is sheltered. The island is accessible by road, and is flat, but interesting for its beachcombing.

Circumnavigation

The island is at the head of a useful round trip with a simple shuttle between put in and out points. Start or finish at Oranmore Sailing Club (well signposted from Oranmore village) at M355-219 on Sheet 46, and at a small pier just W of Clarinbridge at M407-197 Sheet 52. This provides a trip of 18km or so. There are nice

Purple Sandpiper - Séan Pierce

west-going races on the lower ebb off Mweenish Point at M354-175, Sheet 52 (the E point of Mweenish Island) in the S. There are also races off St. Brendan's Island at M326-213, sheet 46 in the N. Under normal winds, the trip is probably best done S to N. There are plenty of convenient escape points.

There are splendid views of the nearby Galway City from the island. Visit Island Eddy village en route.

Mutton Island

M297-233   Sheet 45

Situated 1km immediately S of Galway docks at the Claddagh. The main pier at Galway is named after Nimmo, the great maritime architect of the 19th Century. A non-portageable causeway has joined Mutton to the mainland since 2000. The causeway facilitates a new sewerage treatment plant for the city, the location chosen in controversial circumstances in spite of protests from conservationists. Mutton is useful more as a pitstop than as a waystop. The whole island is taken over by the sewerage works, except for a small swampy portion on the eastern side. Land anywhere on the eastern side. Camping is forbidden... it would be very unattractive anyway.

All Galway bound traffic keeps E of the island, and be careful at night. the low tower on the southern side is no longer a lighthouse.

Connemara South

Conamara Theas

Galway City to Slyne Head

Cathair na Gaillimhe go Ceann Léime

County Galway
Co. na Gaillimhe

This section deals with the coastline from Rossaveel to Slyne Head. There are no islands, and no information available as to the coastline W of Galway City to Rossaveel. For convenience, the section is divided into its eastern and western halves. The eastern section is centred around Gorumna Island (Kilkieran Bay/Greatman's Bay - *Cuan Chill Chiaráin/Cuan an Fhir Mhóir*), and Bertraghboy Bay - *Cuan na Beirtrí Buí* is in the W.

The E section is further divided into three sections: Greatman's Bay, the islands around Lettermullan Island between the entrances to Greatman's Bay and Kilkieran Bay, and Kilkieran Bay itself.

Historical Context

The waters and bays in South Connemara were the realm of Granuaile - *Gráinne Mhaol*, in the 16th Century. Her second husband Richard Bourke, known as the Iron Dick - *Risteard an Iarainn*, had a furnace, an iron works at the head of Camus Bay. Folklore has it that he made armaments there. Then the Royal Navy sailed into the bay and destroyed his furnace. *Gráinne Mhaol* heard about it and destroyed their boats as they were on their way back to Galway.

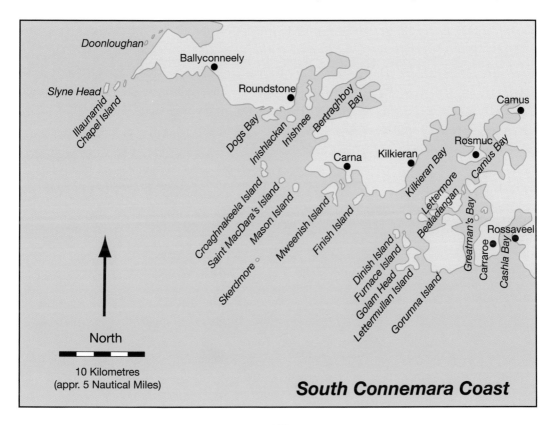

North

10 Kilometres
(appr. 5 Nautical Miles)

South Connemara Coast

In the 19th and early 20th Century, wooden sailing boats, Connemara Hookers, were the workhorses of the waterways. These were a dominant feature of the Connemara - *Conamara* landscape. There were no real roads or road transport. Hookers transported turf to the Aran Islands and ferried goods - tea, sugar, flour and tobacco to small shops in outlying communities on the many inshore islands.

Many of these islands were inhabited in the not too distant past. We walk in the footsteps of the people who have travelled these same boreens before us. We shelter alongside their old walls. We should reflect on the lives of these people and the drastic causes behind these settlement changes.

Have a look at the population changes on the table below.

At the end of the 19th Century, the region was among the poorest in the nation. It was a harsh landscape. With hard labour, people were reasonably self-sufficient. They were providing food and support for their families from farming, kelp gathering, fishing and trades. But there were groups who were very poor. Old people, widows with young children, men with families and no land and families with varying degrees of strength... all were vulnerable. There were years where there was poor harvest in fishing or potato.

The Congested Districts Board was set up in the 1880's to develop schemes to alleviate the poverty experienced in the area. These schemes employed a huge number of men in building roads, causeways and bridges. The Board achieved more than would ever be achieved in the years immediately after Irish independence. The causeways and bridges which joined the islands to the mainland, and between the islands of Lettermullan - *Leitir Mealláin*, Gorumna - *Oileán Gharmna* and Annaghvaan - *Eanach Mheáin*, were built in the years between 1886 and 1891. Many roads in the Carna area were built then also.

The men earned one shilling (about 6 cent) a day. 900 people were working on these schemes from *Ceantar na n-Oileáin*, (*Leitir Móir* and *Leitir Mealláin*) which shows a huge reliance on these relief works to help families survive famine and high rents. About 1900, lace-making industries were set up to create income opportunities for women. It became a way for women to earn the price of a fare to America to escape from a life of poverty, hardship and from the carrying of the '*cliabh*'. A '*cliabh*' is a creel or wicker basket, used to carry turf or seaweed. Carrying it represented poverty.

The population were tenants on the land. It was a struggle to keep their holdings and to survive. Landlords and their agents charged exorbitant rents. If they could not pay the rent, they were evicted. It drove many people to emigrate. There were many schemes in America and Australia at the turn of the century looking for 'white healthy people' to occupy and inhabit the 'new countries'. It was the beginning of an emigration on such a scale that it scourged the West of Ireland until about the 1970's. The emigrants' destination

Island		1891	1911	1981	2001
Finis	Finish	131	100	5	0
Inis Bearacháin	Inishbarra	152	147	5	1
An tOileán Iarthach (Leitir Móir)	Illauneeragh	23	18	0	0
An Chnapach	Crappagh	31	0	0	0
Inse Ghainnimh	Inchaghaun	21	7	5	1
Inis Treabhair	Inishtravin	105	93	7	1
An tOileán Mór	Illaunmore	67	68	6	1
An tOileán Iarthach (Tuarlach)	Illauneeragh West	53	46	0	0
Inis Eirc	Inisherk	40	28	7	0
Daighinis	Dinish	50	52	3	0

South Connemara Coast, Co. Galway - Séan Pierce

changed in the 1950's to England where work was plentiful, due to the efforts to rebuild after World War 2.

In the 20th Century, all the islands in South *Conamara* were ravaged by poverty, emigration, and the hardships of making a living. This contrasted with how these same islands had previously provided people with food when many other parts of the country were starving. From the 1950's onwards, the final death knell for life on these islands came as people chose an easier lifestyle on the mainland. They preferred easier access to housing, health services, education for the children, and opportunities to work and earn money.

These days, islands are a very attractive destination for paddlers and other tourists. Increasingly, many of the small islands have holiday homes. Even the smaller islands with permanent inhabitants have recently had electricity installed, funded by the Department of Community, Rural and Gaeltacht affairs. In 2004, there is a Minister there who seems to actually care. Is the tide turning?

Greatman's Bay
Cuan an Fhir Mhóir

Greatman's Bay is the smallest of the three island strewn bays on the S-facing Galway coast. Greatman's is bounded by the Carraroe - *An Ceathrú Rua* peninsula to the E and Gorumna Island and Lettermore Island to the W. Bealadangan - *Béal an Daingin* at the N connects Greatman's Bay to Kilkieran Bay, for even quite large but unmasted vessels. Only the island free Cashla Bay - *Cuan Casla* just to the E is smaller among the great bays hereabouts.

At this E end of the S *Conamara* coast, information is comparatively scant for the kayaker. This is so even though Carraroe is a famous tourist resort, and that Gorumna is Ireland's fifth biggest offshore island. Let the knowledgeable reader accept the challenge, and furnish information to put matters right.

Tides

Tides enter Greatman's Bay, as others in the region, from about HW Galway -0500 to

125

Kayaking, South Connemara, Co. Galway - Séan Pierce

+0100. Local HW in the furthest regions of the bay such as Bealadangan is about Galway +0100, all much as one expects. The tide floods N and W through the narrows, ebbing S and E. Greatman's Bay is much more open at its northern parts than is Kilkieran Bay, so the tide runs very strongly indeed through the remoter gaps. A flow of 4 - 5kn is reported at Bealadangan, but following this logic, much less may be expected at Kiggaul Bay - *Cuan Choigéil* where Gorumna meets Lettermullan to the W. As with other bays hereabouts, beware when navigating in the narrow places on a falling tide. One mistake and the kayak can be grounded, necessitating a long wait, or a session dragging the boat over seaweed covered rocks in search of open water.

Camus Bay - *Cuan Chamuis*

Camus Bay - *Cuan Chamuis* is the innermost bay among the myriad of islands at the head of Greatman's Bay and Kilkieran Bay. The two bays are joined in places between the islands. Camus Bay is distinctive in that one can meet the tide ebbing from Camus Bay into Kilkieran Bay even as it floods into Camus Bay from Greatman's Bay. This is due to the narrows that occur E of *Cladhnach* - Clynagh Island at L940-340 (off *Rosmuc*) further up the bay.

Cuan Chamuis go Cuan an Fhir Mhóir

The following is a description *i nGaeilge* of a journey from the upper reaches of Camus Bay into Greatman's Bay. This route saw much use and transportation over the centuries. It follows a landscape with some interesting islands, starting at *Risteard an Iarainn*'s (Iron Dick's) old furnace works site at Furnace Bridge - *Droichead na Foirnéise*.

Josie O'Giobúin, sea kayaker from Camus, the heart of the Conamara Gaeltacht , is the contributor. A direct translation is not provided, as any attempt at such would lose the poetry and beauty of the Irish language.

However, some pointers for those paddling Camus Bay are provided in English.

Fadó, baineadh móin ar fud Chonamara le cur ar bháid go hArainn, go Gaillimh agus go Co an

126

Chláir. Talamh chloch aoil a bhí in Arainn agus Co an Chláir agus ní raibh aon mhóin acu ná mórán ábhar tine. Is dócha ar dtús go mbíodh muintir Chonamara ag babhtáil leo, móin ar iasc nó fataí, b'fhéidir. Bhí talamh níos fearr in Arainn, an méid talamh a bhí ann.

Théadh muintir Chamuis agus Rosmuc síos Béal an Daingin agus Cuan an Fhir Mhóir ar a mbealach lena gcuid móna. Tá sruth láidir san gcuisle caol idir Camus agus Rosmuc. Tá áit ar a dtugann siad na léimeannaí ina mbíonn titim maith nuair a bhíonn sé ag trá, go mór mhór ar an rabharta. Tá an chuisle marcáilte le piléir concrete uaidh Snámh Bó síos go Béal an Daingean. Má bhíonn tú ag déanamh an aistear seo in aon bhád ní mór duit staidéar a dhéanamh ar an taoile mura bhfuil tú ag iarraidh bheith ag troid in aghaidh an sruth.

Ag tosnú ag barr Chuan Chamuis san áit a dtéann abhainn na Foirnéise isteach sa gCuan an chéad oileán a fheiceann tú ná Oileán na Scailp. Ta beagán de seanchrainnte Monterey pine fanta ar an oileán seo, ach tá siad ag fáil bháis mar bíonn cailleacha dubha ag codhladh iontu agus maraíonn an acid atá ina gcac na crainnte. Ar an taobh ó dheas don oileán seo, tuairims 100 méadar uaidh, tá carraig atá deas cothram réidh ar a bharr ar a dtugtar Leac an Tobac. D'fhéadfadh go mbeadh scéalta le ninseacht ag an leac seo, dá mbeadh muid in ann í a thuiscint. Le hais an chuain, seasann Teach Scríb, teach tiarna talún.

Uaidh seo leanann tú an sruth atá an láidir ag an áit is cúinge san gcuisle, 100 méadar. Tá oileán beag, Dún Manus ar thaobh Rosmuc den chuisle seo agus tá bóthar déanta istigh air, agus an bóthar ag teacht go cladach chaon taobh. Bhí droichead le déanamh anseo aimsir Bhord na gCeantar Cúng (Congested Districts Board) ach níor déanadh fós é. Deireann an sean dream nuair a dhéanfar an droichead ag Dún Manus go b'shin é deire an domhain. Dhéanfadh muid gan an droichead dhá bhfanadh deire an domhain uainn. Bhí bád farantóireachta anseo fadó ag tabhairt daoine siar go Rosmuc agus aniar go Camus.

Píosa beag tuairims 1km taobh ó dheas de seo tá an t-oileán Inis Aillte. Bhí cónaí ar seo go dtí le blianta gairid. Taobh ó dheas aríst tá Cladhnach, oileán eile agus ar an taobh thoir do Chladhnach idir é agus Camus Íochtair tá na Léimeannaí, an áit is láidre a bhíonns an sruth.

Taobh ó dheas do Oileán Chladhnach, casann tú siar idir Rosmuc ar an taobh ó thuaidh agus Béal an Daingean ar an taobh ó dheas. Feiceann tú oileán Inis Treabhair siar uait. Tá cónaí fós ar an oileán seo. Tá dhá chéibh ann ceann ar an taobh thoir agus ceann ó thuaidh gar don cheann thiar don oileán. Tá sé éasca dul i dtír ar chaon taobh don oileán.

Casann tú ó dheas aríst idir Béal a'Daingean agus Anach Mheáin. Tá droichead concrete anois idir Béal a'Daingin agus Anach Mheáin. Roimhe seo, bhíodh droichead adhmaid ann a bhí le noscailt le h-aghaidh báid seoil a ligeann síos agus suas. Má tá bád seoil ag iarraidh dul faoi anois, caithfidh siad an crann a thógál anuas. Tuairims 3km taobh ó dheas de Bhéal an Daingean tá oileán Inse Mhic Cionnaith. Tá teach saoire amháin ar an oileán seo, tá na tithe eile uilig tréigthe. Tuairims 5km eile ó dheas tá tú ag béal Chuan an Fhir Mhóir ag breathnú trasna ar oileáin Arainn i gCuan na Gaillimhe.

There are a couple of areas to be careful of in Camus Bay.

Upper Camus Bay fills and empties through a very narrow neck at *Snámh Bó*, where there is a very strong fall on springs. This is at L935-360, near Dunmanus Island where roads come down to the shore on both sides. Local HW at the top of Camus Bay can be up to 3 hours after that on the mouth. Pillars mark the channel *Snámh Bó* down to *Béal an Daingean*.

The fastest flow is between Clynagh Island – *Oileáin Cladhnach* and Camus Eighter – *Camus Iochtair* to the east.

Gorumna Island - *Oileán Gharmna*
L897-267   Sheet 44

The grid reference is for Maimin Quay - *Céibh an Mháimín* in the NE, just left of the road as one drives onto the island from Lettermore. This quay does not dry out as much as other local quays that are convenient for exploring the bay. Much of the island is referred to locally as *Máimín* or Maumeen, and parts as *Tír an Fhia*. The island is very much in the heart of the Irish speaking *Gaeltacht* area.

Illaunnanownim (*Oileán an Anama*, literally Island of the Soul, or figuratively Live Island, as it would best be known) off the S side is a prominent navigation marker for passing boats.

Inchamakinna, Co. Galway - Josie Gibbons

There is a roadway along much of the NW side. The quays and bays of the S and E are more isolated from each other. A most attractive pub, *Tí Antaine Laoi,* in the SW at the Lettermullan Bridge serves excellent seafood. Tides flood N round both sides of the island meeting in a lagoon trapped between it and Lettermore.

Lettermore Island - *Leitir Móir*

L902-283   Sheet 44

Lettermore is a large, hilly island. The grid reference is for a quay in the SE, opposite Inishlay, just left of the road as one drives towards Gorumna. This quay does dry out at the bottom of a low tide but is otherwise very usable for exploring the bay. Good facilities may be had in shops by the Gorumna bridge at the SE. Tides meet in the lagoon W of the Gorumna bridge, which is navigable to kayaks at all times. Less navigable is the passage immediately NE of the island, as there are extensive drying areas. At LW, Bealadangan pass may be a better bet, but watch the strength of the current.

Inishlay - *Inis Léith*

L906-276   Sheet 44

A small, low, wet island, with cows, sheep, larks, mergansers, ferns, gorse, rushes, bog pools and an indented, inconvenient, rocky shore everywhere. Camp is possible but unattractive just about anywhere.

Eragh Island
An tOileán Iarthach Theas

L913-264   Sheet 44

Drier than Inishlay, with a more open feel, and good views N to the mountains. Goats. Camp on grass at NW.

Inchamakinna
Inis Mhic Cionaith

L921-263   Sheet 44/Sheet 45

This is the largest and most attractively varied of the islands hereabouts. There are both deciduous and coniferous trees. Houses, some of which are being restored are on the eastern side. Of these, the most southerly is the nicest in a lovely open spot. Tidal peat, bog oak and cows. Landing anywhere requires a carry except at HW. Camp by the houses if they're unoccupied.

Lettermullan Island Group

The next ten or so islands are centred on, and are mostly accessed from, Lettermullan Island - *Leitir Mealláin*, on the E side of and somewhat outside the entrance to Kilkieran Bay.

Tides

The bay fills from HW Galway -0520 to +0105, and achieves 1.5kn at the entrance between Ardmore Point at L818-283 and Illauneeragh - *An tOileán Iatharach* at L838-273. 2kn is achieved inside the bay between North Island - *An tOileán O Thuaidh* and the mainland, just ENE of Kilkieran. In either location, on the ebb, with wind over, quite a race forms. The times are the same for Galway Bay's North Sound, where the flood turns clockwise around the Aran Islands but achieves only 0.5kn at springs.

Lettermullan Island - *Leitir Mealláin*
L826-215   Sheet 44

A sprawling 'mainland', island on the eastern side of the entrance to the main part of the bay. Lettermullan Island is central to more than half a dozen off-lyers on its W, NW and N. To the W, Golam - *Gólam*, Freaghillaun More - *Fraochoileán Mór* and Freaghillaun Beg - *Fraochoileán Beag* surround Crappagh - *An Chnapach*, which is itself attached to Lettermullan by an unmarked causeway/bridge of recent construction. Beware of the passage inside Crappagh at very LW.

To the NW and N, Inisherk - *Inis Eirc*, Dinish - *Daighinis* and Illauncosheen (Illauncasheen locally) - *Oileán Chaisín* surround Furnace - *Fornais*, which is similarly attached to Lettermullan.

Lettermullan is joined on the E to Gorumna Island (and eventually to the mainland) by road bridges to the NE. The bridge between Lettermullan and Gorumna is passable with ease only at very HW but circumnavigators can get through all these gaps with effort at all stages. The gap between Crappagh and Lettermullan has extensive shallows and may be more difficult. Beware when navigating hereabouts on lower or dropping tides. Tides flow strongly, ebbing S or

W through the narrows. Beside the Lettermullan/Gorumna bridge, on the Gorumna side, is a pub that serves good seafood.

The northern shore has nothing interesting. The eastern shore has a number of working quays. The southern shore has a beautiful bay E of centre at L843-216, inside Dog Island - *Oileán an Mhadra*, and a wild, westerly section off which clapotis will always be present.

Camping

Camping for the tourer may be conveniently had at L826-215 on the remote commonage at the SW tip. This is just inside and opposite the signal tower at Golam Head on Golam Island, at the eastern side of a sheltered N-facing bay. The bay is created by Golam Island, which is not totally cut off.

Dog Island - *Oileán an Mhadra*
L846-212   Sheet 44

A small island, about 500m off Lettermullan, Dog Island marks the whereabouts (on circumnavigation) of a beautiful, small beach on the southern side of Lettermullan. Smooth and rounded glacier-scoured, grass-topped rock, which could just about be camped on. Land on the sheltered, rocky, inter-tidal area on the N side at the storm beach.

Golam Island - *Gólam*
L819-214   Sheet 44

Wonderful cattle-grazed, remote, and somewhat short-grassed island, SW of Lettermullan. Camp at the shingle beach by the landing, midway along the E side, facing the WW2 watchhouse and main camping site on Lettermullan. Huge 19th Century signal tower forms the major landmark hereabouts. Very much recommended. Marked 95' on half inch OS map. There is a race on ebb on northern side into a westerly wind.

In fact, Golam Island is accessible on foot from Lettermullan, certainly in wellingtons, for some at least of the lower part of the tide. Golam Head - *Ceann Gólaim* at L817-214 is on Golam Island. Its elevated signal tower is a most prominent feature, which may be used as a visual navigational aid for many kilometres. The land hereabouts in South *Conamara* is otherwise low, confusing and difficult to identify, especially from seaward. This is the spot from which to embark for Inishmore on the Aran Islands, especially if heading for Bungowla at the western tip. More importantly though, coming from Aran, Golam Head is one of the few easily identifiable spots on the coast hereabouts (but in this context see also Croaghnakeela Island).

Freaghillaunmore
Fraochoileán Mór
L823-225   Sheet 44

Granite 'roches moutonées', and boulders. 'Roches moutonées' means 'scoured or scraped rocks'. Geologists can tell which way glaciers moved from the scrapes. Horses grazing. There is a very remote feel to this island. Pleasant. Marked 60' on half-inch OS map. There is a race on the ebb on the southern side into W wind. It can be camped on, just. Land easiest onto sand at sheltered north-eastern tip.

Freaghillaun Beg
Fraochoileán Beag
L825-227   Sheet 44

Granite 'roches moutonées', and boulders. Horses grazing. Pleasant. Land easiest onto sand at sheltered E side between it and Crappagh, where beaches form to either side of the almost drying gap. Marked 51' on half-inch OS map.

Crappagh - *An Chnapach*
L831-227   Sheet 44

The summit is marked as 62' on the half-inch OS map and 16m on the 1:50,000. The 'almost an island' is actually attached to Lettermullan by an unmarked causeway/bridge of recent construction on its E side, built across an extensive area of flats. The tide ebbs S. Be wary at LW. Cattle and an unusual house at E side.

Inisherk - *Inis Eirc*
L832-233   Sheet 44

Inisherk possesses a truly eye-catching feature. A small abandoned cluster of houses is built at the SE corner. These are built right down to the HW mark onto scoured and rounded 'roches moutonées', with a natural 'pier'. The 'village' is reminiscent of similar developments much, much

further N in Norway and Greenland where they also build right down to or over the HW mark.

Land onto slabs at the pier by the houses. Camp between these houses and the narrows to the S. Alternatively, for the oceanic feel, try the sandy beach on the S side of the western tip at L826-234 or the corresponding storm beach N of this tip at L826-234 if conditions insist. Camping may also be possible further N.

Furnace - *Fornais*
L834-234   Sheet 44

Furnace is attached to Lettermullan by a bridge, the water underneath which is passable at all stages of the tide (which ebbs W). A pier at L834-234 at the SW of the island forms a good base for paddling hereabouts. Machair would provide good camping at the northern tip but the welcome is most uncertain, especially if accessed by road, as all the 'Private' signs face this way. The eastern side has several working piers of little interest save as waystops. The gap inside Illauncosheen is barely passable, even to a kayak, at LW.

Dinish - *Daighinis*
L830-254   Sheet 44

Mains electricity is connected to the few inhabited, probably holiday houses on the eastern and northern sides of this beautiful island. Two lovely sandy bays open onto the narrows opposite Furnace. The best beach of all is the E-facing, crescent-shaped beach at L830-254, tucked inside the northern tip of the island. It is backed by machair for camping in comfort, and the single house thereabouts even boasts its own pontoon-landing device. There appears to be mains water at the house.

Illauncasheen - *Oileán an Chaisín*
L841-243   Sheet 44

Known as Illauncasheen locally, but Illauncosheen on the OS map, this little island is situated in Casheen Bay - *Cuan Chaisín*. Ungrazed save by a single donkey, this is a small, unattractive island off the eastern side of Furnace. It provides shelter for the fleet of working boats operating from the pier opposite. Camping is theoretically possible at southern end.

Evening camp opposite Golam Head, Co. Galway - Séan Pierce

Kilkieran Bay
Cuan Chill Chiaráin

The bay N of Lettermore Island is mostly very shallow, giving paddling which varies greatly with the level of the tide. At HW, there are quite a few small islands, some inhabited, some not, and all with reasonably straightforward landings. As the tide falls, the flow between the islands increases and the channels all narrow. Some of the streams reach 3kn, and then the channels dry up, so that the whole area is seaweed-covered rocks and islets. Many of the islets then become linked at lower tides. The area is heavily dredged by fishermen for oysters and bladder-wrack seaweed. The seaweed is collected and taken away in trucks to be processed into iodine and fertiliser. There is also salmon farming.

The local wildlife is spectacular with large numbers of seals, some of which are inquisitive, and otters, which quite definitely are not. Also, there are birds - Common, Herring and Lesser Black-backed Gull, and large numbers of Red Breasted Merganser. Worth visiting in its own right, the area is particularly attractive as a fall-back in time of windy weather. Its combination of races and shelter can combine to give more fun than open ocean water.

Tides

The bay fills from HW Galway -0520 to +0105, and achieves 1.5kn at the entrance between Ardmore Point at L818-283 and Illauneeragh at L838-273. The tide gets up to 2kn between North Island and the mainland, just NE of Kilkieran. With wind over tide (usually on the ebb), a race forms.

Illauneeragh
An tOileán Iatharach

L840-267   Sheet 44

Attractive heather and rock covered island at the eastern side of the mouth of Kilkieran Bay. Landing is on a beautiful sandy beach on the south-western side among rocks. Good camping on grass behind beach. Conspicuous ruined houses. There is an interesting, narrow gorge which is passable at HW, between this and a small island to the E. Note the former ford/bridge. No water found, except in surface water pools.

131

Finish Island, Co. Galway - Séan Pierce

Inishbarra - *Inis Bearacháin*

L860-268   Sheet 44

An attractive, high, rocky and heather covered island, E of the mouth of Kilkieran Bay. One householder lives there, who is a noted builder and sailor of traditional craft. The landing place is at the pier in bay on the northern side. It is also easy to land elsewhere. There is an interesting, very-low-water, artificial causeway to the mainland via several islets to the SE, but do not regard this as a tidal island. Worth a visit. The western part of the passage between Gorumna and Lettermore is easily passable at HW only, but sets up an interesting marine waterfall on the ebb, and then dries.

Inishtravin - *Inis Treabhair*

L893-312   Sheet 44

An attractive, sheltered, low, inhabited island in Kilkieran Bay. There is a landing place at the pier on the eastern end with water in a well behind the house at the pier. For camping, ask at house. Otters.

Beaghy Islands - *Na Beitheacha*

L893-320   Sheet 44

These two small islands lie to the N of Inishtravin and are linked to it at LW. Easily approached at HW, at LW both islands become surrounded by huge expanses of weed-covered rocks. These islands are a favourite haunt of otters.

Illaunard - *An tOileán Garbh*

L877-322   Sheet 44

A small island to the NW of Inishtravin. Land anywhere on rocks, easily at HW, but with more difficulty at LW. Used for grazing. Uninhabited. The best camping is on the northern side. There is a considerable tidal drop and access is probably best at HW. The higher parts of the island are dominated by furze, heather and bracken and sections can be difficult to walk.

North Island - *An tOileán ó Thuaidh*

L873-324   Sheet 44

A small, uninhabited, rocky island to the NW of Illaunard. Land in a small cove on the N coast.

Greeve Islands
Oileáin na Craoibhe

L884-332   Sheet 44

These islands give interesting paddling on an ebbing tide. The entire area is almost surreal at LW. It is very easy to get lost and stranded by a dropping tide, with islands emerging all around.

Illauneeragh West
An tOileán Iatharach Thiar

L888-349   Sheet 44

A low island connected to Illaunmore at LW. There are interesting old ruins and narrow paths through the island, which is quite marshy on the northern half. Land easily at an old slipway on the north-eastern corner at HW. At LW, the mud between the weed-covered rocks is black, smelly, and gets everywhere. This is a popular island with tourists in summer. July can be 'hectic'.

Illaunmore - An tOileán Mór

L896-350   Sheet 44

An attractive, low island connected at its eastern point to the mainland at LW. It is inhabited but there are many abandoned ruins and deserted houses. It is a popular venue with summer tourists for 'camping sauvage' in the fields.

Crow Island - An Cró

L887-353   Sheet 44

A small island linked to Illauneeragh West at LW. Land easily at HW on the eastern side at some old walls. Formerly used for grazing but now covered in briars. A strong flow can develop on the ebb to the S of the island.

Illaunnagappul - Oileán na gCapall

L897-357   Sheet 44

A small island N of Illaunmore. Uninhabited but there are signs of former fields. A flow of about 1.5kn can develop just S of the island. Land anywhere, easily on higher tides, with more difficulty onto weed-covered rocks on lower tides.

Birmore Island - Bior Mór

L804-263   Sheet 44

A low, grassy island, SW of the mouth of Kilkieran Bay. Land on a sandy/rocky shore at the northern end. Formerly inhabited, there are the ruins of a house. Sheep. Pleasant.

Inishmuskerry - Oileán Múscraí

L783-266   Sheet 44

Known locally as Spike Island, this is a low-lying, long-grassed island, WSW of the entrance to Kilkieran Bay. It was never inhabited, and there is no water. There is a sandy beach on its northern side at which one can land easily. It is surrounded on all sides by off-lying rocks and reefs, of which take care. There is a well-sheltered, pleasant, sandy cove on the north-western side, lovely for children. About 300 Barnacle Goose frequent this and other South Connemara islands in the winter.

Finish Island - Oileán Finis

L790-288   Sheet 44

A large attractive island, W of the entrance to the bay. It can just about be accessed on foot at very low springs at its north-eastern end.

There are beautiful beaches along both sides. Long and narrow in shape, the island has extensive machair areas and wetter marshes in low-lying hollows. There are many ruined farmhouses. The island has the distinctive atmosphere of being slowly reclaimed by drifting sands, especially along the original road that runs NE to SW through the central part. The original harbour is still in good condition and is located on the north-western side.

A wide variety of wildlife is on the island, including ducks, terns, waders and otters. Grazed (possibly overgrazed) by cattle and horses during the summer months.

Camping

Good camping all over but probably best on the north-western side, in a little bay at L790-288, a couple of hundred metres SW of the quay. No water found.

Bertraghboy Bay Area
Cuan na Beirtrí Buí

The following half dozen or so islands are in or outside Bertraghboy Bay. Tides of 2kn are reported at the entrance to the bay itself between Inishtreh and the southern tip of Inishnee.

Mason Island, Co. Galway - Séan Pierce

Tides

The bay fills from HW Galway -0520 to +0100.

Duck Island - *Oileán Lachan*

L768-271   Sheet 44

Low-lying and barely grassed islet, with little shelter, and camping only for the truly desperate, immediately S of Mweenish Island. There is a landing that is vaguely sheltered on the north-eastern side in an inlet that is better formed at the lower part of the tide. The highest point on the island is near the landing and has a low cairn, which is generally topped off with a marker to be readily visible for local boats over a wide area. The islet dries to expose quite a large area of boulder beach.

Mweenish Island
Oileán Mhuighinse

L764-294   Sheet 44

A large, well-populated Gaeltacht island, 9km SE of the entrance to Bertraghboy Bay and attached to the mainland by a road bridge to the NE.

The passage under the bridge is always passable.

One Corncrake was heard singing here in 2003.

Mweenish is the home place of the Galway Hooker, the traditional wooden, gaff-rigged, tumble-homed sailing boat of the W coast of Ireland. Hookers very nearly went extinct as a working boat a century ago, but have enjoyed a considerable revival since about 1970 as a leisure craft. There are now 15 or 16 of them on the water.

One such hooker, the Saint Patrick, built on Mweenish in 1906 and skippered by Paddy Barry, crossed the Atlantic in 1986, and has since gone to Greenland. She also sailed to other Arctic destinations including beyond the 80° latitude parallel off Spitzbergen in 1990. Saint Patrick slipped her mooring and sunk at Glandore in 2003... may she rest in peace.

Paddy Barry went on to achieve even more fame by negotiating Canada's North West Passage and in 2004, is attempting Siberia's North East Passage, in each case in 'Northabout', the sailing craft specially designed and built for such purposes by Jarlath Cunnane of Dublin.

134

Saint MacDara's Island, Co. Galway - Séan Pierce

Landing and Camping

There are several working piers and quays, but the points of greatest interest to kayakers are the three beaches. The nicest is at L764-294 in the SW-facing elbow of the island, with good camping on machair in the dunes behind the beach, and good parking. This beach would be the best embarkation point for Mason - *Oileán Máisean* or MacDara's Island - *Oileán Mhic Dara*. More reliably sheltered is the E-facing, smaller beach at L774-284, on the eastern side of the southern tip. Here, there is limited parking but excellent camping beside the ruin of a house at the southern end of the beach. Otherwise camping is impractical as the fields are stocked. There is a tide-dependent beach and machair at the north-eastern side opposite the bridge at L768-299.

Mason Island - *Oileán Máisean*

L745-295   Sheet 44

Mason is 8km SE of the entrance to Bertraghboy Bay. It is an attractive, semi-inhabited island. The pier at the western end is uninviting to pass-

ing kayaks, as it dries out. Water is available in the houses.

Landing and Embarkation

Land virtually anywhere on northern or eastern sides. The best camping is probably in the NE. Camping is possible at other locations, but as cattle graze the island, be sensible.

Embarkation

The best launching point for Mason or MacDara's is the beach in the SW-facing elbow of Mweenish Island at L764-294.

Saint MacDara's Island
Oileán Mhic Dara

L723-299   Sheet 44

A most attractive island, 7km S of the entrance to Bertraghboy Bay.

Named *Cruach na Cara* on the OS 1:50,000 map, but nobody calls it that.

It is uninhabited. 300 Barnacle Goose were found here in April 1994, but whether they were waystopping or wintering is not known. It is a

Saint MacDara's Island, Co. Galway - Séan Pierce

place of annual pilgrimage on the 16th July every year. Saint MacDara is the patron saint of Galway Hookers, which always dip their sails when passing the island. The church is of 12th Century construction. The roof fell in during the 19th Century and was restored in 1977.

Landing and Camping

Land at an attractive, sheltered, sandy beach on the eastern side below the church. There is excellent camping by the beach. There is another landing on the SE, S of the spit, on a pebble beach, necessary perhaps in easterly or north-easterly wind.

Embarkation

The best launching point for Mason or MacDara's is the beach in the SW-facing elbow of Mweenish Island at L764-294.

Croaghnakeela - *Cruach na Caoile*
L690-324   Sheet 44

Croaghnakeela is also called Deer Island. An overgrown heather island, located 7km SW of the entrance to Bertraghboy Bay. It boasts bird

life and an 'oceanic feel'. The island is uninhabited but was once stocked with deer, and hence the name. There is a ruined church, named after St. Brendan.

A small, automated lighthouse near the southern point is a useful distinguishing feature from seaward. It provides the only readily distinguishable feature W of Golam Head signal tower for those on passage from the Aran Islands.

Landing

The landing, onto large boulders on the eastern side of a shallow bay by a bothy, is unattractive. It is better sheltered on lower tides. On higher tides, there is a possible alternative landing in a small rocky cut, midway along the northern side.

Inishbigger - *Inis Bigir*
L741-347   Sheet 44

This unremarkable little island lies off a beautiful beach, 5km WNW of Carna village, on the outer, eastern side of the entrance to Bertraghboy Bay. It is barely circumnavigable at LW. Cattle only occasionally graze it, so the undergrowth is lush. Nevertheless, Willow Herb, Ragged Robin and Self Heal abound.

Embarkation and Landing

It is not really possible to camp and no water was found. The softest landing is on the landward, eastern side. Embark from a car park in the centre of a beautiful beach at L746-339, beside a graveyard and abandoned church.

Freaghillaun - *Fraochoileán*

L735-352   Sheet 44

A surprisingly attractive, small, sheep-grazed island, lying on the outer, eastern side of the entrance to Bertraghboy Bay, SW of Inishlackan. The western side of the island is short cropped grass and very pleasant. The name *Fraoch Oileán* in Gaelic means 'Heather Island', probably the single most common name for an Irish offshore island. Uniquely among such islands, in this case the name is inappropriate, as no heather was found. No water either. Snipe and Common Gull were seen.

Embarkation and Landing

As for Inishbigger, embark from the car park in the centre of the beach at L746-339. Land onto lovely sandy beaches on both sides of a sheltered spit at the eastern point of the island. Camping is immediately above the beach.

Inishtreh - *Inis Troighe*

L739-371   Sheet 44

This is an unattractive, flat, ungrazed lump of heather, gorse and reeds, in a beautiful setting. It guards the eastern side of the entrance to Bertraghboy Bay. Land on the eastern side or walk out at LW from a beautiful quay at 742-367. Periwinkles.

Inishlackan - *Inis Leacan*

L722-377   Sheet 44

An attractive, low island in the mouth of Bertraghboy Bay, it is distinguished by a conspicuous, rectangular, water-tank structure on the island's highest point. There is water in rain barrels outside the houses. Water used to be pumped by a windmill (now ruined) from a walled pond up to the water storage tank. Formerly inhabited, it is now occasionally so in summer. There is a large, shell-midden in sand hills at the north-eastern corner of the island. Inishlackan is a good stopover with easy access to the extremely pretty Roundstone village. Roundstone is a posh tourist centre, with pubs, restaurants, and some shops, but is poorly provisioned. It is the centre for intense tourist use of this stretch of mainland coast. The island is worth the visit.

Landing and Embarkation

Land in many places but it is best at a very sheltered pier with a sandy beach on the eastern side. This is near the north-eastern corner, below a restored schoolhouse. There are rocky shores on the N, W and S, with reefs offlying. There is camping near pier and elsewhere.

The mainland embarkation is from a pier at Erlough at L717-386, in a bay about 1km to the N of the island, reached by taking the first left turn after the Garda Station as one leaves Roundstone for Ballyconneely.

Inishnee - *Inis Ní*

L735-383   Sheet 44

The island has a population of 30. It almost fills the western part of Bertraghboy Bay. The grid reference is for the highest point, which is to the S of the figure-eight-shaped island. The island lies E of Roundstone. Nowadays, it is connected to the mainland by a modern, new bridge, replacing the picturesque relic built by the Congested Districts Board around 1890. Going from the modern and popular holiday village of Roundstone to the island is stepping back a generation or two in time.

The island has a rocky shore all around. There are no sandy beaches. The eastern side is quite interesting in that there are a large number of small, hand-built little harbours and jetties. These are now all disused, and at times, may only be identified at close quarters. One may land on the E coast almost anywhere. The S/SW coast is steeper and landing is not so easy. The northern and western shores may be used to land, but involve carries over uneven ground. Water may be obtained from houses on the island. There are no shops.

Skerdmore, Co. Galway - Séan Pierce

Tides

Tides are strong on the western side and may be up to 1.5kn just at and S of the bridge, where there are some shallows.

Oghly Island - *Oileán an Chlaí*

L748-389   Sheet 44

This very small island inside the bay and E of Inishnee has no evidence of previous habitation or of water. The coast is rocky all around, but totally weed covered, so landings may be effected quite easily. At present, there are two wooden huts on the island.

Illaunurra - *Oileán Ura*

L587-403   Sheet 44

Illaunurra is 15km W of the entrance to Bertraghboy Bay and lies beyond even Ballyconneely. It is about 7km E of Slyne Head and lies near Bunowen Bay and Aillebrack, a pretty holiday spot for the relatively wealthy. A number of attractive islets lie off the shore, largest of which is Illaunurra. Beware the notorious shallows hereabouts, which may leave you stranded on a falling tide. Also, boomers abound in conditions of even

a little swell. Read Brian Wilson's experience, as told in 'Dances With Waves', and be chastened.

Embarkation and Landing

Embark from the E-facing beach, sheltered by Bunowen Bay pier at L593-416, or just W of that from a pretty, W-facing strand at L585-417. The pier is probably the most logical embarkation place for rounding Slyne Head.

There is a sandy beach with camping on the northern tip of the island, and several storm beaches. The landing place of choice must be a sheltered sand/storm beach at the SE. Immediately above it is manageable camping, greater privacy, and abundant firewood.

There are sheep, Dunlin and Mallard.

Strawbeach Island
Oileán na Muiríleach

L578-413   Sheet 44

NW of Illaunurra, Strawbeach is easiest reached from a pretty, W-facing strand at L585-417, less than 1km to the NE. This is a wee gem of a pleasant, sheep-grazed islet, giving unexpected privacy just off a crowded beach. There is a dependable sandy beach landing in a lagoon on the eastern side. Camp anywhere. No water. Ringed Plover.

Skerdmore/Skerdbeg
Na Sceirde

An impressive collection of rugged islets, lying 14km SSW of the entrance to Bertraghboy Bay. The whole area is a network of rocks, bays, narrow channels, cuts, rocky reefs and small outlying rocks, though very much dominated by the bulk of Skerdmore. Well worth the journey on a good day. These islets are said to have the greatest feeling of remoteness of all Irish offshore islands.

As one approaches from the N, the combined mass appears to be one. In fact, the group consists of a series of high, rocky islands, separated by narrow channels. The channels divide the mass into blocks, mainly Skerdmore and Skerdbeg, each with off lying rocks. Outliers are *Dún Godail, Dúleic* and *Dún Pádraig.* Skerdmore is by far the largest and highest block, to the SW, and Skerdbeg next biggest, to its NE. The OS sheet is confusing in this regard. Skerdmore has impressive bulk and climbs to nearly 20m. It is bigger in area than one would at first expect.

Embarkation

The nearest launching point is 11km NW at the beach in the elbow of Mweenish Island at L764-294. It is also practical to set out from anywhere around Roundstone or the Bertraghboy Bay area generally, and break the journey at Croaghnakeela at L690-324.

The layout of the group is quite complicated. Skerdmore is rather horseshoe-shaped and faces E. Skerdbeg lies off the mouth made by its prongs, creating a reasonably sheltered interior embayment. There are rocks and hummocks lying off both islets, including a set that runs E/W from Skerdbeg towards the middle of Skerdmore, thereby dividing the interior embayment into two on its N and S. The northern embayment is accessible from the N, and the southern one is much more easily entered from the S.

The two embayments are joined by narrow channels, the most navigable of which is towards the eastern side. The two large embayments thus produced may not be passable from N to S at extreme LW but are easily so at other levels. Kayaking through the channels is quite possible in calm conditions but the entire area has an aura of danger, and is probably quite hazardous in swell.

A Spanish trawler, the 'Arosa', went aground and was shipwrecked on nearby Doonguddle at L672-243 on 3rd October 2000 in a storm. Of the crew of 13, only one was saved. 2 others were taken off alive but died en route to hospital. Of the 10 that drowned, only 4 bodies were recovered, 6 being lost altogether.

Breeding Herring Gull, Great Black-backed Gull, Shag, Black Guillemot and possibly Oystercatcher. Grey Seals.

Skerdmore - *Sceirde Mór*
L660-248   Sheet 44
Landing

Both islands have deep-water landings, although they are quite manageable as such landings go. Onto Skerdmore, the southern embayment affords the best landing in a long narrow geo or cut that runs deep into the heart of the island, under the highest point. Landing is also possible in a similar cut into the northern embayment.

Skerdbeg - *Sceirde Bheag*
L663-248   Sheet 44

Skerdbeg is split into at least three separate blocks by narrow channels, the widest and most navigable of which lies between the two most westerly blocks. Landing is possible, and probably best at LW to half tide, in the extreme northeastern corner in a narrow cut, although considerable surge has been experienced. This island is a rugged, rocky mass that gains height towards the SW. It is separated from the next islet to the W by an extremely narrow channel that may just be passable by kayak in calm conditions.

Connemara West

Conamara Thiar

Slyne Head to Killary Harbour

Ceann Léime go dtí an Chaol Sháile Rua

County Galway

Slyne Head - *Ceann Léime*

Slyne Head is a major headland and divides the west coast of Galway and Mayo from Galway Bay. It is an island headland. Slyne Head is actually the western tip of Illaunamid, the outermost of a fragmented group of islands lying off the south-western tip of Connemara. There are three main groups of these islands: Illaunamid, Chapel/Duck Island, and nearest the coast, Illaunaleama - *Oileán Léime* and Doonawaul - *Dún na bhFál*. The innermost and outermost sounds are unnamed. The much-fragmented gaps on the inside of Duck Island are Cromwell's Sound, Blind Sound and Joyce's Sound. Tim Robinson's map of Connemara and/or Admiralty chart 2708 are recommended for the detailed navigation required in this area. The area consists of shallow reefs and islets surrounded by deep water and is exposed to Atlantic swell from all sides.

The more interesting route W towards Illaunamid passes through the chain of islands. These are divided by sounds where strong tidal currents and overfalls occur, and are formidable in wind over tide conditions. The area between Chapel Island at L529-409 and Illaunamid at L514-412 is also dotted by reefs, and should be treated with caution, even in small swell. If there are frequent breakers on these reefs, landing at Illaunamid is likely to be difficult, if not impossible. However, if conditions permit, there is scope for exploring and playing in the tidal races outside Illaunaleama - *Oileán Léime* and Doonawaul - *Dún na bhFál*.

Embarkation

The nearest departure point is approximately 3km E on the Galway Bay side, in the bay op-

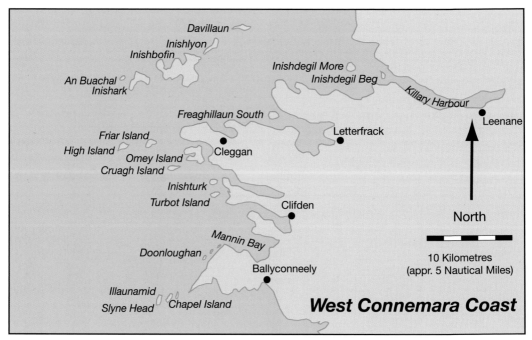

posite Connemara Golf Club, at the NW end of a long beach (*Trá Mhóir*) at L570-432.

Parking may dictate a start further E at the totally dependable Bunowen Bay at L590-417.

A trip N around the headland adds a certain interest and variation to the trip. The nearest alternative landing to the NE is at Stackport at L556-434, 1km NE of the coastal headland inside Slyne Head. This landing is a 1.5km road walk W from the *Trá Mhóir* put-in. Irish Lights used this quay for ferrying goods to the island, but the road is now through a series of gates, and may be private, so please ask for permission before taking your car down to the pier. The landing is difficult to see from seaward, but is close to two small houses.

More dependable is Doonloughan at L569-453, but there is limited parking. Easiest perhaps on this side is at the head of Mannin Bay at L630-460, where the main road skirts the sea and there is plentiful parking.

Tides

HW and LW are as for Galway.

In these sounds, the main W coast tidal stream prevails so the flood makes N at HW Galway -0320, and the ebb makes S at HW Galway +0305. Both streams run at 3kn springs. However, locals say that in this area, the N-going stream is stronger and runs for longer in each tidal cycle. Often, adverse tidal streams can be avoided to a certain extent by using the eddies that develop on the downstream side of the archipelago.

SPA

Storm Petrel, Sandwich, Arctic, Common & Little Tern, Barnacle Goose.

Illaunamid - *Oileán Imill*

L514-412   Sheet 44

This island is best known for its western headland, Slyne Head or *Ceann Léime*, and its lighthouse at L514-412. Illaunamid means 'Wood Island', because of the amount of flotsam washed up here. Robinson also terms it *Oileán Imill* (Edge/Margin Island), which Anglicises as Illaunimil.

The most obvious feature of the island is the two lighthouses. Both were built in 1836. One is unused. The other flashes twice, every 15 seconds.

For the story of these lighthouses and their people, read Bill Long's excellent 'Bright Light, White Water'. Tales include drowning tragedies during the building of the lighthouses, drowning of keepers, alleged murder of Irish Lights' personnel on the island, shipwrecked sailors stealing boats and dismissal of keepers for drunkenness. Three big sets of solar panels are now connected into the lighthouse complex, along the southern wall.

However, other features not mentioned in the book show that the keepers' lives were not all misery. For instance, in the mid-90s, the remnants of a mini-golf course were to be seen, just to the S of the lighthouse. Alas, this is no longer evident. There is also an unusual model of a lighthouse, complete with crane, and very similar

Landing, Illaunamid, Co. Galway - Séan Pierce

Landing on Chapel Island, Co. Galway - Séan Pierce

to Fastnet, on a rock in a (brackish) pond. The elaborate model is the strangest sight here. It is N of the path between the lighthouse complex and the quay. The model also has a small extra and easily missed feature - an outlying channel buoy in the extreme E end of the large pond. The effect of the relatively small model within the large pond/rock pool is quite realistic.

The rock of the island is metamorphic (gneiss).

The island is attractive with a remote feel to it. However, the impression of neglect and decay is strong around the lighthouse complex. This extends to the more modern lighthouse also but a few coats of paint and a general clean up would change this overnight. The quality of the building work in the network of houses and workrooms around the older lighthouse is impressive. Some of the fireplace mantles and capping stones are of beautifully worked granite. The assortment of debris and flotsam and jetsam, both around the lighthouse and on the storm beaches, does provide diversion for avid beachcombers. The island merits an overnight.

Fauna

Wildlife includes seals and rabbits. Breeding birds include Cormorant, Shag, Arctic Tern, Wheatear, Meadow & Rock Pipit, Raven, Skylark, Oystercatcher and Ringed Plover. It is the best seabird and cetacean watching point in Galway. Some excellent work was done here by Davenport in 1979-1981 on spring Skua passage migration, but none appears to have been done on other species since. Pomarine Skua were spotted in nearby Ballyconneely Bay on the southern approaches in May 2003.

Landing

There are two landing areas, both of which are only dependable in low swell conditions.

The first, and more reliable, is at a quay on the E end of the island at L518-410. It is easily spotted by a small pump-house and crane, formerly used to transfer fuel oil to the lighthouse. If the waves are too much at the quay, there is a small gully a few yards S. It leads to a small coral strand, accessible on the top half of the tide. It is accessible at lower water, but only onto boulders.

The gully is very narrow, admitting one kayak at a time. A less attractive alternative is a larger boulder beach on the N side of the quay.

The second landing area is on the N side of the island, close to the W end and the lighthouse itself in a cove at L515-412. This small cove has the attractive name of *Fuaigh na gCaccanai* (Cove of the (Cormorant) Shite)! This landing is only reliable in calm conditions when all weather is coming from the S. There are steps cut in the stone towards the centre of the cove. On the W side there is a rock-choked passage topped by a concrete bridge leading to other steps. In both landing spots care must be taken to lift boats well clear of rogue waves and rising tide.

Camping

There are sheltered flat areas suitable for camping near the outbuildings of the older, disused lighthouse. The walk from the E landing to the lighthouse requires quite a bit of ferrying of gear. Camping is also available S of the E landing over the first hummock. Although not as protected as by the lighthouse, it is fine for reasonable weather conditions.

Chapel Island - *Oileán an Teampaill*

L531-410   Sheet 44

Chapel is a lovely island with pleasant camping and a hint of fresh water in slightly brackish pools. The 12th Century chapel at L531-410 itself is interesting, and boasts a collection teapot. In early 2003 there were no Euro coins yet evident, probably indicating that not many pass this way. There is a somewhat attractive bothy at a tidal lagoon on the S side.

Chapel Island and Duck Island are separated by a narrow channel, open at all stages of the tide. The channel is easier found from the N. It passes immediately under the chapel.

Landing

The main landing on Chapel Island is on the south-western side at L528-408, almost facing Illaunamid. A landing may sometimes be had under the chapel, probably better at LW.

Birds

In March 2003, the following species were seen. An asterisk after the name indicates that they were probably breeding. There were seen 50+ Purple Sandpiper which is a nationally important number. There were also 40+ Oystercatcher*, 30+ Ringed Plover*, 10 Redshank, 1 Merlin, 6 Shelduck*, Raven, Skylark, Black Guillemot, Shag, and 20+ Swallow*.

In March 2003, there were 40+ Grey Seal.

At the same time on Chapel, 3 male and 1 female Eider were seen, and on nearby Horse Island another male, suggesting breeding. This would, if proven, be the southernmost outpost of breeding Eider on Ireland's W coast as of summer 2003. The official such record is Inishkeeragh, Mayo. Eider are expanding southwards year by year, and it is thought that Mink disturbance is the cause.

Duck Island - *Oileán Lachan*

L534-412   Sheet 44

The eastern island of the middle group of islands. It deserves exploration.

Duck is higher and craggier than its immediate neighbours. Tides flow strongly through its many thin channels, which would confuse any navigator.

There are breeding Shag and Black Guillemot on the steep eastern side. 40 pairs of Shag nest in the eastern gully at the waist.

Landing and Camping

Landing may generally be possible onto shelves in a cut on the north-eastern corner. Camping might be bearable, just.

Doonloughan Group

Doonloughan is a beautiful mainland area of machair and beach, with a sprinkling of houses, about 7km NE of Slyne Head. The four islands described here are important as they create a sheltered inside channel. This is useful to know of in the context of a passage from Slyne Head to Mannin Bay to the NE, especially in any kind of wind conditions. The whole area outside the islands is strewn with dangerous booming reefs, and shallows of every kind. Here be dragons! Frightening waves tube, for a long way off, to great height and power, in almost any conditions.

The inside channel is impassable at the lower part of the tide.

Enter from the south-western Slyne Head side via the open bay inside Inishkeeragh. There is a little quay at L569-453 on this side

Enter from the north-eastern Mannin Bay side via the sheltered deep-water channel inside Inishdugga. There is a substantial and sheltered pier at L569-457.

Camping by either pier is excellent, but better at the latter, which suits those heading N (but see also comments on Inishkeeragh below). It is important if arriving at evening time to choose a campsite with open water available in the direction of travel the following morning. If necessary, wait to camp until the channels connect. No water found at either location, but ask at the houses.

The middle channels entering this inner area on either side of Illaunamenara should be avoided in all conditions as they are foul, a vast area of reefs and boomers.

Inishkeeragh - *Inis Caorach*

L557-449   Sheet 44

Lovely grassy, sausage-shaped island that demarcates the entrance to the inside Doonloughan channel from the SW. There is a beautiful little beach at L557-449 with a lovely campsite in a prominent little bay near the north-eastern tip, on the landward side. This is a more private camping option than the mainland at Doonloughan itself.

Illaunamenara
Oileán na Meannán

L555-453   Sheet 44

The most remote and western of the four, this island is pleasant to walk around. It gives awesome views of the crashing waves working the reefs outside in the open ocean. It may be reached on the lower half of the tide on foot across the Calf Islands. Otherwise, this island and its approaches on all sides are best avoided altogether. A large conical cairn on its low summit is very visible.

Calf Islands

L565-453   Sheet 44

A group of fragmented grassy mounds grazed by cattle. Accessible on foot at the lower half

of the tide, and via these islands to either outer island. A sandbar stretches through these islets and divides the navigable inside channel.

Inishdugga - *Inis Duga*

L567-458   Sheet 44

Pleasant grazed island that shelters the north-eastern channel described above, opposite the pier. Landings are numerous all along eastern and north-eastern flanks, some well protected from Atlantic swell, onto sand and gravel beaches. There is some evidence of habitation, now in ruins, at the north-eastern end. There are traces of a small circular building and a few low walls. There were 250+ Golden Plover in March 2003.

Galway West Coast
The Inner Islands

Turbot Island - *Tairbeart*

L580-524   Sheet 37

Evacuated in 1978. Nowadays the houses are mostly used as summer homes. Land on a sandy beach, just E of the sheltered slip. The landing is in a bay on the eastern end of the N side. There is attractive and convenient camping on machair in the dunes behind the beach. There is water in a well.

A road running E to W bisects the island. The former habitation was mostly on the northern shore.

Two Corncrake sang in 2003.

Eeshal Island - *An tOileán Íseal*

L562-529   Sheet 37

A small low, grassy island grazed by sheep, just WSW of Inishturk. Landing is possible onto boulders on the south-eastern side in a shallow bay. 26 Mallard and 4 Common Scoter were seen on 12th September 1999.

Inishturk - *Inis Toirc*

L573-531   Sheet 37

An attractive island, identified by a small hill with an RT mast on the top. It is just NW of the mouth of Clifden Bay. The landing place is at a sheltered, sandy beach and harbour just N of the south-eastern tip. There is water in a well nearby.

In 1991, there was a single holiday home. In 2003, there were 12. Camping is available, but the welcome may dwindle if too many visit. There is an alternative landing place on the north-eastern side. It is secluded, on a sandy beach at the foot of an attractive, formerly cultivated valley. There is limited camping, which is sheltered from the SW.

Formerly a Corncrake island, they were gone in 2003.

Omey Island - *Oileán Iomaí*

L564-554   Sheet 37

This island is accessible to vehicles on all but the highest parts of the tide. A lake dominates the interior of the island. There is a ruined church and graveyard all smothered in sand, on the northern side at L565-563. Human remains are visible which are being archeologically investigated by Dúchas. A lovely, worthwhile island not to be missed.

Landing and Camping

The inside passage at L575-562 dries mid-tide in the north-eastern corner. Landings are possible along much of shore on the northern and eastern sides on either side of the dry area.

Also, at L573-551, there is an attractive small beach in a small cove just W of the SE corner. However, it is a bit exposed, and not very suitable for overnighting. No water.

At L564-554 on the western side of the island, there is a sheltered beach in a deep bay, which is much better. There is excellent, remote, machair camping. There is water in a streamlet 500m NW of the beach.

4 Corncrake were heard in 2003.

Boolard Island

L632-530   Sheet 37

Small, grass and fern covered island in the middle of inner Streamstown Bay, with camping possible at the eastern tip. The most convenient put in point in Streamstown Bay is near the head of the bay on the southern side. This is beside the bridge at L640-525, 1km from the fork off the main road from Clifden to Letterfrack. The road is being widened hereabouts but it is still necessary to be considerate with the parking.

Streamstown Bay empties S of Omey via a narrow mouth, giving a fine bouncy race in sheltered circumstances, worth a play in springs. This tidal race at the mouth is entirely avoidable by those travelling in small boats. Spring tides converge with convenient, midday low tides, giving a good flow for a tour out of the bay and into Clifden Bay to the S, or Cleggan or Ballynakill Bays to the N.

Freaghillaun South
Fraochoileán Theas

L647-604   Sheet 37

An attractive, small island at the mouth of Ballynakill Harbour, just SW of and under Tully Mountain. Once inhabited but the houses are now in ruins. Land on a stony beach on the southern side. There is drinking water at a drip feed from an artificial pool under the cliff by the landing. Camping is available on the bluff

Landing on High Island, Co. Galway - S. Pierce

above the landing. Other landings are possible, including in a lagoon between the main island and a smaller island on the western side, where one may step out onto tidal peat. Freaghillaun South is worth a visit. There are fish cages to the E of the island. There is a significant tide race off Ross Point, 3km ESE. Ballynakill Bay fills from Galway HW -0500. The tides are generally weak, except at the narrows.

Illaunananima - *Oileán an Anama*
L642-657   Sheet 37

The name means 'Live Island', in the sense of the soul or the living spirit. A tiny islet, 1km NNW of Rinvyle Point, to be avoided in any kind of W swell. The waters inshore of this islet can become one seething mass of foam when swell runs, so do not be caught off guard. Otherwise, this island is a superb waystop. Land by a very secluded channel-like entrance on the N-facing shore.

Crump Island - *Oileán Dá Chruinne*
L679-653   Sheet 37

Crump means 'Island of the Sea Inlet'. Landing is best on a shingle beach on the north-eastern side, close to the channel separating the island from nearby Shanvally Beg at L684-650. This landing becomes awkward at LW so time your arrival and departure carefully. There is camping near an old, ruined, two-story house in which some shelter can be had for cooking. Also, one can land on a stony beach in a shallow bay on the southern side. No water found.

The story goes that when deciding where to draw the county boundary between County Mayo and County Galway, the ancient local Councillors threw a sack of oats into the ebbing tide as it spilled out of Killary Harbour. The islands that lay to the N of the oats as they floated out would be in Mayo, those to the S, in Galway. To the surprise of many, the oats floated down S of Crump and then headed out to sea. Hence, Crump is in Mayo.

Editor's Note: Crump is included with the W-facing Galway islands for convenience.

Illaunmore - *Oileán Mór*
L751-647   Sheet 37

A tidal island, just S of the entrance to Little Killary Bay. Though shown on the OS map as well off the shore, it is joined for half the tide by a sand bar to the mainland, at a beautiful crescent shaped, N-facing beach, known locally as Glas-silawn. The island actually forms the outer part of this beach, appearing merely as a headland from most angles. Nice views. It has a holding tank for fish. A PADI scuba-diving school and rescue possibilities are all at the head of Little Killary, the bay opening to the E of this islet.

Galway West Coast
The Outer Islands

Cruagh Island - *An Chruach*
L535-551   Sheet 37

The name means 'The Stack'. This is a large, exposed haystack-shaped lump of a heathery fern and grass island, out west of Omey. At over 63m, it is almost as high as High Island. It has magnificent cliff scenery on the northern side, and spectacular spires in the NW. Deep-water landings only are available, in sheltered creeklets on the eastern side. A holiday home is being renovated just above the most sheltered landing spot.

Friar Island - *Oileán na mBráthar*
L524-578   Sheet 37

This island is split into three or four sections, providing interesting exploration. On the north-eastern side, at the centre of the fragmentation, there is a sheltered storm beach. It is dependably easy to land on, and from which the interior may be explored. A beautiful place. The drying area shown on the 1:50,000 OS map to the E is actually a pronounced heathery/grassy knoll and gives shelter at all times. Well worth the visit.

High Island - *Ard Oileán*
L507-576   Sheet 37

High Island is the jewel in the crown of W of Ireland wild islands. Only Inishtrahull to the N and Inishvickillaun to the SW rival its massive grandeur. Surrounded by high cliffs virtually all around, its overall geography, variety of magnifi-

Inishark, Co. Galway - Séan Pierce

cent and inspiring views, fauna, and other points of interest mark it out as being special.

Landing

The difficulty of landing sets High Island as a prize for all who aspire to come here.

Midway along the south-eastern side is a prominent cove, backed by huge cliffs under the highest part of the island. Landing is best about 200m E of this in a boulder-choked cove. The back of the cove is shown on the OS sheet as having a 'Cross Slab'. The landing cove is where the lower ground to the eastern end of the island begins to rise towards the centre, and where the island is narrowest and most waisted. Scramble airily to the plateau above.

On the eastern side of the cove is a hard-rock landing for boats, at which surge is limited and the scramble to the plateau above is much easier. Kayakers might consider landing even one boat at this spot, in case conditions deteriorate.

There is a second landing point reported, just E of the SW tip of the island at L503-571. Clinker boats might manage better here, but it is a bit exposed for kayaks. If manageable, it is closer to the monastic ruins on the island and might thus be preferred by some. It is directly underneath the smaller of the two island lakes.

Camp at will. Water in the lakes appears stagnant but looks better in the streamlets E of centre.

High Island is uninhabited. It was once owned by Brian Boru, and more recently by Richard Murphy, the poet. There is a (Murphy) stone hut, and a more recent timber Dúchas building. Rumours abound of a ruined copper mine on the eastern slopes near the high point of the island, and of an awesome cavern-like cave on the north-western side.

There are the ancient 7th Century ruins of an early Christian beehive hut, monastery and chapel, said to have been founded by Saint Feichin of Omey Island fame. The ruins are beside the larger of two lakes above the western end. In 2003, these are being refurbished by Dúchas. Raised platforms and planks protect the excavations from workers' muddy boots. There are three impressive inscribed slabs at the back of the chapel, worth finding.

Inishskinnymore, Co. Galway - Séan Pierce

SPA

Peregrine, Chough, Storm & Leach's Petrel, Barnacle Goose.

In 2003, there were Raven, Twite, Black Guillemot, Skylark and Meadow Pipit.

Inishshark - *Inis Airc*

L501-640   Sheet 37

The name means 'Sea Monster Island'. A splendid, formerly-inhabited island. There is an abandoned school, but no modern church. The pier was built in 1937 by Michael O'Sullivan of Ballycastlebeg in Cork, according to a commemorative stone nearby. The islanders in living memory went to Inishbofin of a Sunday for mass. The population dwindled, and the last left in 1961, mainly for Inishbofin. The island is rugged yet pretty.

Birds

The island is home to 70 or 80 Barnacle Goose each winter. Bonxie also breed here.

There is an interesting, small burial ground at the harbour and a small derelict 19th Century chapel, which is called St. Leo's, after the patron saint of the island. The church had a bell, which broke and fragmented, and it was believed that to bring any part of it on a journey would bring good luck. Emigration being what it was in the middle part of the 20th Century, North America is thought to be littered with carefully kept and much honoured little bits of the bell.

Inishshark lies WSW of and is separated from Inishbofin by Ship Sound. The island has large cliffs and sea stacks on the western side. Big breakers and reflecting waves are the norm out the back of the island, providing an interesting and committing circumnavigation. The crossing of Ship Sound can be treacherous with contrary winds and many shallows, which may boom.

Landing and Camping

Land inside a protective but otherwise unusable pier below the abandoned village on the eastern end of the S coast. The landing is onto a steep slipway or stony storm beach beside the slipway. Alternatively, use a very narrow cut providing a dependable soft landing about 100m E of the pier. The camping is excellent. The water in the well looks a little dodgy.

Inishskinnymore - *Inis Scine Mór*

L513-641   Sheet 37

This is the larger of two islands, midway across the south-eastern entrance to Ship Sound. Inishskinnymore is low, sheep-grazed, short-grassed, and altogether quite a pleasant 3/4 hectares. There is a lovely sandy beach on the northern side. A pebble beach in the SE has the best camping potential.

Inishskinnybeg - *Inis Scine Beag*

L512-645   Sheet 37

A small, isolated satellite of Inishskinnymore, Inishskinnybeg lies just to its N. A sandy beach faces SE and other storm beaches lie to the N and W. Long grass testifies that no animals graze, but camping is just possible between the storm beaches.

Inishgort - *Inis Goirt*

L503-629   Sheet 37

The name means 'Bitter' or 'Salty' island. Inishgort is a farmed, grassy island of 10 hectares or so, SE of Inishshark. There are landing places at stony beaches in bays on either side of a waist just N of the southern point.

Sheep grazed. Uninhabited. Good camping. No water.

An Buachal - **The Boy**

L478-645   Sheet 37

An Buachal is a huge vertical stack, lying about halfway along the western side of Inishshark. It is said to have been a target for the young turks of Inishshark, who would come of age climbing it. Certainly, there is a cairn on top. It is nationally renowned as a scuba-diving spot because its walls drop 45m straight to the bottom. Climbers may enjoy the vertical 65m above the high water mark.

Landing and climbing

In the right conditions, one may land easily onto shelves on the southern side. The stack is well sheltered by the cliffs of Inishshark from anywhere E, really from SSE round to NE.

To climb, strike out for the south-eastern ridge. Once gained, immediately follow horizontal ledges all the way to the south-western ridge. Scramble with caution and patience up the south-western side of the summit pinnacle. A more elegant line, but somewhat delicate, is to follow the south-eastern ridge directly to the summit pinnacle.

Inishbofin - *Inis Bo Finne*

L540-648   Sheet 37

The name means 'White Cow Island'. A regular ferry serves this lovely island, out from Cleggan in County Galway at L602-584. The population is 150. There are pubs, hotels, hostel, shops, chipper and restaurant.

Inishbofin is a large attractive English-speaking island, popular with tourists. The grid reference is for the new main pier. The village area is

Off An Buachal, Co. Galway - Séan Pierce

well spread out, ribbon fashion, along the shore of the S-facing harbour and bay area.

Landing

The sea state at the entrance to the main harbour and bay can be very rough for tidal reasons. Two white towers on the island face the entrance to the main harbour, on a bearing of 032° (true), and lead in through the safest entry point. The entrance can boom in heavy swell to either side of the best route. The best landing for small craft is behind the old pier further into the bay than the new pier.

In emergency or on circumnavigation, there are landings on every side of the island, but fewest in the N.

Circumnavigation

Watch for *Dun Na hInine* (Daughter's Fort), an almost detached stack at the NW point. Otherwise, the circumnavigation is interesting if undramatic by local standards. The most turbulence may be expected at Ship Sound and around the Stags of Bofin in the NW at L505-670.

Camping

There is good camping with easy landing and privacy at L537-644. This is by the ruined fort at the harbour mouth, opposite the village. Access to the village area is easiest by sea, given there is a substantial walk around. Any campsite on the (convenient) village side of the main harbour will lack privacy.

For a longer stay, camping is undoubtedly best made around at the eastern end of the island, in the horseshoe shaped bay, which has a very pretty beach for a nice soft landing, very sheltered, but a bit public. The end of the beach where Inishlyon meets Inishbofin used to be popular but is no longer allowed. Coastal erosion defence measures are being put in place in the form of newly planted Marram grass. This landing spot necessitates a long walk to camp or stay at Day's Hostel at L543-653 (095 45855), not to mention the pub and the good shop. The nearness to almost the best seafood restaurant in County Galway, the Lobster Pot, amply makes up for its remoteness.

Corncrake

Inishbofin was always a Corncrake stronghold, but there were only 14 recorded in 1988. By 1994, there were none. The good news is that 5 were serenading in 2003.

Inishlyon - *Inis Laighean*
L560-647   Sheet 37

The name means 'Strip of Land'. A small island, just SE of and separated from Inishbofin at HW. The best landing is onto the beach at the western end of the N side (facing the beautiful E beach of Inishbofin). There is an automatic, small, white lighthouse at Lyon Head on the eastern end, where there is a fierce tidal race on the ebb.

Davillaun - *Damhoileán*
L588-662   Sheet 37

Called locally Ox or Stag Island. Land in small cove on the southern side, E of the middle. The cove is not obvious until close. Alternatively, there is a difficult landing onto rocks on the eastern side at half to full tide. Good camping spots everywhere but most sheltered spots are marshy. No drinking water. Uninhabited. The island is exposed to any swell that is going and often throws up huge waves and breakers off the eastern and western sides. Interesting paddling at the western end where a small channel separates the island from a substantial stack. There are caves on the N-facing side.

Mayo
Killary Harbour to Killala
County Mayo

Inishbarna

L759-659   Sheet 37

Barna means 'gap'. This craggy island is well named, as it lies in the very mouth of Killary Harbour. It has a hillock running WNW/ESE. It is unnamed on the 1:50,000 OS map. The main channel passes through on its northern side, the narrower channel on its southern side being called Smuggler's Gap. There is a tower on the summit, tiled white to seaward. With a similar tower on Doonee Island at L748-662, it forms a transit for safe passage for larger craft through the reefs S of Inishdegil. Doonee is also unmarked on the 1:50,000 OS map, and has a difficult, deep-water landing only.

Landing

Land easily on Inishbarna onto a small stony beach at L762-658 on the eastern side, just under and NE of a ruined bothy. There are great views from the summit.

Tides

The tide runs in for 6 hrs from HW Galway -0500. It reaches 0.5kn until Bundorragha, and then increases to 1.5kn approaching the Erriff River, NE of Leenane.

Inishdegil Beg (Carrignaglamph)

L740-674   Sheet 37

Small grassy island just NE of Inishdegil More. Landing place on sheltered storm beach on SE facing side. Sheep, ruin, views. Purple Sandpiper.

Inishdegil More

L735-672   Sheet 37

A tiny gem of a formerly inhabited island. Grassy and rocky with outliers. Incredibly, people lived here until the 1940s. It lies a couple of kilometres directly outside the mouth of Killary Harbour. The island is privately owned and particular care should be taken to leave absolutely no litter, to ensure continued use for all. There is a good supply of driftwood on the western side, where terns also nest. Well worth a stopover, and a good waystop on an inner coastal tour to avoid the exposed beaches under Mweelrea Mountain.

Landing

The landing place is onto a gravely beach in a cove on the north-eastern side, under ruined houses. Camping is at the houses, with water in a well behind the middle ruin, which may or may not be drinkable. Approach this landing via the main channel through the group. There is also a storm beach just SW of the northern tip. Landing is sometimes possible onto boulders in a creek on the western side. There is a similar landing on the southern side.

Govern Island

L718-690   Sheet 37

Govern Island, just 1km SE of Frehill Island, is inhospitable. Far preferable for waystop or emergency is Inishdegil to the SE. There are plenty of seals but little chance of landing. SW of Govern Island are the Carrickgaddy Rocks (Carraig Gadai-Thieves Rocks). These were named when *Gráinne Mhaol* allegedly chained some thieves to the rocks and spread mackerel on their stomachs for the gannets to dive onto. The ebb tide is often felt here where it turns SW towards Crump after spilling out of Killary.

Frehill Island

L708-698   Sheet 37

Lying 6km NW of the mouth of Killary Harbour, Frehill is a steep, narrow, grassy island running NW/SE. It is about 500m long, with an extensive area of drying rocks to the S.

Landing

Landing on the island itself is all but impossible, although sheep do graze. However, a forced landing is often possible in moderate condi-

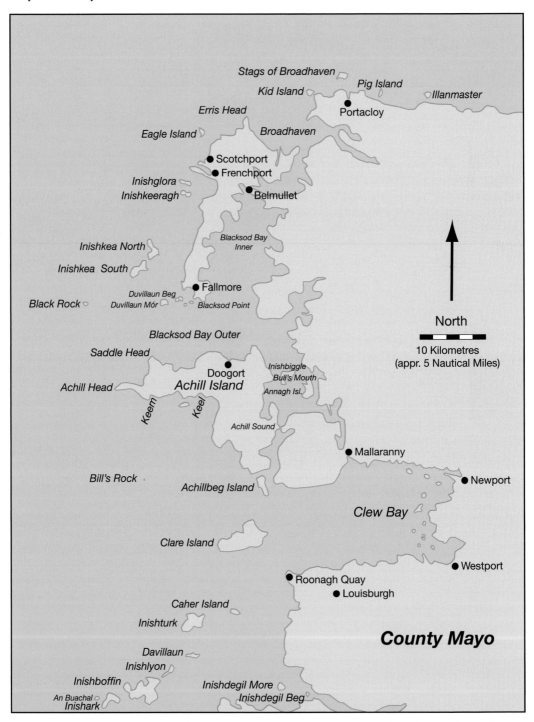

tions on the flat tidal rocks to the S where a low, central lagoon is sheltered by higher, drying rocks to either side. Entrance to the lagoon from either side is via a narrow channel. This landing would be acceptable as a waystop in calm conditions, or an emergency stop in less favourable conditions, but only on the lower half of the tide.

Far preferable for waystop or emergency is Inishdegil. The ground to the N and NW outside Frehill towards Caher Island is shallow and

The harbour, Inishturk, Co. Mayo - Josie Gibbons

breaks in wind. This inshore passage between Killary and Roonah is strictly for good weather only. In any kind of westerly swell, there are many breakers around the island. If paddling past, it's best to keep close to the N-facing shore. Particular attention should be paid to Carrick McHugh, a rock 3 cables N of the island. The island is privately owned and particular care should be taken to leave absolutely no litter, to ensure continued use for all.

Inishdalla

L633-721   Sheet 37

Inishdalla is a small grassy island, lying just 2km SE of Inishturk. The 1968 Pilot says it has a moderately soft landing on a sandy beach. The beach is in a cove at the northern side of the E end. There are also deep-water landings reported in narrow, rocky inlets on the northern side. Uninhabited, its main interest is its large colony of grey seals. No water found, but there is flat grass for camping.

Inishturk

L619-749   Sheet 37

There were once up to 180 people resident on the island, and now there are less than 100. The island children all go away to secondary school as teenagers. This is one of the most rugged and remote of all the inhabited islands off the W coast. Until recently, there was no regular ferry, but long overdue perhaps, Inishturk got a new ferry on September 16th 1997. This is probably the most significant 'Irish Offshore Island Development' for many years, and it's hoped that the needs of islands and islanders are at last being taken seriously.

Operating out of Cleggan and Roonah Quay, this ferry also has a real significance for kayakers, as the homeward trip becomes possible even if the weather kicks up overnight. Those who sail small boats off the W coast of Ireland must occasionally expect to fail to be behind their desks of a Monday morning. Inishturk is now a marginally more dependable objective. We wish the islanders well and hope that all this won't change things for them, other than as they would wish.

There are fantastic high cliffs at the back of the island. The western side of the island can cut up very rough and care should be taken to avoid breakers up to 100m W of the cliffs. In mirror-calm conditions or offshore easterly winds, the back of the island has huge cliffs to explore. Care should also be taken at the N of the island where fierce downdraughts can be experienced beneath the two high points.

There are B&Bs, pubs, and basic shops. There is a splendid circular roadway to walk. This goes inland, up the valley from the harbour, and back anti-clockwise by the southern side. Generally, the walking on the island is very good. The N and W are dramatically cliffy. Near the north-east-ern tip is a blowhole, the seaward end of which emerges through a penetrable boulder-choke, giving a scuba dive of great quality.

Corncrake

Formerly a Corncrake stronghold, there were 26 pairs counted in 1988. Paddlers heard at least one in 1992, but they were all gone by 1994.

Landing

The landing place is in the main village and harbour on the eastern side, which is sheltered. Also, landing is possible at beaches just S of the main harbour, if necessary. Off the mouth of the harbour is a bar, which can give a sporting arrival or departure. But the water inside or outside the bar is well sheltered. In the Great War, the Royal Navy favoured this as an anchorage.

L607-737

A narrow cut in rocks yields a superbly sheltered natural harbour, halfway along the southern coast. Camping is easy, but it is a good walk to the pub.

Ballybeg

L650-755   Sheet 37

A small islet lying SW of Caher. The island is overpopulated with sheep throughout the summer. Deep-water landing is possible through an inlet on the north-eastern side.

Caher Island

L665-759   Sheet 37

Caher is 8km out from the shore and 11km SW of Roonah Quay. On the SE of the island is a brackish lake and on the NW high point is a well - St. Patrick's Well. The island is uninhabited and 'belongs' to Inishturk, the people of which have the commonage grazing here. There is a fine 5th Century monastic ruin and crosses, which are used for the annual pilgrimage to and 'pattern' on the island. A pattern is an ancient rural Irish Catholic prayer tradition. The island is the alleged resting place of Saint Patrick. The 'floating' stone is still there and will always return to the island, even if stolen. And beware the thief, whose boat will sink. There is also an ancient prayer/wishing bowl. A must for the passage maker.

Caher Island, Co. Mayo - Séan Pierce

Landing and Camping

Land on the SE, or at Port Temple in a shallow bay below the ruins of the church, just NW of the eastern tip. There is another, in some ways better, landing on the SW side. It is difficult to find until very close, and consists of a narrow inlet, which turns to the right after a few metres. The land just opposite is probably the best for camping.

Bird life

Bonxie breeding.

Roonah Quay

L744-808   Sheet 30

Situated where Clew Bay turns S, this recently modernised pier is in an exposed cove. There are almost continuous breaking swells over a long rock ledge running out W from the pier. This is the embarkation place for the ferry to Clare Island, with waiting room, public phone, toilets and Post Office nearby. Launching is difficult, from the steps or a boulder beach adjacent. In northerlies, a better spot is the N end of a sandy beach just S of Emlagh Point at L747-797, about 1km to the S, reachable by road. More dependable, but less convenient, on the Clew Bay side is the sand-silted Carrowmore Pier at L794-817. It is just NW of Louisburgh and within walking distance. Another launching point is Oldhead Pier, about 4km further E at L834-824 where there is a hotel but is otherwise remote from facilities.

Clare Island

L715-852   Sheet 30

A beautiful, large, high, dramatic, inhabited island, dominating the mouth of Clew Bay. There is a regular ferry service from Roonah Quay at L744-808. The population of the island is about 150 in winter, and is double that in summer. There are several B&Bs. Basic provisions are available and there are limited facilities - a pub, hotel, hostel, public phone and even a nurse. The island is well worth a special visit. It is the highest of the truly offshore islands of Ireland. Knockmore at 462m gives spectacular views of the Mayo coast and falls almost sheer to the sea. Corncrake have not been heard since 1988 except for a single calling bird in 2002.

Landing and Camping

Land by the pier at L715-852 by the main harbour near the SE tip. The pier is just by an old, square castle, being one-time HQ of pirate-queen Granuaile who ruled the western seaboard. Camping is possible by the pier or in a field behind the beach.

L693-843   This is a significant landing on a gravel beach beside a broken pier. It is about halfway along the S coast at Portnakilly. It is not apparent until close and is situated below a conspicuous church and ruined 12th Century Abbey. This has been recently restored. It is early Cistercian, pre-Norman, pre-English and pre-Granuaile. There is a well-stocked Co-op shop, but it is a long way to the pub at the harbour.

Church offerings, Caher Island, Co. Mayo – Séan Pierce

Off Clare Island, Co. Mayo – Josie Gibbons

L703-877   Near the northern tip of the island, landing is also possible on the north-eastern side, about 1km SE of the tip, in a well-sheltered cove. The cove is about halfway between a prominent boulder beach and the disused but conspicuous lighthouse on the northern point of the island. Landing is onto a steep slip, or onto a sheltered breakwater. This landing is of interest on circumnavigation, or for its green road giving convenient access to the interior.

Circumnavigation

A circumnavigation is a memorable experience, but a serious undertaking. There are long sections without reliable landings, particularly from Portnakilly on the southern side, all the way through the SW and N to the landing spot on the NE. There is an inlet on the southern side of the island, 1km E of the south-western tip. Locally called Lackwee, it is exposed to the SW but otherwise sheltered

Tides

Tides flooding into Clew Bay flow E on the northern side of the island and NE on the southern side. The flood begins a little after local HW and LW, which is Galway +0015. In other words, it runs from HW Galway -0530 to +0040. Note that the flood is stronger than the ebb on the southern side, and the ebb is stronger than the flood on the northern side. In each case, the stronger flow achieves 1.5kn, the weaker only 0.5kn. The ground on the southern side is shallow.

As a result, both passages, and particularly the northern side, kick up when the ebb is against the prevailing westerlies. If on passage N, catching the flood combines well with the tides into and through Achill Sound. But care is needed on passage S for the reasons given above.

The Islands of Clew Bay

L935-863   Sheet 31

A detailed examination of the islands of Clew Bay is way beyond the scope of this guide. Were such included, the size of the guide would instantly double.

Sunset, Clare Island, Co. Mayo – Josie Gibbons

The islands of Clew Bay are easy to get to, and provide an attractive 'last refuge' option for visiting paddlers suffering bad weather.

Essentially, these islands are the most western tip of Ireland's 'drumlin belt', the other end being at Strangford Lough, S of Belfast. The belt wanders through Down, Armagh, and Cavan, and then meanders ever westwards, disappearing into the sea at this point. The islands, just as in Strangford, tend to be grazed, grassy hummocks. Drumlins are the remnants of lateral moraines left behind by the last ice age, covered with grass and gravel.

These islands are in the prettiest of locations. They are sandwiched between the mighty cone-shaped Croagh Patrick to the S and the Nephins to the N. Croagh Patrick is known all over as 'the Reek', a reek being a haycock, or also a stack of turf. The Nephins are probably the remotest and wildest mainland hills in Ireland.

It is widely believed in Ireland that there are 365 islands in inner Clew Bay, 'one for every day of the year'. Pilgrims climbing holy Croagh Patrick get their chance to count them, but must be distracted, as in reality there are slightly less than 100. The barefoot walk to the summit, in late July, is an annual test for the hardier of local Christians.

Only some of the islands are inhabited, and no water has been found on any uninhabited ones. There is probably a connection. Island More and Knocky Cahillaun are the largest. Inishgort has a lighthouse. John Lennon bought Dorinish in 1969 and a commune thrived there for a while. Many of the islands are interconnected by reefs at lower tides, and many others are almost so, making seagoing journeys amongst them less trouble on the top half of the tide. The big worry is being caught on mud on a falling tide, unable to walk or float out of trouble.

Access is from anywhere near Westport or Newport, but perhaps nowhere more central or convenient than the pier at Carraholly at L935-863. From Westport, head northwards on the N59, then turn left at a sign for rugby, golf and sailing clubs. Follow the small road to the sailing club and park at the pier. There is a stand-pipe for fresh water and easy slipway access.

A different island may be chosen each night. Beware that navigation needs careful map reading and getting lost is more than possible, necessitating landing and a stroll to the nearest summit to reorientate. There are a few derelict crofts. Black Guillemot, waders, Grey Wagtails, and all the usual bird and plant life abound. A single Corncrake was heard in 2001.

Tides

There is no committed or exposed paddling, although beware of the tidal race on the ebb at the Inishgort lighthouse at L901-875. Beachcombing on low tides is a must. Local HW/LW is about Galway +0030.

Achill Island Area

Achill is the biggest and most populous Irish island with 2,500 full-time residents. It is connected to the mainland by a bridge at Achill Sound. 'L' shaped, high mountains mark the scenery all along the south-western side. Only in the far north-eastern corner is there flat land.

At Keel, there is a substantial machair, and behind it is the most populated part of the island where there are pubs, restaurants, and all amenities. Two-thirds of the way down the western side is Dooega, a sheltered harbour, and at the southern tip lies Achill's little sister Achillbeg, a wonderful island.

The eastern shore on the edge of Achill Sound is low and boggy. Near the southern end of the sound is a Granuaile castle worth visiting. The RNLI station is close by. Midway up the sound is the bridge at the village of Achill Sound, where there are all facilities.

On the N coast is the hamlet of Doogort, under Slievemore Mountain, with its beautiful beach and pier, backed by machair. During the famine era of the mid 19th Century, Edward Nangle ran the most energetic Protestant ministry ever experienced in Ireland. Generally, the various Christian churches in Ireland do not proactively proselytise (convert) each other's members. Nangle went in hard and succeeded to a degree, but at a price. He opened schools and even a hotel. He stands critically judged by history in that he only offered food to the hungry who would become Protestant. Those accepting this bribe were called 'soupers', a pejorative term all over Ireland to this day. He also operated on Inishbiggle.

Achillbeg Island

L720-924   Sheet 30

Formerly inhabited. Good camping. Attractive. A fertile valley links two ice-rounded hills. There is a row of cottages on the northern slope of the valley and a disused schoolhouse on the southern side. In 1959, there were 8 pupils, all brothers and sisters. The population was never more than 117. There were 100 in 1900, and this was down to 67 in 1936 when the remaining people resisted evacuation and resettlement on Achill. The last 38 people all left during the 1960s.

Dun Kilmore on a forked headland on the western side, is a triple fort with the outer, easterly, section at F709-926. The two inner citadels are on the two branches at F707-927 and F706-926. Dun Kilmore is said to be the most elaborate promontory fort of the W Coast. It was started in the early Iron Age, and was inhabited by many cultures over a long period up to early Christian times. It is somewhat dilapidated through incessant Atlantic assault. Find it by walking W along the northern side of the waist, past a storm beach and under a cliff, until the forked headland is identified.

There are some remarkably attractive (70m) rock climbing cliffs at F714-922.

Landing

The best landing is at a lovely sheltered sandy beach midway on the E side. Landing is also possible on the north-eastern side, but less easily.

The crossing of Achill Sound to the E of the island and Blind Sound to the N are often treacherous as both are exposed.

There are also some storm beaches on the outside (W) of the island for those who favour the oceanic feel to their camping.

Bills Rocks

L551-938   Sheet 30

The Bills Rocks lie 11km due S of Keem Strand (F562-043) on Achill Island. Keem is pronounced 'Kim' locally. This is the nearest launching point for a trip to the Bills. Larger groups might prefer Gubalennaun Beg quay at F623-036 where there

Achillbeg Island, Co. Mayo - Séan Pierce

is easy parking and no surf. This option adds 1km to each leg of the trip.

The Bills comprise three large, steep-sided, grass-covered rocks. The largest rock has a grass covering of approximately half a soccer pitch. The ground is relatively level and could be camped upon, but it is completely exposed and it would probably be foolhardy unless you were sure of settled weather.

Landing

It is possible to land on the largest rock, which is the most northerly. On the southern side is a long, sloping cliff to the top. The gradient here is approximately 50° and while it might be easy for a rock climber, it could be quite challenging in canoeing gear or wet weather. The landing should only be attempted in calm weather and is best at LW, when there is an obvious ledge approximately 2m above water level, which can be accessed by a large, 'easy to climb' crack. It would be prudent to have a light kayak for this endeavour.

There is probably only enough room for three kayaks on the ledge, which limits the size of the landing party. Kayaks can be left on the ledge and tied to the rock face using rock-climbing chocks.

From the ledge, a large fissure runs diagonally from bottom left to top right and the top of the rock face. There are obvious handholds along the crack and it would probably be graded a 'diff' in old rock climbing parlance.

If you have the skills, the climb is worth it. At the top, you really feel exposed, miles from anywhere on a rock in the sea. It is an airy feeling. There are great views back up to Achill while to the SE, the exposed western coasts of Clare Island, Inishturk and Inishbofin are visible. The trip is a brilliant day paddle. It is worth circumnavigating the rocks. There is a beautiful arch to the W.

Achill Island (Outer) - the Round of Achill Head

The round of Achill Head may be done from either side, depending on conditions. The wind direction is everything, but beware of katabatics (downdraughts) on the lee side of the final ridge out to the head, a notorious local feature. The round trip from Doogort to Keem is about 26km.

Achill Island, Co. Mayo – Josie Gibbons

If going to Keel, it is even longer at over 33km.

The round of Achill Island as a whole is about 80km, especially if the beautiful Achillbeg is taken in, and it is worth taking at least three days. This expedition round Achill Head will always be the crux of that trip, and has to be one of the foremost Irish sea paddling trips, to be grabbed when conditions allow, and with caution.

Those on expedition along the coast will find it considerably easier to stick to the inner route through Achill Sound, but the round of Achill Head will be an integral part of the outer route. A trip around Achill and the Mullet Peninsula to the N is a week's unrivalled expedition. This trip involves a challenging open crossing to Duvillaun Mór from Achill Head itself or Saddle Head to its NE.

The Round of Achill Head is described here from the northern side, starting at Doogort.

Doogort

F672-089   Sheet 22/Sheet 30

This is an important launching or finishing point for the route outside the Mullet peninsula

or Achill Head. There is a good beach – it is best to land on at the western end under the hotel. There are also a campsite with facilities and water. It is a bit of a carry from the campsite to the beach. The quay just NW has a landing and water, but no camping. Beware of overfalls to the E of the beach on the ebb. They are just W of Ridge Point at F704-109.

Annagh Strand

F602-077   Sheet 22/Sheet 30

The outer, western part of Achill is dominated by the two summits of Slievemore (671m) at F650-087 and Croaghaun (664m) at F554-058. Between these two, on the northern side, cut off from civilisation altogether, lies the utterly beautiful N-facing Annagh Strand. It is 9.5km or more into the anticlockwise round of Achill Head. The beach is backed by Lough na Keerogue (Lake of the Beatles). From Doogort, the coast follows the cliffs around, with at least one memorable arch, until a truly remarkable pap (teat) shaped hill (269m) at F607-076 lies just SE of the beach. This is a worthwhile trip in itself, either by hill walk or paddle, and a must on the circumnavigation, as 16km lies ahead. The megalithic tomb at F602-076 is easily found as it has a 'modern' *bothán* (hut) built in its middle, anything but a normal sight, probably of Inishkea islander construction.

Achill Head

F517-052   Sheet 22/Sheet 30

From Annagh Strand it is necessary first to travel NW to Saddle Head at F564-094 where a considerable lump may be expected. A reef just offshore adds both technical interest and fear. Then it is SW to the head itself. A few storm beaches litter these impressive cliffs under Croaghaun. Although at least one seems well enough sheltered, conditions would need to be calm indeed to land. The head itself has broken islets off it and the innermost passage is passable under the right conditions. Moyteoge Head at F565-035 lies 5km ESE, behind which is Keem Strand.

Keem Strand

F562-043   Sheet 22/Sheet 30

A beautiful, horseshoe beach at the end of the road on the southern side of the island, Keem Strand is known to photographers the world over. Sheltered in most conditions, it surfs in southerlies. There are parking spots and viewpoints here, and many walks for Croaghaun and Achill Head. No facilities. This bay was the killing ground for the Achill Basking Shark fishery.

Gubalennaun Beg Quay

F623-036   Sheet 30

In trouble, this is the only dependable landing spot for dozens of kilometres in either direction. Keem Strand to the W may dump and Keel to the E is a famous surfing beach. This is a quay with no facilities except water and camping, and the certainty of a landing in any conditions. In nearby Keel can be had most anything - nice restaurants, pubs, provisions. The famous Achill Basking Shark fishery was based here until the mid-20th Century.

Keel Strand

F636-046   Sheet 22/Sheet 30

This is a famous surfing beach to be used by sea kayakers only in calm conditions. There is a camping and caravan site just in from the beach, with a convenient road and water near the village at the NW end of the beach. There is a golf links in the middle. The most remote part is in the SE where the Minnaun (or Menawn) Cliffs begin. Camping is excellent just behind the beach just about anywhere, though watch for golfers in the middle.

Achill Island (Inner) - Achill Sound

Sheet 30

The kayaker on passage can easily manage Achill's inside route. The tide governs entirely only in its narrower places, and the wind mostly prevails.

Achill Sound Bridge at F738-998 and Bull's Mouth at F737-068 are major challenges to larger craft, but kayaks can always manage. Under most conditions, one may paddle under the bridge, even against the flow. This may involve a short sprint, or at worst, a portage. Avoid the bottom of the tide because drying mudflats inhibit the process. All facilities are available here, as Achill Sound is the main town of the island.

At Bull's Mouth, at the northern entrance to the sound at F737-068, the eddies allow one to avoid problems. Wind against tide generates its fearsome reputation.

Tides

The tide flows simultaneously in from both ends to meet on the extensive mudflats just S of Achill Sound Bridge.

Accordingly, the flood flows S under the bridge until local HW, which is a couple of hours after HW Galway.

At the southern entrance to the sound, the tide floods N through the southern entrance of the sound at Achillbeg, from HW Galway -0450 until +0135, and ebbs in reverse. In the narrows at the entrance, especially at the twisty bit just NE of Achillbeg, tides reach 3kn in neaps and 4 - 5kn in springs. On the flood, a major eddy circulates just inside Darby's Point at F723-935 on the Achill Island side, reaching Granuaile's castle at F721-941. Either use or avoid as appropriate.

At the northern entrance to the sound, the tide floods S through Bull's Mouth at F737-068 at 5kn, from HW Galway -0450 to HW Galway + 0120, which is local HW at Bull's Mouth. On the flood, a major eddy circulates just inside the entrance on the Achill side. Either use or avoid this as appropriate. With wind over tide, quite a race is set up to the SSE. On the ebb, the sound empties to the N, which is often benign.

In summary, going either way through the sound, slow boats should start a couple of hours before HW Galway, and enjoy the flood to the mudflats just S of the bridge. Then perhaps break the journey, provision up and have a meal, in time to enjoy the ebb out the other side.

Inishbiggle

F746-067   Sheet 30

The population is 30-40, mainly elderly people. Inishbiggle is a low, boggy island with a dozen or so inhabited houses. The post office is at F746-067. Local information is that the seas on the inner passage between the mainland and Inishbiggle are often treacherous. Although Ballycroy, the local town on the mainland is very near, islanders access the outside world via Achill. There are modern launching facilities either side of the Bull's Mouth.

Embarkation and Landing

Inishbiggle is at the northern end of Achill Sound and is separated from Achill Island by the Bull's Mouth at F737-068. Land on a beach of small stones just E of the Bull's Mouth, between the Bull's Mouth and a pier at F739-069.

Launch from the slipway opposite, on Achill, at F735-071, where there is parking. Another handy embarkation point is on the Achill side of the North Sound at Bunacurry Harbour at F718-044. This is a stone and mud flat area, with a manageable carry even at LW, and plenty of parking.

The islanders have sought a cable car for generations. Boat access is less than dependable, because of the strong tides all round. Without a cable car, they feel their community is threatened. In particular, children cannot be sure they will make school every day. It seems that Eamon O'Cuiv, the Minister for Arts, Heritage, the Gaelteacht, and the Islands in 2004, is serious about providing one at last. He has shown more genuine interest in the islands, even the English speaking ones, than any other minister, ever.

Illancroagh and Heath Island

F786-030   Sheet 30

These two small islands jointly and effectively guard the entrance to the SE corner of Achill Sound North, a water system called Bellacragher Bay. The bay penetrates between the Corraun Peninsula and the mainland almost to Mallaranny, a narrow twisting inlet of great interest and a splendid option for a foul weather day.

The embarkation point at F784-025 is just below the post office at Tonregee, halfway between Mallaranny and Achill Sound Bridge. Limited parking but with a handy stony landing.

Illancroagh at F786-030 is the more interesting of the two islands. It can be landed on anywhere. There is splendid, huge, exposed bog oak on the western side, and a significant Common Gull colony in season. There are tide races all around. The tide runs E and W on either side. Wind over tide in these gaps normally happens on the ebb. These conditions provide a fun race just off the put-in point, and elsewhere at times. The tide also fills and empties round the duller Heath Island.

The passage inwards from this point features strong tides at all the projecting points, and a varying landscape best savoured on the journey SE and inwards. Rhododendrons are followed by conifers, by grasslands suitable for remote yet convenient camping, then by ubiquitous peathags, sometimes close to the road and sometimes away from it. At the head of the bay are salmon farm tanks, always worth a visit to see these brutes leaping and displaying.

The trick is to catch the tide inwards, lunch, and then catch it again outwards. Otherwise eddy-hop. Local HW is about Galway + 0230 in the furthest recesses of the bay, which is perhaps an hour later than local HW at the Bull's Mouth.

Tidal races are to be found at most of the twists and turns. The most playful ones are on either side of Illancroagh, and these are best enjoyed on the top half of the ebb. Being shallow, they do not particularly need a spring tide.

Ancient inscribed slab, Duvillaun Mór, Co. Mayo - Séan Pierce

Inishkeas/Duvillauns Group

F614-183   Sheet 22

This remarkable group of islands is well worth visiting.

Embarkation

Embarkation is from Fallmore, a sheltered, sandy, S-facing beach about 3.5km W of Blacksod Point, and 1km S of a prominent tower on a low hill, known as Glosh. The surf is much smaller at western end. Camping is on machair and there is water at the houses. The southern part of the Mullet peninsula is a stronghold for Corncrake and used to be for Corn Bunting.

Tides

The main W coast flood runs N from Achill Head, past Black Rock, then NNE past the outside of the group, from HW Galway -0320 to +0305.

The flood and ebb pour into and out of what is almost a sheltered 'lake' confined between the group of islands and the Mullet. The flows through the gaps seem to start a couple of hours earlier, at HW Galway −0515 and +0100. It floods generally NE/N through the channels between the Duvillauns, the Inishkeas and the Mullet. Certainly, in Blacksod Bay S of the Duvillauns, the ENE flood runs at these times. The streams are weak inside the lake but achieve 2.5kn in springs off salient points, and flow strongly through the gaps in the inner islands.

Inside the islands, the ebb pours out of the 'lake' the same way, and the timings are the reverse of the flood. Outside the islands, the ebb is more complicated. The main W coast ebb stream outside the group forms eddies and thereby runs weakly NNE immediately outside of the Inishkeas and Inishglora, and keeps going until it rejoins the main ebb flow approximately 3km WNW of Annagh Head, where there is much turbulence.

Black Rock

F483-156   Sheet 22

The rock is known to locals as *Tór Mór*, and to Irish Lights as Black Rock. Like Eagle Island, Black Rock is a prominent lighthouse rock on which landing is impossible in most conditions. This, along with the fact that it is over 11km offshore and steep-sided, makes it essential that any visit is undertaken in (very) settled weather.

Landing

A landing is possible near the steep, carved steps on the south-eastern side of the rock, with very low swell conditions and an unladen (or someone else's, plastic) boat. There are 3/4 options from mid to high tide but only one at lower tides, about 20m from the sea-arch.

There is a jetty at the eastern end, but there is often too much movement there. All landings are very steep, in deep water, with any waves giving a lot of vertical movement. This gives a real risk of a bad bang if the boat hits any rocky outcrops while dropping with the waves. So, even in the calmest conditions, landing cannot be assumed and it is recommended to keep lunch handy to eat on the water before the long, open crossing home.

After a successful landing, the boats must be hauled up the steep rock and tied to the iron stakes near the steps, which were probably chiselled into the rocks in the 19th Century. The walk to the top is steep. Launching is, as always, much easier. Always ask Irish Lights for permission for landing at a lighthouse.

There is rough camping, but this is not advised, as lighthouse keepers have been known to wait months to be taken off after their stint of duty here. Bill Long states that it is reputed to be the 'most difficult of the lighthouse rocks on which to land; totally inaccessible at times, either by boat or by helicopter'.

No water.

On a day trip, embark from Fallmore at F614-183 or Portglash beach at F612-202, for a 12km journey on a bearing of about 250°. If based on the Inishkeas, the distance is 8.5km at 235° from the western end of the sound between the N and S Islands at F556-218.

Tides

Departing from the Inishkeas, the only relevant tide is the main W coast tidal stream, which floods N from HW Galway -0320 to +0305, and the ebb in reverse. For a departure from the Inishkeas, a good strategy might be to leave an hour or more after local LW, taking advantage of the last of the S-going stream, allowing a return after the start of the N going stream. The rate of the streams has not been measured, but judging by the way buoys are dragged down, at least close in to the rock, they do seem to run strongly, possibly 2kn. Paddlers report having to ferry glide when getting close to the rock, to avoid being swept past.

On Black Rock itself, the light character is FL WR 12s 86m 22/16M, i.e. flashing, white & red sectors, every 12 seconds, height 86 metres, visibility 22 nautical miles in the white sector and 16 nautical miles in the red sector. It was, until recently, an acetylene gas light, one of the very few in Ireland or Britain. It was converted to acetylene from incandescent paraffin vapour in 1974 when it was automated. The acetylene system was decommissioned to a museum in Wexford in 1999 and replaced by solar power.

In 1940, the S.S. Macville was attacked by a German bomber close to the Rock, shattering the lighthouse panes and damaging the roof.

There are impressive, recently renovated dwellings of cut stone which was quarried from the rock. Amazingly, lighthouse keepers and their families lived here for 29 years until 1893. Then, dwellings for the families were built at Blacksod and the keepers would stay in shifts on the Rock in the years until the light was automated.

Duvillaun Mór

F579-157   Sheet 22

Landing

There is an unreliable landing place on a somewhat sheltered sandy beach (bouldery at LW) on the southern shore at a point marked Gubnageeragh. The scramble up is awkward, but tired paddlers from Achill Head may take advantage. There is camping above the beach. Water is available in small lakes at the top of the island. Otherwise the much more reliable landing point in calm conditions is in a shallow bay on the north-eastern side, almost facing Duvillaun Beg. Land onto flat rocks, in a sheltered cut, best just NW of a ruined dwelling.

The island was abandoned in the early 20th Century. In the 1821 census, there were 19 people living on the island, and a community existed

Rusheen Island seen from Inishkea South, Co. Mayo - Séan Pierce

here up to at least 1917. The ecclesiastical remains on the brow of the hill at the western end are of a small anchorite settlement being an eremitic establishment from the 6th to 10th Centuries.

The square ruin is a killeen, a children's' graveyard. A carved flat stone on the summit depicts a Greek crucifixion on one side and a pre-Celtic cross (with a circle surrounding the cross) on the other. Well worth the visit. The western end is wild and dramatic, with small sea stacks and islets lying off the shore. The E end boasts a beautiful arch.

SPA

Storm & Leach's Petrel, Barnacle Goose, Peregrine, Chough, Arctic & Little Tern.

Lapwing and Greater Black-backed Gull breed and there is a colony of black rabbits.

Duvillaun Beg

F588-164   Sheet 22

The landing point is on a storm beach just N of south-western tip. Otherwise, land on rocks just N of a long spit at the eastern tip.

Gaghta Island

F600-174   Sheet 22

Land onto stony beaches, midway along the north-eastern side in a cut.

Leamareha

F608-175   Sheet 22

Land at shingle or rocks on the northern side. Greater Black-backed Gull breed.

Inishkeas

These islands are not named for Inis Gé (the 'islands of geese' in Gaelic), despite their ornithological significance. Instead, they are named for 'Insulam Gedig' in Latin, or Naomh Géidh or Saint Gé in Irish. The first written reference to the islands was in a letter from Pope Innocent III appointing a local Bishop in 1198.

There was a thriving and stable Irish speaking population here from the late 18th to the early 20th Century. Nevertheless, no native writer ever emerged to record their lives from their own perspective, as happened elsewhere. Their story is

Inishkea South, Co. Mayo – David Walsh

pieced together from outside records. The population was stable at about 300 between the two islands for much of the time, though the South Island nearly always held more people than the North Island.

They ran out of turf by the 1830s, importing it thereafter. They survived the 1840's famine better than the nearby mainland, partly through fishing and piracy. Circumstances suited piracy because calm weather conditions in April and May becalmed many a sailing boat hereabouts. This all got out of hand so the coastguard placed a presence on the island to stop the practice.

Ravaged always by storms, the islanders were almost beaten by a big one in 1857, and were finally defeated in 1927. As protection against the wind, they developed a special style of lazy bed for the potatoes, 2m across and 30cm higher on the windward side, to protect the fragile young plants. The climate being milder than the mainland, potatoes could be sown in February or even January, giving the islanders a huge competitive advantage at the market in Belmullet.

They kept cows for milk, pigs for meat, and sheep for sale and for wool. They even kept horses to work the land, but more so on the N island where the widespread machair is more equine friendly. They also grew barley and their *poitín* was well known over a wide area, being favoured by the Boycotts, a well-known but not particularly popular local landed family. Their *poitín* was despised by the artist Paul Henry who visited in 1909. The boat crew got sozzled and gave him a trying journey back to Westport.

A pier was built on the North Island in 1863 but it was blown away within the year. A sturdier model was built on the South Island beginning in 1888, which is there to this day and looking well, sheltering the strand in front of the village. Schools were established on both islands about 1899. Three policemen were stationed on the North Island about the same time to try to stop the worst of the illegal distillery industry. Relations between the islands were never good, except when absolutely necessary. Burials took place only on the North Island. The North Island also took in the Coastguard in 1849 and a police barracks fifty years later.

Perhaps all this influenced things so that the North Island took the pro-Treaty side in the Irish Civil War of 1922/23, and the South Island the Republican side. On one occasion, they all drew up on their own side of the narrow channel between the islands and pegged stones at each other.

In 1927, the two islands were united in grief when, on the 26th October, their young men were cruelly taken, ten of them lost in one storm. A big low came in and they were fooled by the lull at its centre. The fishermen were yards off the North Island when the westerly winds struck suddenly and strongly. Many couldn't retreat, and the last to drown were almost on the mainland well to the E. Each of the five currachs contained two brothers, mostly in their late teens. The community spirit was broken and another drowning a couple of years later emptied the islands by 1939.

SPA

Peregrine, Barnacle Goose, Golden Plover, Common, Arctic & Little Tern. Corncrake numbers have dwindled to nothing, and the last bird heard singing was in 2000.

Inishkea (Inis Gé) South

F558-210   Sheet 22

The S island is perhaps the more attractive. It is renowned for its winter population of Barnacle Goose and Snipe. There is also a large population of seals. The landing place is at the ruined village onto a sandy beach beside a stone pier. The beach is sheltered between the pier and Rusheen Island, which is accessible at LW.

Approached from the SE, the island is seen as low lying, with a white tower on the summit of a low hill, which, when aligned with another on the shoreline, gives a bearing of 120°. The two towers transit to the gap between Duvillaun Beg and Gaghta Island, useful to yachts. The ruined building on the skyline is the village school at the northern end of the village.

Water

Good reliable water can usually be had in a small well, 100m S of the pier, just above the first beach, Porteenbeg, where sand meets grass.

Camping

Good camping may be had at the village behind the houses.

Beaches in rounded bays to the S of the village give good landings and camping, but not water. On circumnavigation, escape is possible on the Atlantic side at the head of at least three deep channels almost dissecting the island towards the southern end.

Climbing

There is what appears to be unlimited and excellent rock climbing on steep gneiss at the south-eastern end. Stan Pearson and Ian Stevens have been working here since 2002. There is a clean crag at the southern tip, and other crags on the outside as one moves N. Grades vary between severe and E1, 10m to 25m. Routes can look improbable, but the rock is fantastic with hidden finger jugs. On balance, the crags here are not as comprehensive as Gola, but it is quiet, for now anyway.

It is an outstandingly beautiful and pleasant island, not to be missed if in the area.

Rusheen Island

F561-212   Sheet 22

Rusheen is a small tidal islet off the strand in front of the South Island village. One may walk out at HW. It appears as an undistinguished islet, and one may land anywhere. Rusheen might not even have achieved individual mention here, save for its extraordinary history. It was a major centre of the whaling industry in Ireland in the first years of the 20th Century.

Then as now, the Norwegian whaling industry wanted to do things its own way. Seasonally controlled at home, they established out-stations in other countries to bridge the gaps. They set up one such station in 1908 at Rusheen. They rented the island from the Congested Districts Board who had bought out the whole of Inishkea. It appears they also paid rent to the islanders, who liked to think they owned the place, and wouldn't be persuaded otherwise. This may have been a Norwegian solution to a Norwegian problem, but was more likely an Inishkea solution to an Inishkea problem.

Within months there was a thriving industry, with modern buildings, piers and slips, though made of wood, Norwegian style. Three whaling boats killed an average of 60 whales per annum, of all main types but mostly Fin. The Norwegians kept themselves to themselves, living on their boats, but some learnt Irish to deal with the workers. Steam power helped with the hauling and boiling of the whales to reduce them to oil and fertiliser, but water was in short supply. Hence the dam to be seen behind the houses on the South Island.

The S islanders coveted all the employment for themselves, and wouldn't let N islanders work for the Norwegians. This actually suited everyone in a roundabout way. The southerners could afford to employ mainlanders to till their fields and harvest their crops for them. North Island fishermen thrived because less fishermen meant better fishing. Also, lobsters seemed to thrive on the discarded whale offal. So did the pigs of the South Island which all went feral. Cray and lobster were plentiful and valuable, and were transported live. The cray went to Paris and the lobsters to faraway London.

The whaling only lasted until 1911 when a combination of events ended it. There was a major strike. Further, the stench was unbearable. Even the mainlanders many kilometres away to the E complained. Finally, a fall off in demand for whale products ended the enterprise. The rusting and rotted remains of this endeavour are still to be seen as litter all over Rusheen.

No drinking water was found.

Inishkea North

F565-223   Sheet 22

The North Island is separated from the South Island by a narrow sound. The most visible feature is a huge, prominent burial mound just E of the village at the south-eastern tip, known as the Baily Mór. Its humpbacked shape is dominant from most angles, and it boasts carved stone slabs said to relate to St. Colmcille. The dead of both islands were buried on the North Island.

Landings

Land at sheltered sandy beaches in the rounded bay in the SE, underneath the abandoned village. There are landing points also in many other spots. These include the northern side of the south-eastern tip, and a beach on the north-eastern side, just short of the northern tip, where there is a seal colony. Escape is also possible on the Atlantic side, at the head of a deep cut behind the village, and probably other spots.

Water

Water has been found in a well that may need a little tidying, at the N end of the houses, in from the N end of the larger beach.

Camping

Camping in the bay in good weather is best at the Baily Mór mound, which is open but scenic, and otherwise attractive. In bad weather, some shelter may be had at the village.

Little Tern were seen acting territorially in 2004 (fighting), which may indicate that they are starting to breed.

Carricknaweelion

F565-240   Sheet 22

A large, flat, grassy, sheep-grazed companion to Inishkea North, just off its northern side. In fact, the camping is the more attractive on the main island opposite, on machair, for those seeking the truly remote experience. The two islands are connected at the bottom of the lowest tides. Land easiest at any of several small sandy beaches on the south-eastern side.

Carrickawilt

F568-249   Sheet 22

The southernmost of three remote rocky islets separated from Carricknaweelion and Inishkea North by a modest sound. The three are collectively perhaps more interesting to paddle round than to land on. Carrickawilt is a small, low-lying, flat, grass-topped rocky islet, with a large concentration of Atlantic Grey Seals. Land at a sheltered boulder beach in a cut on the south-eastern side.

Carrigee

F567-254   Sheet 22

The middle of the three separated islets. Barren, with some patches of grass and thrift. Many seals. Easy landing on the ESE side with shelter

Village seen from the pier, Inishkea South, Co. Mayo - Dave Walsh

from swell by offshore rocks. It is easiest to land at LW. One deep inlet is best. Many gulls' nests.

Carrickmoylenacurhoga

F572-257   Sheet 22

Carrickmoylenacurhoga is a large, low-lying and very rocky island, the northernmost of the three separated islets. Rather inhospitable, especially at the northern end. A series of deep cuts along its eastern side provide landing onto rock shelves or into rock pools at LW. The best-protected landing is in a narrow gap in the southeastern corner. More than 80 Grey Seal were present in May 2002.

Erris Head Area

F701-418   Sheet 22

The 'head' of Erris Head is on a small, grassy island separated from the Mullet peninsula by a narrow, dramatic channel at F699-416, which is a useful escape from the Atlantic side. On the Broad Haven side, about 2km to the SE, is a good little harbour called the Danish Cellar at F706-397, useful on passage, with water in the house and camping.

Tides

The main W coast stream touches land hereabouts, so the flood runs NE/E from HW Galway -0320 to +0305. Races occur on the Broad Haven side where returning eddies meet the mainstream. On the flood, a clockwise eddy comes back N along the Broad Haven coast from about 2.5km SSE of the head.

On the ebb, anticlockwise eddies happen in two places. One eddy comes back N along the eastern side of Broad Haven bay, and rejoins the mainstream W of Kid Island. The ebb also sets up anticlockwise eddies on the Atlantic side, SW of the head. During the ebb, a race occurs off Erris Head, and ripples or overfalls occur NNE and ENE of Eagle Island, where the eddies running N along the coast between Eagle Island and Erris Head rejoin the main flow. Local paddlers report that the tide always seems to be going N inside Eagle Island, on both flood and ebb.

In combination, all this seems usually to favour a clockwise passage on a circumnavigation of the Mullet, given a south-westerly wind direction.

Embarkation

Embark from either of two locations, safe anchorages both, important to yachts on passage:

1. A working pier at F644-344 with good parking, on the northern side of Annagh Head, in a good big bay known as French Port, *Port na Francagh*.

2. A wonderfully sheltered, isolated storm beach just further N, called Scotch Port at 647-361. The Commissioners of Irish Lights have a building at Scotch Port, for servicing the lighthouse on Eagle Rock and Black Rock. Here is a Corncrake reserve (one bird in 2003), and where Quail are not unknown.

These are also excellent embarkation places for a round of Erris Head, linking with Belmullet for a manageable walk-back of about 8km. The paddle is about 32km. For a shorter trip, shuttle to the Danish Cellar at F706-397 for about 16km paddling. Either trip enjoys the Atlantic side of the Head, which is as scenic and committing as any.

Passage

On passage, there is camping manageable opposite the French Port pier, but no water. For water, ask in the house nearest the pier. This is the house once owned by Danny Gilboy, the late warden of the nearby Birdwatch Ireland reserve. Do not go onto the reserve without permission, or unless accompanied by a member of the Gilboy family. Do not camp at the head of the bay unless intending departure near HW, because of the extensive flats which severely dry out. Camping at Scotch Port is convenient and uncomplicated.

The islands off the NW of the Mullet peninsula share common access and tidal information. They vary from low and grassy to huge and rocky, with a significant lighthouse.

SPA

Storm Petrel, Arctic & Little Tern, Barnacle Goose, Corncrake, Quail.

Inishkeeragh

F607-303   Sheet 22

A low, uninteresting island just S of Inishglora, where a landing is possible on a beach of small boulders on either side of the eastern tip. Note that small half-tide reefs between Inishkeeragh and Inishglora are unduly prominent on the OS 1:50,000 map. They show as small islands, which confuses the navigator.

The island is almost cut in two by a ravine. Land at the head on either side.

Inishglora

F616-308   Sheet 22

Inishglora is a long and narrow low-lying island. It is interesting for its monastic ruins at the eastern end, and for its beehive stone formations. The church roof collapsed in 2003 after standing for centuries.

The Children of Lir

The cairns on the island are said to be the resting places of the children of Lir. The children, Finola and her brothers Aedh, Conn and Fiachra were changed into swans by a jealous stepmother, Eva. She was jealous of the love of the children for their mother Eve, her eldest sister, who had died. The swans would keep the wit, the nature, and the speech of humans, as well as the power of music. This would last until a prince from the N married a princess from the S, and they heard the voice of the Christian bell bringing the light of the new faith over the land.

In all, they spent 300 happy years on Lough Derryvaragh in County Westmeath, 300 desperate and stormy years around Rathlin Island off the NE of Ireland, and finally 300 years at peace around Inishglora. Then, Saint Kemoc changed them back into humans. Alas, they were elderly crones. Here on Inishglora, as Christians, they ended their days at last. This is the saddest tale of ancient pre-Christian Ireland, well worth reading up on.

Storm Petrel extensively colonise the eastern end of the island.

In the 1821 census, 7 people were living on the island.

Landing and water

There is a landing place opposite Inishkeeragh on a sandy beach on the southern side, just inside the eastern tip. Landing might also be possible on a storm beach in a shallow bay, midway along the northern side. There is a disused well at the eastern end, but the water is not good. Wells need use.

Eagle Island

F641-392   Sheet 22

A prominent, rocky lighthouse island, on which landing without swimming is almost impossible in nearly all conditions. The sound immediately inside the island to its SE is always lumpy and best avoided in difficult conditions. Local paddlers report that the tide in the sound always runs NE, and that it is usually best to pass by further inside altogether, along the coast.

As with all lighthouses, always ask Irish Lights for permission to land. There were two lighthouses, which form a transit, clearing obstacles nearby. The eastern light was discontinued in 1895, and the western light was automated in 1988. Its character is 3 white flashes every 10 seconds.

The lights have a troublesome history. Storms wrecked the towers during construction and again afterwards. The keepers' accommodation was washed away. A wave 68m high washed over the island in 1861. The tower filled with water and the keepers had to drill holes to open the door.

The grassy top of the island feels sheltered, and appears to have once sustained the lighthouse personnel well enough. There is a substantial walled garden just above the northern landing steps. The lighthouse is powered by solar panels. Great Black-backed Gull abound in the long grass.

Landing

There are two landing spots. Each is at or alongside a small landing stage, each either side of the SE sound. Each is just outside the sound, one at the eastern tip, and the other at the southern tip, behind a stack. Steps are cut in the rock either side of these landing stages, where it is probably best to drag up heavy boats.

Camping

There is no water, but there is plenty of camping on the grassy plateau. However, an overnight stay runs a huge risk of stranding, should swell

height increase, even a little. See Bill Long's 'Bright Light, White Water' for descriptions of the huge seas which give this island it's bad reputation. A short visit is recommended.

Belmullet

F703-325   Sheet 22

Sheltered and easy access from Mayo's western and northern coasts may be had through Belmullet. A lock-free canal is navigable to kayaks on the 2 hours either side of local HW. This gives easy passage from Blacksod Bay into Broad Haven. Belmullet is a most useful town on passage. A market town, all facilities are available.

Tides

The tide flows simultaneously into Blacksod Bay and Broad Haven, meeting on the drying mudflats on the Broad Haven (eastern) side of the town. The flow in the canal is usually from Blacksod towards Broad Haven, and reaches 4kn in springs. The mudflats on the Broad Haven side are severe, so don't miss the tide. Approach and leave Belmullet near HW.

Local HW is Galway HW +0040.

An excellent evening meal is available in the hotel, and a handy B&B is with Eileen Gaughan, Mill House, American Street, Belmullet, tel. 097-81181. Her garden backs onto the canal just on the Broad Haven side. Kayaks can be left here conveniently and securely, which is otherwise a problem.

Camping locally is unattractive.

Kid Island   - *Oileán Mionnán*

F787-438   Sheet 22

Kid Island is a massive lump, 86m high, more than matching the local mainland cliff-top, 250m to its SE. Kid Island guards the northeastern approaches to Broad Haven - *Cuan an Inbhir Mhóir*. To pass NE inside the island is to be transported instantly into the surreal world of the N Mayo coastline. High and sheer cliffs dotted with huge caves vie with jagged stacks everywhere. Transcending everything are the Stags of Broad Haven. This is scenery worthy of any James Bond boat chase.

Embarkation, Camping and Water

Launch from the beach inside Binroe Point pier - *Barr na Rinne* at about F802-406. There

Stags of Broadhaven, Co. Mayo – Alyn Walsh

is no water or camping on the island but there is excellent camping on machair at the launch point, on either side of the road approaching the pier. Excellent water is available from a pipe exiting the cliff at the northern end of the beach, N of the pier. This area is known locally as Carrowteigue - *Ceathrú Thaidhg*.

Landings

There are two. Land more easily in a cove in the NE, below some metal stanchions placed there long ago to aid getting sheep onto and off the island. However, the scramble from here is long and needs care, up rock slabs and then grass. Marvel at the thought of yapping dogs industriously herding sheep on such terrain. Many of both species must have had an unexpected swim or worse. The landing at the western tip is more exposed, but there is an easier scramble to the summit.

The grass top is extensive and sheep-grazed. It was the sight of sheep in 2003 that tempted an ISKA party to try to find a landing. A long, interesting ridge runs out N, worth the scramble for the view. A cave appears to run right through

this ridge, 20m above the water line. Light can be seen. Rumour has it that scuba divers climb up there and scramble all the way through.

Breeding sheep, Puffin, Guillemot, and Great Black-backed Gull.

Stags of Broad Haven - *Na Stacaí*
F838-479   Sheet 22

No amount of forewarning prepares the visitor for the reality. Only a few places truly merit this assertion. One thinks of Skellig, Moher, Aran, but these Stags are worthy of inclusion on any such list. Unlike the others, these Stags are little known, greatly enhancing their fame among the few fortunate enough to have visited.

There are five stags in all - huge, dramatic, pointy topped rocks usually circled in foam. They lie 4km from the beach and 2.5km from nearest land. They are best seen from the SW. All but one have arches, and one is entirely bisected by a long narrow dramatic cave. The passage through and around the Stags is one of the significant Irish sea kayaking experiences.

Embarkation

The embarkation place is at Portacloy - *Port a'Chlóidh* at F840-440, a sheltered, sandy beach, attractive and N-facing. There is good camping just behind the beach on commonage, but ask for permission. Water is available in local houses. Launching and landing is easier at the pier NW of the beach under most conditions, but the camping there is less satisfactory. There are no provisions available locally - this is a very remote spot. A watchtower on the headland marks the western side of the entrance to the bay.

The whole coastline hereabouts, particularly from Portacloy W, has arches, caves, channels and passages second to none anywhere. These are easily enjoyed in plastic boats. Bring good headtorches for the caves, which are very deep.

Local HW is Galway +0040.

SPA

Puffin, Storm & Leach's Petrel.

Landing

Landing on any of the Stags without swimming is not normally possible.

The central Stag (*Teach Dónal Ó'Cléirigh*) is highest at 97m. Land at the south-western tip at F840-478.

To its S is *An Teach Mór*, second highest at 94m, on which the landing is easiest on the northern tip at F839-479, but the climb to the top is harder. Or, land at the more exposed southern tip at F839-476, which has the easier looking climb.

E of centre is *An Teach Beag* at about 85m, which boasts the tunnel, running E/W. Land at the south-eastern tip at F840-478, or at an equally sheltered spot just outside and NE of the tunnel at F840-479. A little rock to the E of *An Teach Beag* is *An Bád Bréige*, which is often mistaken for a boat when seen from a distance.

No kayaker is known to have landed on either of the Stags NW of centre, *Carraig na Faola* and just further out, *an t-Oighean* (78m).

Pig Island - *Oileán na Muice*

F880-440   Sheet 23

Named for its amazing porcine appearance when seen from E or W, the island is splendidly bisected by a sea arch at the centre. The landward side of the roof of the arch is the jowl of the pig. The view of the arch in itself warrants a visit. The island, when viewed from the sea, appears to be attached to the land behind.

Embarkation and Landing

The embarkation place is Porturlin - *Port Durlainne* at F885-425, which is a small fishing village. At the harbour in Porturlin, the camping is unattractive, but there is water out of a pipe on the roadside. Launching and landing is easy. No provisions. Beware that the lights on the quayside are not a transit for entry. The mouth of the harbour is narrow, and the ground outside is steep, blocking sight of most land features. If however, the features can be seen, entry is looking good. While there is obvious evidence of sheep grazing, no landing was found on the island. A deepwater landing might be forced on the landward, southern side. Scramble up at the SW.

Local HW is Galway +0040.

Illanmaster - *Oileán Maigheastar*

F935-432   Sheet 23

High, square, block-shaped island located very close to the mainland but separated from it by a dramatic rock canyon. The channel is easily navigable by kayak and perhaps by other small, seaworthy boats, in good weather conditions. When entered from the western side, the passage through the high, steep, rock walls is impressive. The passage opens on the eastern side into an attractive bay, at the head of which (F936-426) lies a fine storm beach. The area provides an ideal lunch spot for kayakers en route from Portacloy to Belderg - *Béal Dearg*.

Landing

The island is steep and precipitous. Landing is difficult but possible on the sheltered eastern side onto shelving rock platforms. The climb to the summit is a good scramble, best negotiated from the NE corner.

SPA

Puffin and Storm Petrel.

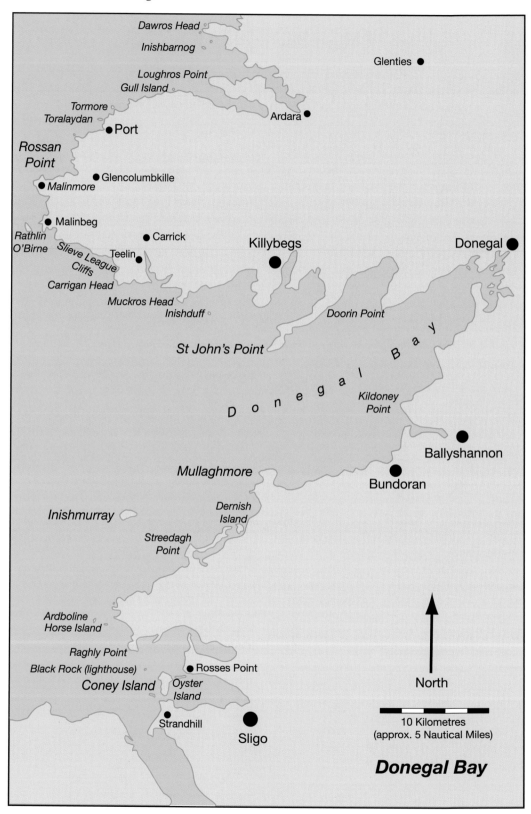

Dawros Head

Inishbarnog

Glenties ●

Loughros Point
Gull Island

Tormore
Toralaydan
● Port

Ardara ●

Rossan
Point

● Glencolumbkille
● Malinmore

Donegal ●

● Malinbeg

Rathlin
O'Birne
Slieve League
Cliffs
Teelin ● Carrick

Killybegs
●

Carrigan Head

Muckros Head
Inishduff

Doorin Point

St John's Point

D o n e g a l   B a y

Kildoney
Point

Ballyshannon ●

Mullaghmore

Bundoran ●

Inishmurray

Dernish
Island

Streedagh
Point

North

Ardboline
Horse Island

Raghly Point
Black Rock (lighthouse)
Coney Island
Oyster
Island

Rosses Point ●

10 Kilometres
(approx. 5 Nautical Miles)

● Strandhill

Sligo ●

Donegal Bay

The North-West
Sligo to Malin
County Sligo

Sligo Bay

Sheet 16

Sligo town has commercial and fishing boats trading from its harbour. Sligo Bay is really in two parts, an outer bay called Sligo Bay and an inner bay called Sligo Harbour. The two are separated by a narrow entrance, between Coney Island and Rosses Point, about 7km WNW of Sligo Town. The islands next described lie in the general area of this narrow entrance separating Sligo Bay from Sligo Harbour.

SPA

SPA designation attaches to nearby Ballysadare Bay to the S, (Whooper Swan, Golden Plover, and Bar-tailed Godwit), Sligo Harbour (Great Northern Diver, Whooper Swan, Golden Plover, and Bar-tailed Godwit), and Lissadell Strand in Drumcliff Bay to the N (Barnacle Goose, Whooper Swan, Golden Plover, and Bar-tailed Godwit).

Tides

In Sligo Bay, as is common on the west coast, slack water occurs about an hour and a quarter after Galway HW and LW. The flood runs from about HW Galway −0450 to +0115 and ebbs in reverse. The flow rate does not exceed 1kn. The direction of the flow is E/W south of Raghly Point at G583-416 in the outer part of Sligo Bay. A part of the flood branches off into Drumcliff Bay to the NE and the main flood continues ESE all the way to Sligo Town.

Closer to Sligo Harbour the flow rate increases, peaking about 1km inside Sligo Harbour, N of Oyster Island, at up to 6kn in springs. The flood divides at the Metal Man, mid-harbour entrance. The main flood flows E through the shipping channel N of Oyster Island and on towards Sligo. A strong secondary flow passes between Oyster and Coney and circulates anticlockwise around the deep pit just S of the W point of Oyster. The ebb reverses all this.

There are significant danger areas hereabouts. With wind over tide, which usually means the ebb, quite a sea state is generated in the main channel N of Oyster Island, and between Oyster and Coney Islands, in the region of the Metal Man. There is a submerged spit curving out from the N end of Coney Island at about G615-399 to Black Rock at G598-401. This is partially exposed at LW. In any sort of sea, there are big breaks here and on the sandbanks on its N side.

Embarkation

For all these islands, launch from Deadman's Point at G626-399, at the end of the Rosses Point road at the sailing club or nearby at a bathing area from a small sandy beach on the north-facing Drumcliff Bay side, if conditions allow. If using the sailing club, remember that this is private property. Park off-site and do not block access for others, especially at the slipway.

It is also possible to launch from the main beach, though this involves a carry, other than in high summer when the whole area is infested with people, so that parking becomes impossible. At these times, it is possible to launch from the pier at G630-397, a working fishing pier but with less tourists. The disadvantage for the kayaker is that the requirement not to block others becomes absolute, and it is further up the channel.

Black Rock

G598-401   Sheet 16

2.5km W of Deadman's Point, this is a major lighthouse on a minor piece of rock. While there has been a beacon on Black Rock since the 18th Century, the current lighthouse was designed by George Halpin Senior and was established in 1835. Intriguingly, the stairs are up the outside, to half height, a feature unique among Irish lighthouses. The light is 24m above sea level and flashes once every 5 seconds. It was automated in 1934. Land E of the lighthouse, N or S sides, conditions dependent, in either case into rocky but sheltered harbourlets.

Coney Island

G613-388   Sheet 16

0.5km SW of Deadman's Point, this is an attractive, low-lying and varied island with a truly remote feel. It is reachable by car with difficulty from the mainland to the SE. If driving, leave the mainland 1km off the Sligo/Strandhill Road at G641-369. Posts mark the roadway across 2km of sand. If circumnavigating by kayak (strictly top of the tide) the passage is between the 3rd and 4th posts from the island.

Landing

Land easiest at a pier in a small bay at G623-394 facing the mainland and Oyster Island, just N of Wards Pub at G623-391. For kayaks, the nicest aspect of the island is the west-facing beach along its W side, in the middle. Camping is possible at the N end of this beach in a lay-by at the end of the island road. Dunes cover the S end of the island. Beware of the seas off this beach which can be dangerous.

Oyster Island

G631-394   Sheet 16

0.5km SE of Deadman's Point, this is a privately owned, residential farmland, semi-grazed by horses. Landing may be easiest by the house on the N (landward-facing) shore, though it is possible to land just about anywhere. Limekiln on S side. No suitable camping found.

The small lighthouse is a rear leading light with the Metal Man to guide ships into the channel. It was established in 1932.

Metal Man

G626-396   Sheet 16

0.3km S of Deadman's Point, the Metal Man was originally destined for the unlit tower that stood on Black Rock. However, once it was decided to build a proper lighthouse there, the Metal Man was established where it now stands on Perch Rock in 1821. Four metal men were cast by Thomas Kirke in London in 1819. One of the others stands on a headland near Tramore

in Waterford but the whereabouts of the remaining two is unknown. The Metal Man is dressed in the uniform of a Petty Officer in the Royal Navy and, with right arm outstretched, he points to the safe channel to Sligo.

Horse Island

G560-440   Sheet 16

7km WNW of Deadman's Point, this is a small island just off Yellow Strand (no easy vehicular access) to the NW of Raghly Point, at the N side of outermost Sligo Bay. The island is low-lying, ungrazed, and there is a suspicion of rodents present. Such merit as the island possesses lies in its position, especially in its feasibility as a waystop on passage, for instance to or from Inishmurray out of nearby Rosses Point. Camping would be unattractive.

SPA

Internationally important numbers of Barnacle Goose in season.

Landing and Embarkation

Landing is quite manageable onto storm beaches along its S side, either side of a sheltering off-lying rock, or in a cut at the E point. Embarkation is easiest from the N side of the horseshoe bay, 1.5km to the NE at G564-456, called locally Ballyconnell West.

Nearby, lovely Dooneragh Point at G557-447 boasts an ancient promontory fort with multiple rampart defence systems in good condition. Knocklane Hill 1km to the ESE provides fine views of these islands, a World War 2 lookout recently knocked down, and an older military building with musket firing slots, of uncertain age.

Ardboline Island

G550-444   Sheet 16

A small island 1km outside and to the W of Horse Island, taller, with steep sides, and altogether more substantial. The central plateau has steep sides, is ungrazed and is given over to nettles. Camping would ordinarily be entirely out of the question. Around the edges are sloping limestone pavements, wider on the seaward side.

Marvel at the remains of part (mostly propeller shaft and housing) of a 248 ton iron steamer lodged near the SSW tip, said locally to have

Dernish Island, Co. Sligo - Séan Pierce

been driven deliberately on shore, successfully saving the crew. Local lore is that the captain was from Sligo, knew the ground, and in a rising gale, drove the ship up on the island, because he knew he could. Objectively, it is known that the 'Sligo' sank here on 5th February 1912, carrying coal inward to Sligo from Garston. Public records show that Captain Devaney and his crew of 13 escaped ashore from a ladder at the bow at LW.

Worms up to half a metre long are fossilised in the rocks around the island, some quite raised by erosion.

SPA

Internationally important numbers of Barnacle Goose in season.

Landing and Embarkation

Landing is quite challenging, especially at HW. The island is sausage shaped lying NNE/SSW. Landing will always be entirely unappealing on the outside due to permanent swell. A deep water landing may be had at a choice of spots along the inside. At lower water there may be available storm beaches, simplifying things.

Embarkation is easiest from the N side of the horseshoe bay, 1.5km to the NE at G564-456, called locally Ballyconnell West. Yellow Strand to the E has no easy vehicular access.

Dernish Island

G677-524   Sheet 16

A medium-sized island located close to the coastline 5km ENE of Streedagh Point. The island is a pleasant mixture of stone-walled fields, patches of scrub and small copses. A green road cuts across the centre of the island connecting several ruined farmhouses with the only inhabited house at the southern landing place mentioned.

The island is separated from the mainland by a narrow channel of 100/200m on its NE and SE sides. On the western side, an extensive boulder beach at LW connects the island to a spit of land known as Conors Island, at the extreme N end of Streedagh Strand. This is entirely impracticable to cross.

Landing / Embarkation

The island's main landing is (easily onto mud/

177

Stone slab with carved cross, Inishmurray, Co. Sligo, (Benbulbin in the background) – Séan Pierce

shale) at the S tip. The closest launch is from a small pier just opposite at G677-519. At LW, landing elsewhere is made difficult by extensive boulder and rocky foreshores on both the N/W sides. Landing is easier along the E inside channel though there is a good tidal flow from the inner bay area. Good camping on the NW peninsula on machair, for which land on the N side of the spit of the peninsula. No water found.

Inishmurray

G580-539   Sheet 16

About 6km WNW of Streedagh Point, this is a lovely, remote, low-lying, formerly inhabited island, with a most interesting history both ancient and recent. Its monastic ruins are excellent and worth the visit in themselves. A row of fairly recently abandoned houses lines the SE side above the unsatisfactory pier/slip. Fields, bog, lake and scrub comprise the rest. The NW point has interesting small cliffs and passages.

Tides

Local HW Galway +0040. Tidal movements are not strong.

Embarkation

Inishmurray lies about 6km NW out from the nearest and most common embarkation points, either side of Streedagh Point. Choose depending on conditions between the NNW-facing beach at G637-510, and a smaller SW-facing beach at G631-502. Otherwise the position is a bit more complex. By far the most convenient embarkation place for bigger boats or larger groups of kayakers is the harbour at the village of Mullaghmore at G709-576, about 15km from the island. Here there is parking and dependable shelter. There are several other possibilities 7/8km S of the island, at Ballyconnell North, a N-facing beach at G566-462.

Landing

From the S/SE direction, there is a roofed building prominently visible at the E end of the island. This is the schoolhouse, which lies just above the pier wall. The shoreline generally is slippery boulders and slab. Landing with kayaks can be difficult, even at the pier wall, which is not very sheltered and distinctly open to the SE.

Beehive hut and monastic ruins, Inishmurray - Séan Pierce

The village is a single line of houses just above the shore just W of the schoolhouse. Landing can also be had further W on the S side in the often more sheltered deeply indented coves at G571-537, W of the village, onto rocks. This spot, though sheltered, is more suited to boats that can be tied or anchored, such as dinghies or ribs where one can hop or step onto rock. For those overnighting, a landing here leaves a good distance to carry gear to the better campsites near the schoolhouse.

Camping and Water

No drinking water was found though there is a lake in the centre. Camping is perhaps best at the schoolhouse.

Wildlife

The Eider and Common Scoter ducks are sometimes found here in summer. This was until recently considered almost the most southerly breeding area of the Eider.

Local History

Of special interest on the island is the monastic ruined settlement, founded by Columba in 550 AD. It is inside a Bronze Age fortification, the walls of which were once about 4.5m high, but now half that. The enclosure of cells, beehives, churches, altars, cursing stones and carved stones, which in themselves make the island a must for a visit, are in better condition after 1400 years than the village houses after 100. The menfolk of the island were buried inside the enclosure and the women outside, at Teampalnamban about 150m distant.

The island was pagan until Columba built a new monastery inside the fort and installed St. Molaise as Abbot. The monastery obtained fame almost immediately. Columba, back on a visit, borrowed a book from the library. Without telling Molaise, he copied it. A furious Molaise demanded the return of the copy. Denied, he appealed all the way to the High King, Diarmuid, who was then like the Supreme Court is today. His judgement was 'to every cow its calf, to every book its copy', probably the first ever recorded copyright decision in Western Europe.

Worse was to come. Columba still wouldn't return the copy. Diarmuid, feeling he was being challenged, set out westwards with an army of 3,000 to punish Columba and his followers. Columba was resoundingly beaten near Culdrennan outside Sligo, with the loss of all his men.

Columba was upset by all these unanticipated downstream consequences of his thievery. He relented, and presented himself to Molaise in confession. As penance, Molaise banished Columba to Scotland, never to return until he had converted to Christianity as many pagans as the 3,000 killed in the battle. Columba sailed, and didn't settle until he could no longer see Ireland. He landed at Iona, and there founded his greatest ever monastery. He never returned to Ireland.

The Vikings raided Inishmurray in 795 and 802, and the Black and Tans in 1921. In 1915, a British warship, mistaking the island for a submarine, torpedoed it. It is thought the fort was mistaken for a conning tower. The islanders were unhurt.

The island was infamous for poitín making. There being no natural embarkation point for access to the island, and no easy landing, visits by the authorities were few. This enabled the undisturbed islanders to distil the best illicit whiskey in the country, marketed as 'Old Inishmurray'. When the Revenue officials did come, they had to hire boats locally and word would escape. Then, in the absence of any one truly sheltered landing spot, it seems it was always necessary for the local boatmen to circle the island looking for the easiest landing place. The illicit brew was normally well hidden by the time anyone got ashore.

The school was built in 1889 when there were 102 people living here in 15 houses. There were only 46 in 1948 when the last people left.

The islanders were renowned for a combined rowing/sailing technique unique in Ireland which made them the safest, fastest and bravest sailors around.

Kayaking under
Slieve League Cliffs
Co. Donegal
David Walsh

County Donegal

South Donegal

Inishduff

G648-724   Sheet 10

Also called locally 'Shalwy Island', this small islet is very visible from the south Donegal coast road just 3km ESE of Muckros Head, about 2km out from land. Inishduff forms a useful leg-stretching waystop on passage, perhaps the island's greatest contribution to the scheme of things. The island was once grazed but nowadays has gone wild and is given over to nettles, brambles and seabirds.

SPA

Storm Petrel, Barnacle Goose.

Embarkation Points

Inishduff is 3km from the nearest beach on the E side of Muckros Head, where there is poor parking at G627-742. Closest is a small pier just opposite Inishduff on the mainland, but down an uncomfortably steep roadway at G640-747. Not recommended is Fintragh Beach to the NE at G685-764, as many cars will not cope with the steep descent here either, and the road boasts a kayak unfriendly barrier which sometimes operates.

For those on passage, the island lies in a straight line along the coast, 6km from St. John's Point. There is a sheltered slipway just S of and under the lighthouse at G703-689, but cattle graze here so camping can be a problem. Also available is a beautiful sheltered beach 2km NE of St. John's Point at G717-702 where there is excellent camping, but be discreet as this land belongs to the Commissioners of Irish Lights.

Landing

Land at either of two well-sheltered east-facing storm beaches on the very indented E side.

Slieve League Cliffs

G523-785   Sheet 10

This is one of the truly mighty excursions of Irish sea paddling, yet is quite manageable. It consists of 13km of majestic cliff scenery from Malinbeg at G494-799 to Teelin at G593-753. There are numerous waterfalls coming off the cliffs to shower under, some up to 100m high. The shuttle is tedious so consider doing the expedition there and back. There are several beaches well spread out along the base, for breaking the journey should conditions allow, none of which is attainable from the land. One stony beach is reasonably sheltered at G523-785 and is important, being one third of the way from Malinbeg. It is just E and somewhat in the lee of a vaguely prominent headland, the other beaches being nearer Teelin, at Bunglass and just W of it. Sail Rock, for hard climbers only, is just E of Carrigan Head. Deep caves along the way add excitement for those who like their adrenaline pumped.

Tides

Local HW is Galway +0040. Nothing is reliably known about tidal movements along the north coast of Donegal Bay, or when they start, but they are considered to be weak, except off salient points.

Malinbeg

G494-799   Sheet 10

A most important embarkation place for kayaking. Landing, while safe at the sheltered pier and steep slipway, is a little awkward and involves a steep carry. There is excellent camping on commonage immediately above the pier, by a white house with three chimneys and a garage. The nearby beach is splendid. Drinking water is available at a tap external to an outhouse beside a dwelling, near the crossroads in the village on the road to the beach.

The rock climbing hereabouts, mostly under the prominent signal tower, is nationally important. Malinbeg's situation makes it a most attractive venue for paddling to Rathlin O'Birne Island, E along the Slieve League cliffs, or N to Glen Head. Basic provisions may be had in the village, as may B+B, and the hotel at Malinmore (3km) is excellent for eating and drinking.

Local HW Galway +0040.

Finding the harbour from the sea needs care. Once close, the white house with three chimneys in a line is prominent atop a low cliff and is just above the pier, which can then be made out. At night, the pier is lit. From out to sea to the SE, aim between the beach and the prominent square signal tower. Coming from the E, pass the prominent white strand, well to the E of the tower until the white house appears. Coming from the N, the spread out village disappears as one paddles past the promontory with the obvious signal tower, off which are two prominently visible (actually there are more) rocks. Turn in left (E) after the rocks. Follow around until the white house appears.

Malinmore

G493-827   Sheet 10

A modern, well maintained and protected slipway is located near Malinmore, named Oughig. There is camping available above the slipway with parking available for small groups. The area is quiet and undisturbed, being well away from local houses. No water found. The area is within easy walking distance of the excellent nearby Malinmore Hotel.

Rathlin O'Birne Island

G467-801   Sheet 10

2km W of Malinbeg, this is a low-lying, grassy island indented all round with channels, bounded by cliffs and even bisected by a sea arch. It has a major lighthouse, now automated. While the building was completed in 1846, the light was not fitted for another 10 years. Lighthouse keepers and their families lived here from 1856 to 1912, when the families moved to shore dwellings in Glencolumbkille. There is a rumour that a battery pack of nuclear power was used here at one time for about 20 years, but proved uneconomical. I have been unable to substantiate this. Two parallel cut stone walls, 6 feet high and 12 feet apart, enclose a roadway, once used by the lighthouse keepers as protection against the Atlantic winds on their journey from the beach to the lighthouse.

N of the walls lies the kayak landing, and beyond it across the 'moraine', lies the remains of lazybeds, a house, and what looks like the evidence of monks' dwellings.

No drinking water was found, but the lighthouse roof drains into a barrel.

There is camping, but not very conveniently.

SPA

Storm Petrel, Leach's Petrel, Barnacle Goose, Terns.

Landing and Embarkation

Best landing is at a stony beach visible from the mainland in the NE in a somewhat sheltered bay, where the island appears to be almost dissected. The pier at the SE is unsuited to kayaks. Out of Malinbeg, the crossing is only about thirty minutes.

Tides

Local HW is Galway +0040.

Tides in the Sound run N strongly for nine and a quarter hours out of the twelve, starting at HW Galway -0300 and run S weakly for the other three from about just before LW Galway. The spring rate of the N going stream is about 1.5 knots and the S going stream is very weak. The main west coast tidal stream runs along the coast from Rathlin O'Birne to Aran, the NE flood starting HW Galway -0320 and the ebb at +0305, mostly 0.8 knots but achieving 1.5 to 2.0 off salient points.

West Donegal

Toralaydan

G544-897   Sheet 10

Located about 750m N of Port at G547-890 this is an impressive, square, precipitous island block. No obvious landing. The passage between the island and headland is navigable in good conditions. The island is a reliable navigation aid as it stands out well from the coast especially when approached from the S. The island marks a useful escape point on this wild and beautiful section of the SW Donegal coast. Breeding colonies of Fulmar, Kittiwake and Guillemot.

Tormore

G555-908   Sheet 10

2km NE of Port G547-890, Tormore is located just off a headland and is the most seaward of a broken triangle of islands. The sea has breached this group of islets in several places and one can enter a narrow stretch of water through a sea arch in the most southern islet of the group.

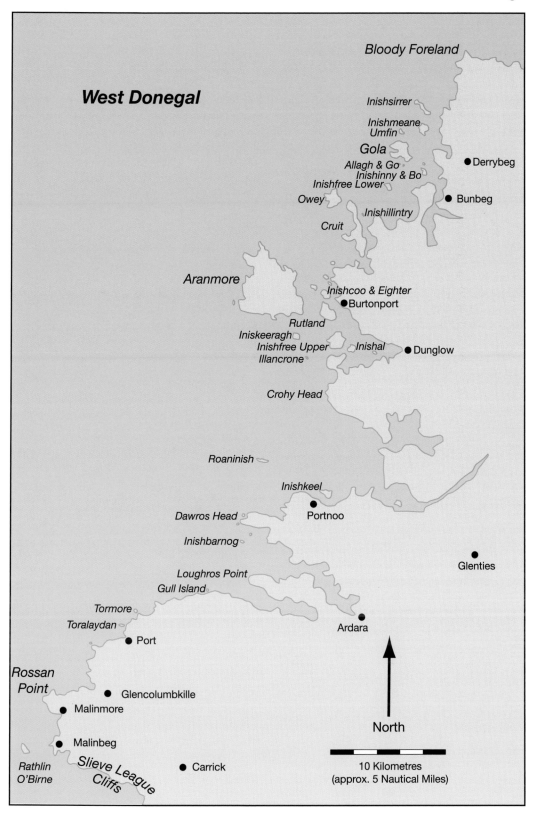

Bloody Foreland

West Donegal

Inishsirrer

Inishmeane
Umfin

Gola

Allagh & Go
Inishinny & Bo
Inishfree Lower

Owey

Inishillintry

Cruit

● Derrybeg

● Bunbeg

Aranmore

Inishcoo & Eighter
● Burtonport

Rutland

Iniskeeragh
Inishfree Upper
Illancrone

Inishal
● Dunglow

Crohy Head

Roaninish

Inishkeel

Dawros Head
● Portnoo

Inishbarnog

Glenties ●

Loughros Point

Gull Island

Tormore

Toralaydan

● Port

Ardara ●

North

Rossan
Point

● Glencolumbkille

● Malinmore

● Malinbeg

Rathlin
O'Birne

*Slieve League
Cliffs*

● Carrick

10 Kilometres
(approx. 5 Nautical Miles)

High cliffs all round make it a dramatic place, as all entrances are narrow and a tricky place to be in heavy swell. The north-facing breach is too narrow and dangerous for kayaks at LW. Tormore is high and precipitous. No landing was found. Breeding colonies of Kittiwake, Guillemot, Razorbill and Fulmar.

SPA

Peregrine, Chough, Grey Seal.

Gull Island

G613-924   Sheet 10

2km NNW of the summit of Slievetooey, this is a massive big lump of rock, 95m high with cliffs all round, barely separated from the main Slievetooey cliffs at only the highest spring tides, and easily missed as it merges with the cliffs behind. Land on sheltered storm beach at SE. Situated about 4km W of the slip at Loughros Point at G653-928. The cliffs E of the island are less exposed to the WSW swells and are thereby the more comfortably explored for their dramatic arches, canyons, gaps, caves and waterfalls, giving a most worthwhile excursion in this beautiful and little explored area.

Inishbarnog

G640-963   Sheet 10

1km south of Dawros Head, this is a small, low-lying island in Loughros More Bay. There are rocky cliffs on the western side and an attractive sandy beach on eastern side named as Bealanillan Port on 1:50,000 OS map. There is good camping at the landing and a possibility of water at a wet marshy area about 200m west of the landing area, if sufficiently desperate. The island is grazed heavily by sheep and by Barnacle Geese in winter and spring. When approached from the S a small cairn marks the highest point. On the northern side, rocky platforms are exposed at low tide. Bird life includes breeding Herring Gulls and Common Gulls. The following species were seen in April 1999: Eider, Barnacle Geese, Oystercatcher, Ringed Plover and Snow Bunting.

Inishkeel

B711-002   Sheet 10

An attractive island lying just N of Portnoo, half joined to the land at its SE. There are the remains of a farmhouse, a collection of early Christian churches (in ruins), and a walled graveyard, just above the beach on the E side. Some of the land appears private. Cows graze. The island is heavily grazed in winter by a flock of 300+ Barnacle Geese. There are some small wet marshy areas containing stands of Yellow Iris. No definite source of water was found. There is good camping at the landing. Large glacial erratics are found on the higher ground west of the landing. Breeding bird species include Herring Gull and Common Gull, Lapwing, Ringed Plover, Oystercatcher, Meadow Pipit and Skylark.

SPA

Barnacle Goose, Tern, Chough, formerly Corncrake.

Landing

Land at a fine beach on E side.

Roaninish

G658-027   Sheet 10

A lovely, remote, low-lying, short-grassed island, 6km WNW out from Portnoo. Land and camp at a sheltered sandy beach in an east-facing little bay on the E side. Beware on arrival that the entrance to the bay is subject to swells and boomers can catch the unwary. A small lake by the campsite should be treated with caution as sheep graze the island. No other water spotted. In 2001, we found no sign of the remains of a wreck of the Greenhaven on the W side.

SPA

Storm Petrel, Tern.

Aranmore Group

This group extends from Illancrone in the south to Aranmore itself in the north.

Embarkation

The normal embarkation place for the Aranmore group is from Burtonport at B717-152 which has good facilities in terms of pubs, restaurants and shops. Launch from the wide slipway. Be sure though to park 150m away in front of the pub. This will keep the slipway and pier free. Also, be aware that the sea in the immediate vicinity of Burtonport is very protected and is no indication of what may be happening outside. The North Rutland Channel runs SE to NW

Torneady Point, Aranmore, Co. Donegal - Mike McClure

and is the narrow sound between Eighter and Rutland which gives access from Burtonport out to Aran. The SE entrance to the Channel is difficult to identify from Burtonport. Aim for the two-story house on the Rutland skyline WSW of Burtonport pier. Navigation locally is far more challenging in windy conditions than any casual glance at the OS 1:50,000 map might suggest. Accordingly, some considerable nautical detail is given for this area, and a proper nautical chart is recommended to any visiting group.

Maps and Charts

Chart 1883, Crohy Head to Bloody Foreland (1:30,000) covers the area. The details of the seabed give a good indication of what to expect on the surface in bad weather and in this respect it is much better than the OS 1:50,000, sheet 1. However, many of the beacons on the approaches to Burtonport are not marked on the chart but can be worked out from the Pilot or Sailing Directions. This is a complicated area. The Sailing Directions (South and West Coasts of Ireland) give a good sketch map of Aran Sound, shows most of the beacons and all of the shoals. The

Pilot gives detailed information but needs to be used with a map or chart. The older half-inch, (1:126,720) sheet 1 OS map is virtually useless (unusually perhaps) for bad weather navigation in this area.

Tides

Local HW and LW are Galway +0100.

Tidal streams in the locality flow strongly and can cut up rough in contrary winds. The direction of the tidal streams coincides with local flood and ebb, or at worst begins half an hour later. The flood tide starts at local LW (HW Galway -0500) and the ebb starts at local HW (HW Galway +0100). The tide floods into Aran Sound from both ends N and S, meeting near the Carrickbealatroha Upper beacon at B695-147, midway between Rutland and SE Aran. This is also sometimes known as Stream Rock, and the beacon is a wide square tower, 5m high. On the E side of Rutland, the tides meet halfway up, at Teige Rock, a large white beacon, at B713-145.

The tide floods SE through the North Rutland Channel and strongly, up to 2-3 knots in springs. But it is not a problem going against, if you keep to the side of the channel, out of the main stream. This is one of the very few channels on the west coast of Ireland where the tide floods southwards. Other examples are mainly north-facing bays such as at Achill Sound and Valentia Harbour. Similarly, the tide floods logically into Dunglow Bay around both sides of the more southerly islands in the group.

Illancrone

B695-103   Sheet 1

3.5km SSE of Aranmore. Unremarkable twin grassy tufts atop drumlinesque stony mounds, separated by the sea except at LW. Breeding Eider. The grid reference is for SE top. Land just NW of SE top.

There is a beacon light on the SE. The ruin on the NW top was the holiday home of Saint Crona Beg, who summered here.

SPA

Barnacle Goose, Tern.

Inishal

B726-113   Sheet 1

In Dunglow Bay 5km SE of Aranmore. Overshadowed perhaps by Inishfree, this turf and boggy island with ruins has no particularly attractive camping spot. Land anywhere sheltered. There are the remains of a small village at the bay on S side.

Inishfree Upper

B715-126   Sheet 1

2km SE of Aranmore, at the mouth of Dunglow Bay. Large interesting island worth exploring. Homes on the NW apparently result from recent settlement by English and Welsh families. The island was electrified August 2000. The island is developing a tradition in art that yet may rival Tory. The shipwreck of the 'Mallrin' is to the W. There is tidal peat with bog oak (some say giant cedar?) in the baylet W of the S point at B714-114. The old schoolhouse is at the E end of the island.

Landing and Camping

Land easily on sheltered sandy beach just SW of N point of island, where there is a slipway, if preferred. The landing point is backed by mach-

air that is friendly to camping. Cows grazing. No water found. You may land and camp also at a beach to the SW at B711-114.

Tides

Tides flood strongly E past the N point.

Iniskeeragh

B685-125   Sheet 1

1.5km S of Aranmore. This is a fine island, not to be lightly missed.

Schoolhouse

View the remarkably located schoolhouse to W, where the novelist Peadar O'Donnell (1893 - 1986) taught for many years. Born and bred in nearby Dunglow, he wrote of island life - 'Islanders' 1927 and 'Proud Island' 1975. He also dealt with his political phase in 'The Gates Flew Open', a reference to his escape from internment as a Republican during the Irish Civil War in 1923. He was the leader of IRA militant agitation for land reform in the 1930s. This led to the withholding from Britain of land annuities by the fledgling Irish government of the new state. These annuities were due as the repayment (mortgage fashion) of the capital investment in agricultural land made by the Congested Districts Board pre-independence in 1921. The economic war with the UK that followed brought Ireland to its knees. Strangely, when the dispute was settled in 1938, as part of the deal, the UK handed back to Ireland its maritime ports. After independence, Britain had continued to occupy and utilise deep harbour naval facilities at Cobh, Bearhaven and Lough Swilly (Rathmullen). The UK would regret its folly almost immediately, as they could have well done with these ports during the Battle of the Atlantic that followed during World War 2. Ireland could hardly otherwise have remained neutral in such a conflict. One side or the other would surely have invaded. The association of such a remote place with such momentous events is amazing!

Landing and Camping

Land easily at E end of the N side onto a gravel beach, or on the ESE side of the island, on N side of the projecting Portnamweela, where there is a sandy beach. There is good camping by the ruined houses on short sheep-grazed grass. Good water is to be had in a well, found behind 'main street' along the north side. N.B. Wells need use, so you may need to clean it out and let the sediment settle before you take water from it.

SPA

Barnacle Goose, Tern. Also, Brent Goose, Eider, Greylag, Shelduck and Lapwing seen in May 1999.

Rutland Island

B704-151   Sheet 1

The largest of the outer islands immediately inside Aran, SW of the North Rutland Channel. There are a fast-growing number of newly built holiday homes on the NE quadrant of the island facing Burtonport. West of a line from the NW tip to the SE tip, the entire island is a desert of prickly sand dunes. This is a most attractive island, accessible yet quiet, whose main tourist feature must be its magnificent beach running the length of its W side and where few others would ever be met. Absolutely worth a visit.

Landing and Camping

Landing on the main beach would involve a lengthy and difficult carry, easily avoided by accessing a small, hidden, sandy cove through a short, narrow channel just inside the mouth of the North Rutland Channel (beside a sign warning of a Power Cable). A 100m carry then accesses splendid machair short-grass camping in the shelter of the dunes and near the north end of the beach.

Alternatively, land 150m further SE into the North Rutland Channel, onto a steep, sandy beachlet at B705-150, just seaward of a new house with new steps to the sea and just inside a green navigation marker. This gives a shorter carry to the same camping, but the beach, although sheltered, is steep at most points of the tide.

The island has long been electrified, but there is no mains water.

Tides

Beware strong tides all around, and foul ground off the SW tip. There are many landings possible all around the island.

History

Rutland Island has a remarkable history, having been the commercial capital of NW Ireland 200+ years ago. The herring industry thrived so strongly in the 18th Century that the local landlord Lord Burton Conyngham invested heavily in providing access via Burtonport to a major new town on Rutland Island. By about 1785, the island had a Post Office, hotel, harbours, fish handling facilities and a population of hundreds. Then the herring shoals declined and disappeared altogether in 1793. The town degraded somewhat but was still occupied in September 1798 when the second wave of French invaders to Ireland that year landed on Rutland. Napper Tandy, commander of the United Irishmen on board, raided the post office. He found out that the first wave of the invasion of the previous month under General Humbert, which had landed at Killala and had some early successes, had been beaten. The 1798 Revolution was as good as over. Tandy retreated towards France, was caught, but not executed. Wolfe Tone would accompany a third wave of invaders a couple of months later but they were beaten by the Royal Navy in a battle just off the back of Aranmore.

Later the cancellation of the island's hotel liquor licence would make legal history in the 20th Century.

The island remained the administrative capital of the region for a century. A channel to the nearby mainland was dredged out, so that Burtonport became eventually more important and took over the marine industry hereabouts. The island was inhabited until the 1960s. Nowadays there are holiday homes on all these inner islands. In 2003 a marina for pleasure yachts has been planned, but lack of funds has frustrated progress. The main fishing hereabouts is now out of half-deckers, for crabs and lobsters. Trawling is very much in decline. This area may thus become principally a tourist destination, but that is the way of things.

Inishcoo

B706-153   Sheet 1

1.5km E of Aranmore, situated on the NE side of the North Rutland Channel, the second largest of the outer islands inside Aran. A huge granite wall zigzags across the island. The biggest of the holiday homes is the former coastguard station at the SW. There are nice sandy beaches midway on the SW side and even a small lake in the interior. There is a highly attractive, secluded, family type, swimming sandy beach in the NW channel at B703-158.

This attractive island lies just SE of Oileán Eighter and is joined to it by a footbridge at B703-157. The dividing channel is passable by kayak at HW.

There is also a passage between Inishcoo and the smaller Edernish just SE of it. Land at a small quay at the SW corner at B706-153.

Eighter Island

B703-157   Sheet 1

1km E of Aranmore, NW of Inishcoo. The most northerly of the outer islands inside Aranmore, Eighter is the small rocky low-lying island at the NW end of the North Rutland Channel. The North Rutland Channel runs SE to NW and is the narrow sound between Eighter and Rutland which gives access from Burtonport out to Aran. There are a number of holiday homes clustered in the SE quadrant. These have the distinction of appearing very unchanged from the original construction. Landing is most convenient at the southern tip of the island onto a sheltered SE-facing beach in the North Rutland Channel. Camping is all around. The houses collect water, not all of them in sealed tanks. There is a rumour of a pitch and putt course on the island, unauthenticated. There is at least one highly secluded, beautiful sandy beach, facing NE at the N exit from the cut with Inishcoo.

Edernish

B710-150   Sheet 1

Edernish is the smallest of the four outer islands inside Aranmore, barely detached from Inishcoo to its NW. Seen from Burtonport, it is dominated by a large house with a boathouse to its S. The house has a tidal swimming pool beside. The entire island has a perimeter fence. Most such fences are to keep stock in; some keep people out. This fence is unique in keeping stock out. Cattle graze the extremities of the island. Every little projection or headland boasts short

grass and cow manure. The inner core of the island is utterly ungrazed, wild as can be. It does have contorted pines and other tough bushes and trees, for shelter. This approach is unique among Irish offshore islands.

An tOileán Leathan

B708-169   Sheet 1

This is the most northerly of the inner islands inside Aranmore, and by far the most attractive. Anglicised as 'Lahan', the term means 'broad' as opposed to 'caol' meaning 'narrow'.

A beautiful stone cottage dignifies this island. Whoever painted its doors and windows blue deserves some sort of medal. The result craves a camera or easel. There is a slip below the cottage, but it is quite steep. The easiest landing for a kayak is 100m just ENE below the stone outbuilding, also pretty. Here on a storm beach there is also a sunken bog, at a cut. The top is 20m high. The views from the summit are the best of any hereabouts, N to Owey, W to Aran, S to Glencolumbkille.

There are other islands within those inside Aran. These are sometimes named, sometimes not. They include one large such just SSE of Leathan at B710-165, Eadarinis Fraoigh just further SSE at B715-158, Inishmeal at B722-138 (inside Rutland Island), and Inisheane at B746-111 (in Dunglow Bay). None of these demonstrate any particular merit to the leisure activist, or demand individual attention.

Aran Sound South

The South Sound of Aran on the E side of Aran is a fearsome place with a high swell, particularly if the swell is from the N. The safest N/S passage goes approximately 200m east of Aileen Reef. Aileen Reef extends SE for 1km from Cloghcor Point at the SE corner of Aran. Boomers may be experienced over the shallows on the E side of the sound at a point E of Cloghcor Pt., off the beach on Rutland. You may also encounter boomers immediately west of the Carrickbealatroha Upper rocks beacon B695-147, which is shown but not named on the 1:50,000 OS map.

If you plan to paddle from the village (Leabgarrow) on Aranmore to Burtonport via the S end of

Aranmore, Co. Donegal - David Walsh

Rutland, with swell about, it is best to follow the channel S to Clutch beacon, marking the S end of Aileen Reef and then turn E, aiming for the beacon on the S end of Rutland. This should avoid any of the breaks on the E side of the Sound.

Aran Sound North

A large swell runs through the Sound of Aran in strong north-westerlies. At the N end, Blind Rocks at B686-166 and Ballagh Rocks at B693-170 are places to be avoided. Blind Rocks are just E of Calf Island and Ballagh Rocks (marked on the 1:50,000 OS map) are 0.6km NW of Eighter Island. In these conditions, the North Sound is virtually closed. Waves frequently break *over* the Ballagh rock light (10m high). This lighthouse was built in the autumn of 1875 and was originally known as Black Rock. It was converted to electric batteries in 1983. Waves also break over the Black Rock beacon (red) just off Leabgarrow pier. If in doubt, follow the ferry route around the N end of the beacon and then down to the beach and the landing described in the Aranmore section.

Aranmore Island

B685-156   Sheet 1

Mostly known more simply as 'Aran'. The island is mountainous at 227m high and about 6.5km square. Day trippers can enjoy a circular walk called Siúlóid Aran Mhóir, almost entirely on roads and good bog tracks and rivals the necklace walk on Great Blasket. The island has a stable and prosperous population of about 650, considerable by island standards.

Landing and Camping

The main landing is onto a sheltered sandy beach in front of the main village, midway up the E coast. The strand is bounded on the N side by two piers and on the S by a gentle point, where there is excellent camping near the new school, beside a football pitch. The more northerly pier is the busy ferry pier. In normal conditions, land at the extreme S end of the beach at B685-156, from which there is a very short carry. The best landing in N winds is at the N end, in the shelter of the smaller, S pier. This avoids the surf farther down the beach but carrying to camp is then a problem. Water in the village. The S end of the beach is the best semi-private camping convenient to everything. Remoter camping exists elsewhere as described.

Accommodation and Services

A many-times-a-day ferry services the island with a sheltered run from the mainland at Burtonport. The ferry runs punctually during peak (usually summer) times but less so in the off-peak. The car ferry can take up to 8 cars, is regular and well run. Information can be had from Annie Bonner at 074 9520532 who also runs a restaurant and B&B on Aran at the pier. There is a hostel by the beach which also appears well run, 074 9520515. Glen Hotel is just above the beach for those seeking comfort at 074 9520505.

Circumnavigation

From the paddler's point of view, the entire W side is challenging. Great cliffs reflect huge waves, especially at the steeper cliffs and mighty headlands. There would often be no real stopping point between the two waystops midway on the S and N coasts next described. That involves 14km of committed paddling on the outside stretch. With 'pottering', allow almost 20km around the whole of the island altogether. Factor in the foul ground off the SE corner and this adds up to an achievable yet demanding circumnavigation.

Rannagh Point B666-136. This is the spit of land jutting S from midway along the S coast. On the E side, there is a lovely sandy beach, a pier with water on tap, a football pitch and short grass camping which is much more private than at the main strand on the E side. This is a working pier with associated advantages and disadvantages. Camping here is perhaps the most attractive on the island, with about a 4km walk to the main village, though there is a pub locally, which does excellent grub. Sheltered in almost all conditions.

Storm beach B643-154. There is a substantial storm beach just N of the SW point of the island, which in calm conditions might give a landing, being somewhat protected by the off-lying islet Illanaran. It is feasible to scramble to the moorland above by a watercourse in a gully at the S end of the beach, if really necessary.

Lighthouse B642-186. In very good weather, a landing might be had at the foot of the concrete steps. These were constructed down the cliff to service the lighthouse at the far NW of the island at Rinrawros Point. A tiny landing spot has been cut into the rocks at sea level in a deep narrow SE-NW cleft. This might serve as a lunch spot or a base to explore locally. A lighthouse was first constructed here in 1798 and functioned until 1832, when Tory light was established. George Halpin Jr. designed the 'new' lighthouse, which was rebuilt in 1865. It is now automated. The steps are due S of the lighthouse, near where the straight wall reaches the cliff edge and inside a number of small off-lying stacks.

Look for the Big Giant and the intriguingly named Small Giant, two stacks on the N side of the lighthouse, to its E.

Ballachreesh Bay B674-176. A deep bay near the E side of the north coast. Attractive looking on the map, this is a sheltered (NB - not from N swells) storm beach with possible camping. There is water in nearby houses and this beach will appeal to some for its sense of remoteness. Its importance is its status as a jumping off point, providing conditions are suitable, for the round trip.

Natural harbour B683-171. A small extremely sheltered natural harbour near the N end of the east coast, where there is a quay and the former lifeboat station. The lifeboat is now moored inside Calf Island 0.5km to the south. Camping is inadequate. Worthy of waystop mention only.

Calf Island

B685-166　　Sheet 1

On the Aran side of Aran Sound North, this small island gives shelter to the mooring place for Aran's modern lifeboat. This is a truly magnificent beast, too large for the lifeboat station that previously served the community here from the land station just NNW. The island is campable, for those for whom privacy is everything. It is grazed by sheep and quite unexpectedly attractive. No water. The landing is at the E end, onto north or south-facing beaches to taste, where an off-lying islet is barely disconnected.

North West Donegal - Tidal Overview

For Aran Island to Bloody Foreland, Horn Head, Tory Sound and the Inishbofin Group, local HW and LW are Galway +0040. The main NE tidal stream in the area generally starts at HW Galway -0350 and the SW flow at +0235, half an hour ahead of the main west coast tidal stream. However, it is important to note that this general statement does not hold good close in to Tory or amongst the inshore islands of the Cruit, Gola and Inishbofin Groups, where the details are given individually. The streams here tend to turn an hour or more earlier. In Tory Sound, the maximum spring rate is 2 knots. At Bloody Foreland itself, as might be expected, usable eddies form inshore downstream. Further E, inshore past Horn Head, Melmore Head and on towards Malin Head, the stream runs ENE from HW Galway -0350 to +0235. The bays tend to start to fill an hour or more earlier, from HW Galway -0500 to about +0100.

Owey Group

Admiralty Chart 1883 covers Crohy Head to Bloody Foreland and is well worth having for a visit to this area. The main offshore tidal stream from Aran to Bloody Foreland starts and finishes half an hour earlier than the main west coast tidal stream further S. The NE flood starts at HW Galway -0350 and the ebb at +0235. In this region however, it merely brushes off the outside of the islands, eddying. The streams in the channels tend to be from HW Galway +0130. These tidal streams are not said to be significant throughout the whole group except in Owey Sound.

Cruit Island

B734-205   Sheet 1

An attractive inhabited island, inside Owey, joined to the mainland by road. The island runs N/S, is narrow, being 4km long and 1km wide, and achieves a modest 26m in height in the middle. A golf links is spread out over most of the N end of the island. The clubhouse is just above a sheltered beach and slipway at B724-224. In the middle of the island, just SE of the highest point, is a most pleasant caravan/campsite at B734-205 on commonage, with water on tap. Rock climbing has been developed nearby, mostly on the W side, in the elbow just W of the high point. Although on good granite, it is small and a poor relation of the climbing on Owey.

Landing and Camping

The sand flats on the E side of the island dry out and extend to just beyond this campsite so arrive and depart at HW. Circumnavigation is possible only on the very top of the tide as the S/SE parts dry. No shopping or similar facilities were found on the island but the mainland is accessible on foot.

Local HW and LW are Galway +0100. Tidal streams in Owey Sound coincide with local ebb and flood, or half an hour later, flowing very strongly indeed and can cut up very rough in contrary winds.

The landing, Owey Island, Co. Donegal - S. Pierce

Owey Island

B719-229   Sheet 1

Owey is uninhabited since about 1980, with a deserted village. Some refurbishment seems to be in progress, and some of the houses may be occupied in summer. There is neither mains electricity nor water. A pleasant island, square shaped, tilted a bit anticlockwise, with granite sea cliffs all along its N half. Well worth a visit. A distinctive type of curragh was found in this region which was sculled over the bow and was used by islanders for access to and from the small pier on Cruit.

Embarkation

The nearest launching place for Owey is at the N end of Cruit, opposite Owey. Launch from a sheltered beach and slipway at B724-224, just below a golf clubhouse. Park in the clubhouse car park. Beware of flying golf balls when crossing to the slip as you're on the 18th fairway and the golfers are unsighted at that point.

From a car, the more convenient embarkation point is from a harbour about 1km NW of Kincaslough, where the parking is convenient, which is sheltered, and is free of aerial bombardment.

Landing and Camping

The landing place is at a slipway on the E side in a small sheltered cove at the N end of the narrows opposite Cruit Island. The slipway in the cove is easily found coming from the N but can be missed coming from the S, as the cove opens ENE and is low lying. The markers are a large rock in the Sound, the cove itself and a prominent schoolhouse on the island all in line. There are lights on Cruit at 070º leading into the Sound from the south.

Water and Camping

There is water in the stream through the village. Camping at slip.

Rock Climbing

There is excellent rock climbing on good granite, relatively undeveloped. It started in 1991, began in earnest in 1993 and there are now a few dozen routes. Some routes just 300m north of the landing place at the S end of 'the Canyon' do not need an abseil for access. With an abseil there are more in the Canyon itself at its N end, in the first cove N of the Canyon, and on slabs at the NE point. The N coast of the island has not yet begun to yield its unlimited climbing potential, though it will, well into the future, especially to access from the water.

The 2002 Donegal climbing guidebook edited by Alan Tees and published by the Mountaineering Council of Ireland www.mountaineering. ie in 2002 has all the Owey climbs. Look it up also on www.climbing.ie.

Circumnavigation

Circumnavigation gives good caves, canyons, channels and stacks. Owey in Irish - 'Uigh', means 'Caves'. There is a through cave with a right angle turn going through the N tip. There is a passage on the NW side of the island which is entered from the land, leading to a large underground cavern. There are deep sea caves along the NE side, including one with connecting chambers. These are easily accessible when the wind is from the S/SW.

Tides

Local HW and LW are Galway +0100. Tidal streams in the sound with Owey turn with the tide by the shore, or half an hour later, flowing very strongly indeed and can cut up very rough in contrary winds.

Inishillintry

B737-218   Sheet 1

Off the E side of Cruit, this island consists of high heathery separated mounds. Never inhabited. See the fish-holding tanks in offshore rocks off the SE side. The grass is a bit long for camping. No grazing. No water.

Embarkation and Landing

Land in a sandy cove in a cut on the SE side. There is a good embarkation point from a harbour about 1km NW of Kincaslough, where the parking is convenient, and which is sheltered.

Gola Section

This section stretches from Inishfree Lower in the S to Inishsirrer in the N.

The generally most convenient embarkation point for all the islands of the Gola Group and certainly for Gola Island is from a pier at B793-266 just N of the entrance to Gweedore Bay. It is

The pier, Gola Island, Co. Donegal – David Walsh

the more northerly of the two such piers locally. By road from Derrybeg, go past the graveyard and fork right. There is good camping beyond the graveyard along the access road but no water.

Ferry

An all-year-round ferry to Gola is run by Jimmy Sweeney 087 6607003. It leaves from Bunbeg Pier B802-235. The Tory ferry is based here, as the harbour is very sheltered.

Nearest provisions are to be had in a shop at the main road, 2km or more from the pier. Full provisions are available in Bunbeg, just S of Derrybeg. Bunbeg harbour is accessible to kayaks at all stages of the tide. There is a hostel 1km up the road from Derrybeg in Magheragallon, 07495 32244. Ensure the tide is with you in the estuary, local HW being Galway +0100.

For the N part of the group there is also an excellent pier right opposite Inishmeane at B799-284 known locally as Carrick Pier. Here there is an extensive sandy beach, good camping on machair grassland or in dunes behind the pier, but no water. By road, drive 3km N out of Der-

rybeg, then (1km N of a significant junction), follow signs left for 'Beach', and continue past an enclosed soccer pitch.

Inishfree Lower
B759-240   Sheet 1

2km SSW of Gola. An unexpectedly pleasant island. Landing is possible on the E side of the island in a wee bay, onto sheltered boulders. There are the remains of a house on the island, which was occupied until the 1960s. The island is generally low-lying and now (probably only occasionally) grazed by sheep.

Inishinny and Bo Islands
B785-255   Sheet 1

1km SE of Gola. These two islands are almost one and together shelter the S side of the entrance to Gweedore Bay, which is the estuary leading to the town of Bunbeg. There are many good safe beach landings on Inishinny on the S and E. The gap between Inishinny and Bo is navigable at most stages of the tide. A very at-

Departing for Inishmeane, Co. Donegal - David Walsh

tractive thatched cottage is sited on the adjoining Illancarragh B782-252 to the SW.

Go and Allagh Islands

B765-258   Sheet 1

Just off the south side of Gola. Of little interest, landing is possible on both. Useful shelter on passage on E side.

Gola Island

B773-271   Sheet 1

This is a truly beautiful island, a must to visit. The island is now uninhabited, though the houses show signs of being kept up, and an increasing number of summer homes have been built. Mains water and electricity are scheduled to be supplied to the island in 2004. In a remarkable feat of co-operation, the water and the electricity will be placed in the same trench.

A book 'Gola, the Life and Last Days of an Island Community' by Aalen and Brody was written in 1969 and a film 'Terminus' was made by RTE at the same time. Gola is famed also in song, 'Baidín Fheidhlimi, d'imigh go Gabhla...'

was about a drowning tragedy involving a Gola boat on passage to Tory. It was written by Felim's brother, the renowned seanchai of Rannefast in the nearby Rosses.

Landing and Camping

Land at the modern concrete pier and sheltered beach on the E side, the main landing point for the island. The main village, called Portacrin, is on the S side and is exposed to south-westerlies. A number of sandy beaches exist at the SE corner of the island, which provide soft landings in any conditions. There are a number of other landing places available which are sheltered from different sea and weather conditions. A south-facing beach, near the E tip, has good camping on grass by its W end. A storm beach landing is possible at all stages of the tide in Magheranagall Bay at B764-269, the deep indented bay on the W. Camping is possible here but departure may be difficult if the sea gets up. No dependable drinking water has been found, though there is a large freshwater lake at Magheranagall. Mains water is planned for 2004.

The pier and slipway on Inishmeane, Co. Donegal – David Walsh

Circumnavigation

Circumnavigation offers spectacular views of cliffs, arches and caves. Tororragaun Sound on the N side, between Gola and Umfin, can be lumpy at times, being shallow, and a lot of clapotis can be expected on the W side. A tunnel penetrates through the tip of the N side of Magheranagall Bay at its seaward end, which is worth looking out for if there is not too much swell. The entrance is not obvious from either end.

Rock climbing

Gola has excellent climbing on good granite, more developed than Owey and very popular. Climbs have been put up on the N side of Magheranagall Bay and on the sea cliffs of Mweelmore, the hill S of Magheranagall Bay, facing S towards Owey. The 2002 Donegal climbing guide book edited by Alan Tees and published by the Mountaineering Council of Ireland www.mountaineering.ie in 2002 has all the Gola climbs. Look it up also on www.climbing.ie.

Umfin Island

B767-284   Sheet 1

Umfin is 1km N of Gola and although much smaller, Umfin has superb granite coastal features of caves, cliffs and shoals. There is a dependable landing point onto a very sheltered storm beach in a channel on NE side, which can be entered on most states of tide, but which dries to the SE at LWS. A small ruin of a bothy remains tucked away in the hollow by the landing, where there is the most possible camping.

Inishmeane

B786-283   Sheet 1

1.5km NE of Gola, Inishmeane is a dependably accessible island. Landing is always possible at a slipway under a cluster of old houses at the SE corner, or on the beach just E. There is a new pier and some houses are occupied in summer. The houses by the slipway are still used in summer by fishermen, and are well kept. Permanent inhabitation was abandoned in 1974. There is neither mains electricity nor water. The houses form

Lake and village, Inishsirrer, Co. Donegal – David Walsh

a distinctive tight group. A Corncrake was heard singing at the beach in 2001. There is good camping in a hollow in the dunes behind the beach, just W of the E point, known as Gobacurrane.

SPA

Barnacle Goose, Tern, Chough, Corncrake.

Inishsirrer

B785-300   Sheet 1

3km N of Gola, Inishsirrer is the most northerly of the chain. Inishsirrer is a most attractive island, formerly inhabited (abandoned 1943), but now only occasionally. The village is SE of the middle of the island. No drinking water found, the lake E of the village is brackish, but contains good cockles. Many deserted houses, old fields, paths and walls. A walk to the automated lighthouse in the NW is worth the effort, as this end of the island has quite an 'oceanic feel' to it.

SPA

Barnacle Goose, Tern, Chough, Corncrake.

Landing

From the SE end of the island a boulder-strewn spit juts out E, ending at a prominent rock, Damph More. On passage from the S, at LW it is necessary to keep close to the mainland, E of Damph More. Only cross the Damph More spit at HW, with care. There is a landing point by a pier/slipway at B791-297, just N of the spit. At LW when the slip is too high to use, the landing is onto boulders/sand.

A more secluded landing point can be found in a bay at B782-306 on the SW- facing side, the first bay SE of the NW tip. This is near the highest point of the island and onto a storm beach, and drying shoals at the entrance can be a problem in south-westerlies. Also, at HW, a landing may be had just further SW at B784-304 in a sheltered inlet just NW of halfway along the SW side, at a place called locally Slodanawaud. Here there is a rusty windlass and a ruined boathouse, but beware that Slodanawaud is a tidal-pond which forms on the lower half of the tide and may trap your escape.

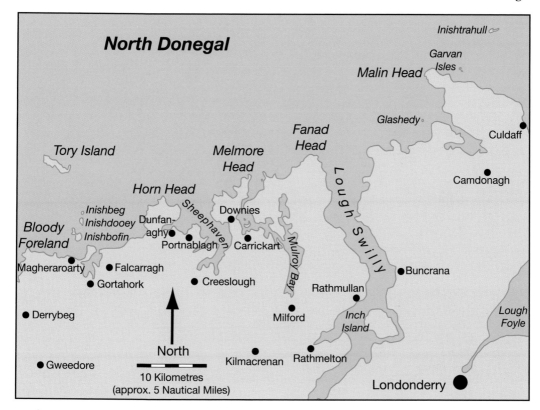

North Donegal
Tory Group

Inishbeg, **Inishdooey** and **Inishbofin** together form a worthwhile group for a day trip or for an overnight camp, or just for shelter on passage out to Tory. Embarkation for all the islands is from the sheltered strand E of pier at Magheraroarty at B889-333.

SPA

Storm Petrel, Greenland White-Fronted Goose, Barnacle Goose, Tern, Chough, Corncrake, Peregrine.

Tides

Local HW and LW are about Galway +0040. Tides flow strongly through the sounds and off the points, nowhere more so than over the shallow bar off the SE point of Inishbofin. The causeway here dries in springs and there is a fair race. Tides in the channels amongst the islands and in Tory Sound close in to Inishbeg turn about an hour after HW/LW by the shore. The E making flood runs from HW Galway -0450 to +0135. The stream further out in the middle of Tory Sound turns an hour later at HW Galway -0350 and +0235.

Inishbofin

B896-360   Sheet 1

2km N of Magheraroarty, an attractive island, the innermost of the three inner islands.

Mains water and electricity were supplied in 2002. Now there is even a hostel to welcome the visitor, tel 074 9162070 or visit www.teach-johnny.com. The island is very pleasant and every summer the former residents come back to live and work so that a vibrant community thrives for half each year.

Landing

There are many landing points and two landing places. One landing place is at the pier B896-360 at the inhabited village in the SE where it is important to ask for water and campsite. The second is at the lovely beach in remote Toberglassan Bay B 890-367 to the N.

Corncrake

Inishbofin represents a unique part of the success story for the frustrating efforts of Birdwatch Ireland to halt the Corncrake decline in Ireland. Here there was a huge increase in numbers and the first such in the country. There were 12 calling males in 1994 and more than double that in 1995. This was the first return for their policy of grant-aiding eco-friendly harvesting methods.

Inishdooey

B895-385   Sheet 1

1km N of Inishbofin, this small uninhabited island, the centre of the three inner islands, has the ruins of a church (Saint Dubhthach, or Dooey) and is especially noted for its magnifi-

Rock arch, Tory Island, Co. Donegal - David Walsh

cent arches and caves on its E side. Landing is perhaps best at the sheltered storm beach in the SW where there is good camping but no water. The three masted 'Loch Ryan' was shipwrecked here in 1942. Landing is also possible in a sheltered but messy narrow zawn to the NE, or onto any of several tiny storm beaches in cuts on the E/SE.

Inishbeg Island

B896-396   Sheet 1

1km N of Inishdooey, the outermost of the inner group, this is a pleasant small sheep-grazed uninhabited island. It has a well sheltered but concealed landing onto a storm beach at the head of a dog-legged cut at the SSW tip. This is in the sound to the S of the island and the landing is onto the low-lying rocks just E of the SSW tip. It must be searched for, though it's worth it.

Tory Island

B856-464   Sheet 1

12km NNE of Bloody Foreland, Tory is named for the dramatic appearance of the high tors at its E end as seen from the mainland; this is the most remote inhabited Irish island and holds a special place in history.

SPA

Storm Petrel, Corncrake, Tern, Chough.

Facilities

The main pier on the island is at Camusmore Bay serving West Town at B855-465. In the village there is water available, two shops, a new hotel, hostel, cafe, pub and post-office.

Camping

Camping is possible at West Town, but a bit public. A more remote landing can be had onto a storm beach at Port an Dúin on the E end of the island at B877-454. This is the dramatic square-shaped indent in the skyline, just E of the last house on the island. Camping may be dramatically had on the flat ground just above the cliffs. The disadvantage of camping here is that all visitors walking to the Anvil and Tormore pass directly by. For larger groups, or those requiring privacy or greater security, perhaps in high season, a well sheltered landing may also be had hereabouts at a small storm beach (HW) /

North coast of Tory Island, Co. Donegal - David Walsh

sand beach (LW) just 500m W of Port an Dúin. There is good camping at the shore directly SW of the last dwelling on this side of the island at B874-453. In either case, there is good water at a spring beside this house, where asking would be respectful.

Tides

Tory is a challenging trip, at almost 13km out from Magheraroarty Pier at B889-333. However, the Inishbofin Group shelters half of this, and the trip out can be broken. Local HW is Galway +0040. In the middle of Tory Sound, the ENE flood runs from HW Galway -0350 to +0235. Close in to Tory and to the islands of the Inishbofin Group, (as well as in and around and through the Inishbofin Group), the tidal streams turn one hour earlier. The E making flood runs from HW Galway -0450 to +0135. Slack occurs about one hour after local HW/LW. As the exposed part of the passage between Tory and Inishbeg takes an hour or so, and as another hour is needed for the passage between Inishbeg and Magheraroarty, it is impossible to organise slack water all the way across. Local advice is to

emphasise the later 'middle of Tory Sound' tide for planning purposes, accepting some wind over tide as necessary in the first or last part of the trip, to taste.

Circumnavigation

The N and E sides of the island are sheer for their entire length and offer no rest other than as mentioned below. A landing may be had at three places on the north side.

- Immediately behind Port an Dúin at B876-456 onto a sheltered storm beach.
- A very sheltered landing onto a sandy beach 300m N of West Town at B855-468, at the head of a deep cut, but regrettably, under grassy cliffs.
- Onto a slipway near the W end of the N side at B849-471, just south of a prominent house. This is a former Lloyds signalling station and was later the residence of the artist Derek Hill who did much of his work on Tory.

The scenery on the N/NE sides is magnificent. The whole E end from Port an Dúin outwards

West Town, Tory Island, Co. Donegal - David Walsh

is a prehistoric promontory fort known as Dún Balair, once the stronghold of Balor of the Evil Eye, the baddest of Fomorian bad guys. He ended up being killed by his own grandson, Lewey, who penetrated his one good eye with a huge wooden stake. Lewey hailed from Dunlewy at the foot of Errigal mountain on the mainland to the south. Lewey was mean and was nicknamed 'Lewey Lamh Fhada' meaning 'long arms', a reference to his habit, when he came to visit, of having one arm as long as the other i.e., empty handed.

The remains of Balor's four outer defensive ramparts may still be seen. His citadel is the mighty Tormore, an unapproachable pinnacle at the end of an alpine rocky ridge, called The Anvil, sticking N out to sea. Note the cairn on its summit put there by local kids for a dare. The Anvil may be bypassed on circumnavigation by going though a majestic arch at B878-460.

The cliffs change from quartzite in the E to granite in the W. The cliffs at the E end of the N side are unsurpassed anywhere for unyielding verticality. Arches and offshore reefs abound for the more daring paddlers. Clapotis may be al-ways expected on the W side, by the lighthouse and S of it. A shallow reef sticks far out to sea at the SW corner, which must be given a very wide berth.

The S side is less dramatic, being flat, but the ground inshore at the W end is shallow for some way out and boomers may catch the unwary. Best to keep well off.

Local History

Tory's most famous shipwreck is that of HMS Wasp in 1884 when the ship struck in daylight just near the lighthouse. 51 men died and only six survived. The incident is hard to explain, as the visibility was good so the lighthouse must have been visible for hours and the ship struck just after dawn. It has been attributed to a curse having been put on the ship with the aid of local cursing stones. There were also personality problems in the ranks of the officers and men of the ship, whose attitude to their work of carrying out forcible evictions up and down the west coast varied greatly. At the time of the wreck, Wasp was carrying policemen to evict the inhabitants of Inishtrahull.

Much has been written about the myth, legend and history in which the island is steeped, especially 'Stories from Tory Island' by Dorothy Harrison Therman and Wallace Clark's 'Sailing Round Ireland'. There are remains of a Columban church and of a round tower in West Town. Beside the tower is a very unusual tall cross, 'T' shaped, called a 'Tau', almost unique in Ireland. The cross is 3,000 years old and was adopted into Christianity. Colmcille himself founded the monastery here in the 560s.

There are three types of curragh associated with Tory, the smallest of which was the smallest in Ireland, at eight feet, handled by one oarsman, kneeling at the bow. Nowadays there is only one type, the two-man curragh found all over North Donegal. Of note locally also is the more modern type of double-ended (i.e. transomless) clinker boats somewhat peculiar to Tory, usually white, said to be livelier handlers than transomed boats and with a mast that is purely for the radio. They are the subject of a book by Dónal MacPolin, entitled 'The Drontheim, Forgotten Sailing Boat of the North Irish Coast'.

Rare birds turn up frequently on Tory and those breeding include Corncrake, Storm Petrel and Little Tern.

Legal affairs are carried out most informally on the island, with land being transferred without anything at all being put down in writing by the parties to the deal. Instead, they let the resident priest know and he keeps a track of who owns what.

Tory was once renowned for its Poitín making and it was the turf burned in its illicit stills that accounts for the barren look Tory now presents. Its huge tracts of bog, once rich, are now barren desert, home mostly to rabbits.

There is now a modern hotel in West Town and some modern housing beginning to appear, but most streets and roadways on the islands present a somewhat 19th century appearance. A salvaged World War 2 torpedo marks the high point of the road between the two villages, East Town and West Town.

The island has its own king, Patsy Dan Rogers.

Permanent population approximately 175.

Horn Head

C012-423   Sheet 2

The mainland coastline from Bloody Foreland to Horn Head (Sheets 1/2) is mostly sandy beaches. Horn Head is a local 'big' paddle, well worth the shuttle for its magnificent coastal features on a grand scale.

Other than as mentioned below, the paddle is a non-stop 15km. Pollaguill Bay at B990-388 is the obvious rest-stop enroute, midway between Horn Head and the Back Beach, about 4.5km from each. Also, less obvious, though dependable in all but bad W/NW winds, is a well sheltered storm beach in a deep west-facing cut, 1km SW of Horn Head itself at C006-413. From here, there is at least the theoretical possibility of human escape (in dire emergency) up the tall cliffs

Dún Balor, Tory Island, Co. Donegal - D. Walsh

Horn Head, Co. Donegal - Séan Pierce

of Coastguard Hill, which lean back slightly in the gully. This storm beach probably represents a more convenient way stop for those on more serious passages.

Shuttle

Put in or out on the W side at a beach unnamed on the map but known locally as the 'Back Beach' at B948-350 (Sheet 1). Turn N off the main coast road 1.5km E of Falcarragh, following signs for 'Trá', eventually to a good car park where the River Ray flows into the sea. This beach involves a carry and may surf. Better perhaps to start on this side, to be disappointed before, rather than after, a long paddle. If it is surfing badly, try Magheraroarty Pier further W at B889-333. A last resort option might be Ballyness on the E side of Ballyness Bay at B923-336, NW of Falcarragh, but watch the bar on the way out.

On the E side, there is a good, sheltered, dependable 'in-all-conditions' pier C047-372 near Portnablagh, 3km E of Dunfanaghy, just off the main road.

Tides

A sustained lump may be expected, as this is a significant headland, so avoid any wind over tide. The Round of Horn Head is thus perhaps best done W to E on the flood in calm or light westerlies. Tides are as Tory Sound, ENE from HW Galway -0350 to +0235. This is half an hour ahead of the main west coast tidal stream, or a couple of hours behind the rise and fall by the shore.

SPA

Peregrine, Chough.

Melmore Head

C136-457   Sheet 2

The 19km round of Melmore Head is one of the classic paddles of Donegal sea kayaking, principally because of the splendid rock scenery along the W side of the Rosguill Peninsula, yet less committing. Also, the shuttle between Downies at C101-382 in the W and Fanny's Bay pier at C118-390 to the E is very convenient, being only about 2km. Parking is freely available at both, but please be considerate as both are working piers.

There are many escape points even on the west side, but the beautiful Tranarossan Beach at C117-424 is a bit far in except for the hungry or the incontinent. Many of the other more NW projections boast convenient deep cuts en route, with storm beaches or better.

Tides

Expect a bump off the head itself, where strong tides run. Judge the entry or exit of Mulroy Bay correctly, where to fight the tide exhausts the already weary. Beaches inside Mulroy are more plentiful and accessible, E or W side. Both Sheep Haven and Mulroy Bay fill and empty much with the rise and fall of the tides by the shore, i.e. from HW Galway -0520 to +0100.

The inner sections of Mulroy Bay behave differently and are dealt with later. The main west coast tidal stream affects the outer parts of the journey, between Rinnafaghla Point (at C086-426, 3km E of Tranarossan Beach) and Melmore Head itself. This stream runs ENE from HW Galway -0350 to +0235, about an hour and a half behind the bays. The round is probably therefore better paddled clockwise. A suggestion is to start before or at local LW to achieve a favourable LW slack (an hour or two later) at the exposed outer parts of the journey and enjoy the filling tide into Mulroy Bay.

Mulroy Bay

Island Reagh

C129-390   Sheet 2

This low, grassy island is the furthest to seaward in Mulroy Bay and was surrounded by a barbed wire fence in 1999. The flooding tide flows strongly E past the N side. Tides flow into and out of this outer part of Mulroy Bay consistently with the rise and fall of the tides by the shore, from about HW Galway -0520 to +0100.

Mulroy Bay, Inner

Inner Mulroy Bay is a lovely place, and a splendid paddle on blown out days. The tides run strongly at the various narrows and, as is normal with such configurations, the flood and ebb each start later as one penetrates further into the bay. 7km SE of Island Reagh at C184-357 is the most significant narrows of the bay, opening S into the inner bay proper, called Broad Water. Here the flood starts 3 hours later, at -0220 and the ebb at +0335. These timings can be one hour later in springs than neaps. So constricted is the rush of water that the height difference can be as much as 0.5m, producing huge turbulence and a current up to 8 knots.

There is also a strong flow at Moross Channel at C183-393 which gives access from Broad Water to North Water. Here the flood and ebb start up to an hour later still.

Within Broad Water and North Water, the tidal flows are not significant. For a day trip, there are good shuttle points. To the south, there is a car park / picnic site in a wood at C190-305 on the main Milford / Carrickart road. To the north there are multiple choices, including Fanny's Bay pier at C118-390, a working pier east of Downies.

Inishowen Peninsula

Inishowen Peninsula lies between Lough Swilly to its W and Lough Foyle to its E, and is almost totally in the Republic of Ireland.

Inch (Inis) Island

C310-265   Sheet 2/6

Situated at the head of Lough Swilly, Inch is now attached to the mainland due to extensive drainage and reclamation works on the SE side. Inch can be accessed by two-lane roads, and lacks all island feeling. The population is about 350 but there is no village, pub or shop. The whole SE of the island is an extensive farm that featured infamously some years ago in a major legal battle during the 1980s depression. Its owners were evicted by a bank for failure to meet mortgage repayments. The channel along the S and NE sides dry at lower tide levels to reveal extensive 'glár', a local term for unpleasant grey knee-deep silt. Only enter these channels on a rising tide! The SE 'channel' contained within a barrage at each end is actually a fresh water lake, constantly pumped out to keep the salt water at bay. Circumnavigation is therefore impossible. Only the W side has any real interest to small boats. The highest point on the island is Inch Top in the NW at 222m high, a pleasant walk.

At the extreme S tip of the island lies Inch Castle, now in ruins. Built about 1430 by Neachtain O'Donnell for his father-in-law, Cahir O'Doherty, who jailed a rival chieftain Dónal O'Donnell in it. O'Donnell managed to escape and take over the castle, but in 1454 his enemy Rúairí O'Donnell laid siege to the castle and tried to burn him alive in it. The remains of Inch Fort, a later fortification, are at the extreme N tip.

Embarkation

- By road, a left turn off the R238 from Letterkenny towards Buncrana, after the village of Burnfoot.
- From the E side of Swilly at a small pier near Fahan C333-266 near the sailing club.
- From the W side of Swilly at Rathmullan pier C295-274 or the beach beside it.

Landing and Camping

Land at the island pier, C310-265 at the NW of the island. Some occupied houses make the limited camping above the small beach at the pier a bit public. Inch Fort is nearby.

Otter may be found on the island. In winter there are Whooper Swans on the lake, and Greenland White-fronted Geese. Sandwich Tern breed in summer.

Glashedy Island
C383-526   Sheet 3

3km W of the mouth of Trawbreaga Bay, into and out of which washes a strong tide, this is a squat tower of a rocky island with access to the top limited to an airy scramble on the west side. It is said that sheep once grazed here, but certainly not now. Land easily on a gravel spit to the SE. Eider breed. Beware the skerries to E and NW. This island fits nicely into a round of Malin Head. Mind the tide flowing in or out of Trawbreaga Bay, which operates about 3 hours behind Lough Swilly and which can affect navigation approaching from north or south.

Famed for its wintering geese, and its poitín-linked history.

Round of Malin Head
C381-590   Sheet 3

Malin Head is popularly but incorrectly known as the most northerly point of Ireland. In fact nearby (2km ENE) Dunaldragh Head at C398-598 is the most northerly point. Malin Head faces west and is small, low-lying and thoroughly undistinguished, except for the seas off it. Dunaldragh Head faces north and is a high rocky headland, complete with a Lloyds Signalling Station since 1805, an Eire sign from 1939, and lookout sheds from the same period. There is a nice non-waymarked trail around the immediate area.

Tides

The tidal streams in the area are complex and require careful study, after which passage close inshore is perfectly feasible. The diagrammatic hour-by-hour sketches in the Sailing Directions are highly reccomended. Paddlers have studied these for days at a time and found them remarkably accurate.

- Local HW is approximately HW Galway +0100.
- Belfast HW is approximately Galway LW.
- Belfast HW is Dover HW -0015.

Beware that HW at Malin village can be as much as 3 hours behind HW in Lough Swilly outside.

At about an hour before local HW, which is HW Dover -0600, the flood stream starts hammering eastwards and is split by its collision with Malin Head. This gives associated turbulence, initially off Dunaldragh Head, followed (after about an hour or so) by Malin Head itself, until about HW Dover -0400. Then there is slack for about an hour until HW Dover -0300. Then until about HW Dover the inshore flow around the Head favours a passage S to N, but beware wind over tide. From about HW Dover +0100 until about +0400 the stream is hammering west, so that eddies are set up inshore and these turbulently collide with the main flow, mostly at Dunaldragh Head and to the E of it, making things difficult indeed. Therefore the only reliable window of opportunity is at about Dover -0400 or -0300, an hour or two after local HW. If travelling anticlockwise, aim to pass the danger zone closer to HW Dover -0400 than -0300, and if going clockwise, there is slack at HW Dover -0400, followed by several hours of mostly favourable flow until HW Dover.

The really troublesome times are as follows:

- Dover HW -0600 to -0500, which is local HW −0100 to local HW and
- Dover HW +0100 to +0400, which is local LW to local LW +3000

In calm conditions, paddlers will succeed anytime, but do respect that there is significant turbulence hereabouts at other times.

Short Option

A worthwhile half-day trip around the head is between Malin Pier at C423-586 in Slievebane Bay and the small pier in a sheltered bay locally named as Port Ronan (or West Town on the OS 1:50,000 at C406-573). A 2km walk saves a shuttle. One and a half hours in all, quite leisurely. There are regular escape points along the route, so the only committed section is the 2km section between Malin Head and Dunaldragh Head, where you also have the best cliffs, scenery, caves and waves. There is a 400m long passage, only a boat width in places, at Dunaldragh, which is thought might be passable at higher water.

The nearest escape point on the N side is at C404-595 where a stream falls onto the beach and on the S at C387-589 in Breasty Bay, or more leisurely in Ineuran Bay at C390-584. There is a newly upgraded pier facility at Port Ronan, which is hard enough to spot, but there are now half a dozen or so holiday homes clustered above. It is almost at the E end of the high ground. There is a useful hostel in a prime position just at Port Ronan, for a kayaking meet or for the weary passer-by.

Longer Option

A longer trip at 35km with a short shuttle is from the bridge in Malin village at C470-498 (or from Port Ronan, a longer shuttle, paddling distance 23km) to Portaleen Pier at C525-528 or a small pier near Culdaff at C538-507. Departing Malin village has the disadvantage of a long trip through Trawbreaga Bay, which needs an appropriate tide. Beware that HW at Malin village can be as much as 3 hours behind HW

in Lough Swilly outside. Any of these longer options include the committing 11km section of escape-proof cliffs from the Garvan Isles to Glengad Head, which are quite stunning and highly recommended.

The stretch from Malin Pier to Culdaff is unremitting with high and brooding cliffs. An early morning paddle perhaps! The stacks add interest along the route but caves and arches are very few and far between. There are good numbers of breeding Fulmars along the high cliffs and the stacks hold Kittiwakes and Auks.

A flood tide on this section is noticeable between the stacks at Reaghillan at C459-580 and Glengad Head at C526-547. Interesting tidal races set up quite unexpectedly at times. There are beaches of shingle and small pebbles under these cliffs but these may be exposed to a northerly swell. There is a small, well sheltered, east-facing shingle beach at C526-541 just S of Glengad Head near Burren, but at that stage it would probably make more sense to go on to the pier at Portaleen.

Culdaff itself is an attractive place. There is a fine landing at Portaleen pier. You could also try a small picnic site up the Culdaff River at C537-499. There is a track from the picnic site to the river but at low tide getting up the narrow channel may sometimes be a problem. Alternatively, there is a gap in the sand dunes on the beach C540-500 with access to a car park behind. The coast from Glengad Head to Culdaff gets progressively lower in height and for the paddler the pier and river channel stay hidden from view until you are very close.

On the S side, the extra journey has almost continuous escape potential.

SPA

Trawbreaga Bay is an SPA. Whooper Swan, Barnacle Goose, Golden Plover, Bar-tailed Godwit.

Garvan Isles

C436-602   Sheet 3

About 2km NE of Malin Pier, which is 4km E of Malin Head, the Garvan Isles are widely reputed to be no more than inhospitable, weathered quartzite rocks, named from the Irish 'Na Garbh Oileáin' meaning 'Islands of the Rough Sea'.

There are three small islands, White Isle, Middle Isle, and Green Isle, all three names logical, as one has grass atop. Middle Isle does too actually, and is the easiest to land on. The landing is on the N side through a tiny keyhole slot onto stones, strictly one at a time. Local fishermen say that to land sheep to graze Middle Isle, they used to manoeuvre a boat right up to the mouth of the slot and throw the sheep overboard. The sheep did the rest.

Tides do run awfully fast through the Isles, setting up mighty races that must be fun to play in under the right circumstances and should be very much avoided otherwise.

Inishtrahull

C482-652   Sheet 3

About 9km NE of Malin Pier, Inishtrahull is the most northerly 'big' island of Ireland. The passage by kayak takes about one and a half hours.

Inishtrahull is a mighty island, about 1.5 km in length E/W and somewhat hourglass shaped. Hills form the E and W ends, joined by a low flat piece of ground where the abandoned village and farmland lie. It is thought monks were here in the early Christian era, but there is no sign now. Uninhabited since 1928, except for visiting lighthouse personnel, there are ruined cottages and lazy beds, and some rabbits. Beside the old schoolhouse there is a cross inscribed rock, possibly a Mass Rock? There is at least one grave.

Geology

Ireland's oldest rocks are to be found on Inishtrahull and the off-lying Tor Rocks. The rock hereabouts was formed 1780 million years ago (during the Palaeoproterozoic Age), which is old, apparently. Consider that the last Ice Age occurred only 1.6 million years ago. On Inishtrahull and the Tor Rocks, the rock is gneiss, coarse crystalline banded metamorphic rocks, produced by a strong metamorphism of igneous rocks, predominantly Metasyenite Othogneiss.

The gneisses hereabouts are predominantly coarse grained metasyenite with minor intrusions of metagabbro and assorted dykes. Metasyenite is a medium to coarse grained pink and grey foliated gneiss which forms about 95% of Inishtrahull and the Tor Rocks. Metagabbro is a medium to coarse grained green and white rock which has intruded the metasyenite.

The whole Rhinn Complex was affected by mountain building during the Kitilidian Orogeny, which lasted from 1900 to 1700 million years ago.

Metasyenite Othogneiss of the Rhinns Complex of Inishtrahull is the same as appears in Greenland or Scandinavia. It also crops out in the Rhinns of Islay in Scotland, where it is called Lewisian Gneiss.

Lighthouse

A massive automated lighthouse stands at the west end, 23m high, flashing white 3 times every 20 seconds, built in 1958. There is a white accommodation block attached. A disused stub of a lighthouse stands at the east end, built in 1810. It has a very visible base surrounded by large cogs, bits of machinery and derelict living quarters which could provide shelter if stranded. Because of its pivotal position, Inishtrahull Sound is a major route of passage for all sorts of living creatures and Basking Shark and Sunfish have been seen. Perhaps because of the strong tides, no debris is found on Inishtrahull, most unusual for such an island.

In 1994, a herd of 5 Sika deer was brought onto the island, and it is said 4 now remain, all does. They are very shy, and very efficient at keeping out of the way. It is more than possible for a small party never to find them on a visit. In summer 2001, a huge party of 200 or so visited the island for a commemoration. The deer could not evade so many forever, took flight, jumped into the sea, and swam for it. Fortunately, they were spotted leaving by some scuba divers walking about the island. A rescue mission was mounted. By the time they were found, they were two thirds the

Looking W across Portmore, Inishtrahull, Co. Donegal - Séan Pierce

way to Malin Head. In the rescue efforts, unfortunately one drowned, the only stag. The remaining four were saved, and were returned at very high speed to the Hull.

SPA

Barnacle Goose, Peregrine, Arctic Tern, and a significant breeding Eider population.

General Area

Malin Head, pier, and the very pretty village are all on the well signposted coast road tour around the headland, the Inishowen 100. Malin Head Radio Station (VHF channel 23) has a very positive attitude to interaction with canoeists and a visit is very educational.

Embarkation

Embarkation is from Malin Pier C423-585 in the small harbour in Slievebane Bay, 4km E of Malin Head. The pier faces the Garvan Isles C436-602 at 2km out to the NE across Garvan Sound and Inishtrahull is 7km further out beyond them across Inishtrahull Sound in the same direction, 9km in all. Park so as not to obstruct fishermen. This recently improved pier supports

the fishermen's co-op for the whole area and is quite busy.

Inishtrahull Sound

The tides in Inishtrahull Sound itself, reaching about 4 knots in Springs, are notorious with wind over tide and are said to get steeper more quickly than in Tory Sound, but are otherwise quite manageable. It tends to cut up rougher just W of the Garvan Isles than to their E. It is strongly advised to keep east of the Garvan Isles, bound inwards or out, in any wind.

Landing

The most convenient landing on the island is in the waist at the W end of the S side of the island just under the W lighthouse, where a narrow SW-facing cut leads to a jetty and steps, called Portachurry. The landing is said to be a problem as it can be exposed to swell. A much more sheltered landing is also possible in the waist of the island midway along the N side at Portmore. There is a jetty and an impressive 15m raised shingle beach. There is less of a carry at Portachurry. The well at Portmore seems well maintained.

Tides

- Local HW is approximately HW Galway +0100.

- Belfast HW is approximately Galway LW.

- Belfast HW is Dover HW -0015.

Tides run strongly, are very complicated, and deserve respect. With wind over tide, the sea sets up steep waves more quickly in Inishtrahull Sound than even in Tory Sound or Rathlin Sound.

At Inishtrahull itself, there is shallow foul ground at the SW, tidal races flood and ebb at the NW, and the island even boasts a whirlpool off the NE corner, a circular eddy that gets ferocious in springs, from HW Dover +0100 to about +0430. Fortunately, this whirlpool seems always avoidable, as Gull Island at the NE is navigable inside by very small craft. The stream through Inishtrahull Sound on its S side runs at full strength to within 3m of the shore off Portachurry, and a 300m wide race guards the entrance to Portachurry during all the ebb.

The main ESE flood stream passes outside the Garvan Isles, in Inishtrahull Sound itself, for 8 hours from HW Dover +0315 to -0115, and the WNW ebb runs for only 3, from HW Dover +0015 to +0315. There is virtually no slack at the start of the flood. There is an hour and a quarter of slack at the start of the ebb, from HW Dover -0115 to +0015 (much less in springs, half an hour).

At the Garvan Isles and in Garvan Sound to landward, the position is somewhat more complicated. The mainstream of the flood tide passes further out, through Inishtrahull Sound. Therefore, in Garvan Sound and through the Garvan Isles, the tide never runs with much strength ESE at any time, because of the eddying effect of being bypassed. What happens is that for the last couple of hours or so of the flood, the flood stream eddies back around and runs weakly WNW, from about HW Dover –0300 to before HW Dover. So the inshore ebb stream runs continuously WNW altogether from Dover -0300 to +0300. It is stressed though that while it runs relatively weakly while an eddy (say Dover -0300 to HW), it runs very strongly indeed on the main ebb from Dover HW to +0300. The Garvan Isles must (please believe their reputation in this particular regard) be avoided during that period as the streams set strongly through its shallower channels and outlying rocks. To look is enough, and do not go there. Best keep well east of them altogether on passage in or out and choose the timing carefully.

It might seem soundest to leave the mainland at HW Dover -0130 or so and ferry eastwards for a while against the weak ebb, until slack water outside permits an untroubled trip across Inishtrahull Sound. Returning after multiples of twelve (not six) hours later, depart the island at HW Dover -0030 or so, as soon as it looks right. Then bear up eastwards a little while, traversing the Inishtrahull Sound to be carried westwards home across the Garvan Sound, once close to land.

There is also the 'non-slack' at about HW Dover +0300, when the direction of flow changes, they say instantaneously. In calm conditions, bite it. It really must be stressed that in calm conditions, both Sounds are quite manageable, and timing becomes more a matter of navigation and convenience than safety or necessity.

For advance planning of trips, be aware of the significance of a (neaps, predictably) HW Dover falling during hours of darkness, which can mean (every 12 hours) convenient slack waters forcing the choice between a dark leg and windows of opportunity once every 24 hours only, increasing the commitment levels somewhat.

Realistically though, it is better to go spontaneously, when conditions invite. Inishtrahull really is not a forward calendar entry candidate.

Tor More

C474-668   Sheet 3

Tor More is the biggest of a group of isolated rocky islets, skerries and sea stacks called the Tor Rocks, 1.5km NW of Inishtrahull, all consisting of the same rock type. Tides run very strongly in the sound between the Tor Rocks and Inishtrahull and indeed through the gaps and channels amongst the smaller rocks and skerries hereabouts.

Tor More, as the name suggests, is the highest in elevation of the group, rising to 35m. Tor More is high and craggy, especially so on its S flanks. Narrow channels divide it from three smaller outlying stacks.

Garvan Islands with Inishtrahull in the background, Co. Donegal - Séan Pierce

The angle of slope on its northern side is less, and landing is possible onto rock shelves in calm conditions. The summit can be reached easily enough from the northern side, the reward being a fine view of Inishtrahull from almost the most northerly points of Ireland.

Evidence of breeding Shags and c.30 Grey Seal present in August 2003. Oystercatcher, Purple Sandpiper, Turnstone and Eider.

Tor Beg

C479-673   Sheet 3

Tor Beg is the most northerly possible landing in Ireland, save Rockall. Land on the more sheltered S side, where the rock is less steep. Seals abound.

Further Information

www.oileain.org

Oileáin in simple text form was first published on the WWW in 1995. It is constantly evolving, expanding, improving and being updated. Readers researching a particular area should be aware that that area may well have been substantially added to or altered since this publication. Especially before undertaking a trip, look up the relevant area and print the bit you need. Paddlers have had this practice for years.

Oileáin as a webpage also extends to subjects beyond those dealt with in *Oileáin* the book. These relate mostly to sea kayaking issues. For example, "Recommended Excursions", details on "First Known Kayak Landings", "Kayak and Guide Hire" are all dealt with there.

www.irishseakayakingassociation.com

Irish Sea Kayaking Association was formed on 4th June 1991 at Gartan Outdoor Pursuits Centre in County Donegal on the initiative of Ursula MacPherson. It has ever since fulfilled its intention of being a conduit for information, both amongst Irish sea kayakers, and as between Irish sea kayakers and sea kayakers abroad. It also runs national meets once a month in summer, newsletters quarterly, a library, and a web-based discussion board.

www.irishcanoeunion.com

The Irish Canoe Union is the national governing body for the sport of canoeing in the Republic of Ireland. Its webpage contains useful information on all canoeing related matters.

http://homepage.eircom.net/~caoim/oileain/oil1.html

"Islands of Ireland". Well worth a look for the photos. The webmaster John Chambers has long been a friend of *Oileáin* and both have benefited from the collaboration.

http://islandsoftheworld..tk/

Alex Ritsema wrote "Discover the Islands of Ireland" in 1999, and this webpage introduces the reader to the islands that he has explored in many other countries, as well as Ireland.

Glossary of Terms

Boomer	Sailors say 'blind breaker'. An enormous wave, significantly larger than others, even than those in sets (see below), passing a given point.
	The surface above a reef or shallows may appear quite calm most of the time, with no visible warning of the reef underneath, normal waves and even bigger sets passing unaffected. When very occasionally an exceptional wave or wave set comes along, it feels bottom, raises way up in seconds and breaks. With no warning to the unwary, there can be disastrous consequences. Such a wave is a boomer.
Bonxie	Great Skua.
Borreen(s)	Tracks and paths.
Brackish	Of water, half fresh - half salt. In context, not drinking water.
Cable	Old nautical unit of measurement. There are ten cables in a nautical mile (see below). Thus a cable is about 200 yards, or 200 metres.
Clapotis	A confused sea state caused by wave systems colliding into each other, usually experienced where waves reflect off a steep shore and meet incoming waves head on or at an angle. Their peaks and troughs combine to exaggerate wave steepness and height, and generally agitate the surface. Unpleasant.
Coum	Terrain feature, armchair-shaped hollow, as in Cwm or Corrie.

Curragh	Traditional Irish boat. Made from canvas stretched over a wooden frame.
Dúchas	Dúchas – the Heritage Service. It is responsible in the Republic of Ireland for ancient (over 300 years old) buildings and sites. Part of the Department of Arts, the Gaeltacht, Heritage and the Islands. Responsibilities include areas of scientific interest, such as wetlands, wildlife habitat, and SPAs. Dúchas means 'heritage'.
Ebb	The falling tide, or the tidal stream associated with the falling tide.
Flood	The rising tide, or the tidal stream associated with the rising tide.
Gaeltacht	Areas where Irish is spoken predominantly. Most Gaeltachts are in Donegal, Mayo, (particularly) Galway, Kerry, and to a lesser extent Cork, and Waterford.
Grid references	A letter and six digits, e.g. A123-456 that pinpoints position on a map, accurate to 100 metres. It designates a square area 100m by 100m (a hectare). It is the standard OS map-reading method, and is the method used in the text of this guide. Grid references refer to landing spots, except where the small size of an island makes this impractical, in which case the grid reference just identifies the island.
HW - LW	High water, Low water. The highest and lowest points of the height of the sea caused by the flood and ebb of the tide, or the time at which HW or LW occurs.
Inis	In English, 'Island', as is 'Oileán'. Island place-names in English often include 'Inish' or 'Illaun'.
Katabatics	Katabatic winds occur close inshore, often in conditions otherwise calm. Cats paws are immediate local indicators. Lenticular clouds on hill-tops (like cotton wool eyelids) may indicate suitable conditions. Katabatics consist of down draughts, often sudden and violent.
Knot	A knot is one nautical mile per hour, written 'kn'. A Knot is a wading bird.
Laying off	Laying off a course involves plotting a course to steer which makes allowance for any tide or wind which would otherwise sweep you off your desired route.
Lazy beds	Where soil and drainage were poor, beds of soil were built up by piling up sand and seaweed. So called because they didn't involve deep digging, the work involved in establishing them meant that they were far from 'lazy'.
Lee shore	Shore onto which the wind is blowing. Boats losing power would be blown ashore.
Lough	On the sea this refers to a long, narrow inlet of water.
Machair	*Machaire* is a common coastal feature consisting of an exposed sandy beach immediately in front of a raised dune system. Behind the dunes there is often a flat well drained short grassy area, much favoured nowadays by sheep (who call the feature 'grazing'), golfers (who call the feature a 'links'), birds (who call the feature a 'roost'), and kayakers (who call the feature a 'campsite').
Nautical mile	A nautical mile is one minute (one sixtieth of one degree) of Latitude, or about one and one sixth (1.15) land miles, or just less than 2km.
National Trust	In Northern Ireland, as elsewhere in the U.K., the National Trust owns old buildings and conserves land, as Dúchas does in the Republic.
Oileán	In English, 'Island', as is 'Inis'. Island place-names often include 'Inish' or 'Illaun'.
Oileáin	In English, 'Islands'.
OS	Ordnance Survey. In Northern Ireland – OSNI. Ireland's official cartographers or bodies with the job of mapping Ireland. Sheets are available, at scale 1:50,000. They are produced by the modern highly accurate process called photogrammetry.

There are 89 sheets altogether, and the numbering system is the same in Northern Ireland as in the rest of the island. The overlaid 1km square grid has the significant advantage that grid references can easily be given and read, pinpointing locations accurate to 100 metres, more than sufficiently accurate for sea kayaking purposes.

Plastic More usually 'plastics', a kayak made from the substance plastic. Most sea kayaks are made from fibre glass. Reference in this text to plastics usually means that a landing might require risk of violent contact with rock.

Polder Low-lying reclaimed land, usually surrounded by dikes.

Poteen Poteen or Poitín is illegally distilled home-made whiskey.

Scend When a wave stops rising against a shore and drops away. The opposite of Surge.

Set A group of waves, usually three or four, larger than those that went before or after. Surfers wait for sets to catch the bigger and better waves. Sea kayakers wait for the intervals between sets in order to be less challenged when they land, launch or go through a gap.

Shuttle The process of leaving a vehicle at start and finish of an excursion, the difficulty or ease of which often determines the route.

Skerries A Viking word given to groups of large rocks that rise steeply out of the sea .

Slack/slack water The absence of lateral movement of water caused by the flood and ebb of the tidal cycle, or more usually in context, the time at which slack water occurs. Slack can sometimes mean not just a point in time but a period of time during which such water movement is negligible. Slack is often associated with a local HW or LW, particularly in bays and estuaries, so there can be reference to 'the HW slack …'.

Slingshot A trip planning process that involves going somewhere with the benefit of a favourable tide, and coming back later, again with a favourable tide. This requires being at the objective when the tide reverses itself. The slower the craft or the stronger the tides, the more this technique is required. Kayaks typically cruise at 3.5kn, so this is a common enough feature of kayak trip planning.

SPA Special Protection Area. The European Union adopted the Birds Directive, a resolution for the conservation of wildbirds, in 1979 (79/409/EEC). Nations in the EU have to establish SPAs for the conservation of wildbirds that are rare, in danger of extinction or vulnerable to habitat change, mainly breeding birds. Migratory birds count too. Wetlands and seabird sites that support 20,000 birds or 1% or more of any migrant species get designated as internationally important.

Steep to A steep shoreline which may or may not be a cliff. This usually implies that the water remains deep quite close to shore.

Storm beach A beach comprising (often quite large) rounded stones rather than sand. Nature constructs storm beaches where minimal shelter is found in otherwise exposed locations, typically in a small cove on a headland or any wild bit of coastline.
The stones forming a storm beach are often much bigger lower down and smaller nearer the top, making it much steeper near the high water mark. On wider storm beaches the stones are often larger on the less sheltered side. They tend to be more user friendly at lower tide levels, and it is often necessary to pick your spot.

Souterrain An underground chamber (antiquity).

Access – The Legal Issues

Access is not yet a major issue as regards the remoter Irish offshore islands.

Land ownership and accessibility issues seem almost irrelevant in such places, even in these modern times. In comparatively attractive locations all over mainland Ireland, landowners suffer a "honey-pot" effect that sometimes makes them intolerant of visitors. Out beyond the surf-line however, numbers are so few as to make those who do go there, normally, truly welcome.

Mainland hill-walkers have managed in the last 40 years, by sheer numbers, to erode their traditional welcome. The many who go to sea in yachts or other large craft are restricted as to where they can land conveniently. Few enough can and do land on small wild islands in small boats. Therefore there is as yet little problem for them. Nevertheless they are in danger of, sooner or later, repeating history, unless they are respectful of who and what they find out there.

Islands may contain people, stock, and/or fencing. Even if the land is unfenced, it does not mean it is not someone's valued asset. Do not disturb people, stock or fencing. Others who come after you will be judged by what you do or don't do. Respect is the key.

So best be clear about the legal issues. Every square centimetre of Ireland is privately owned, from the HW mark to the top of the highest hill or remotest island in the country. Therefore access, water, and particularly camping, may not be taken for granted. You are there at the sufferance of the landowner, and there is always a landowner. Because people may have 'always' gone there gives no rights there.

Always respect land, its rights, and its owner. Even in the remotest spots on the remotest islands, you are on private property. In my experience, nothing irritates landowners more, or causes them more to strictly exercise their landowning rights, than lack of that respect.

Where in this guide there is reference to "camping possible" or "water in tap" or the like, that is entirely without reference to whether the landowner objects or is agreeable, or, given the likely remoteness of the situation, probably isn't bothered. All description of access, water availability, and camping possibility, means only that these physically exist. In every case it is a factual statement of a physical possibility, not a legal assertion.

It is in the nature of this guide that most places dealt with are so remote that checking ownership would be impossible. This guide has made no effort whatever to make such enquiries.

More populated areas tend to be more regulated in a visible way. Working piers and harbours command their own respect. It is outrageous for holidaymakers to prevent locals doing a day's work by any lack of consideration.

Inhabitation affects the welcome one may expect -

- Only about 10% of Irish offshore islands are inhabited all year round. Almost all of these welcome visitors, in fact all of them do so far as I am aware, except Lambay, County Dublin.

- Increasingly, some more are inhabited in summer only, often by members of their former community, for example in Donegal, Owey and Inishbofin. Such summer communities are often elderly, and are quite welcoming places.

- More islands again now boast holiday homes, used a few weeks in summer and otherwise shuttered. These are almost irrelevant on most islands, if the island is large and there are several houses.

- Holiday islands that are small enough to be owned by one person give the more unpredictable access difficulties. The single owner thereby guards the whole island and not just his site. Access permission problems normally only arise when the owner is resident, but how can one know when that occurs ? It is a good bet to be cautious in August.

Such holiday islands tend to be in or about sheltered bays, modern building works requiring accessibility. West Cork tends to have more than its fair share.

Such limited access difficulties as otherwise exist arise in a number of logical and predictable ways.

- Nature reserves tend to be found in remote places, such as islands, and some discourage access because their work would be disturbed - Lighthouse Island in the Copelands, Rockabill or Keeragh Islands in season.

- Dúchas discourages overnighting on the heritage islands it controls - Scattery, Great Skellig - but otherwise encourages visitors subject to strict regulation.

- Irish Lights does not encourage access onto its lighthouse properties, and certainly discourages overnighting. Lighthouses are intensively maintained during good weather in summer and the last thing such personnel want is to have to share their provisions if the kayaker becomes storm-bound.

- Sometimes private tourist interests discourage all but those on approved (i.e. paying) access methods - Carrickarede, Garinish, Great Skellig.

When landing in a remote spot, be sensible and conduct yourself reasonably. Do not cross wire fences if avoidable, and be very considerate if you do. Leave gates as you find them. Be ultra careful with fires. Respect the privacy of others and particularly, keep well away from occupied houses. No litter ever. Do not disturb livestock. No dogs. Leave nothing but footprints – take nothing but pictures.

As an aside, in Ireland where any paying campsite exists, it would be considered very bad form to wild-camp nearby. The neighbour to neighbour relationship expected of nearby landowners erodes the welcome for strangers otherwise reasonably to be expected. Pay the few euro and camp inside the site.

Place Names - The Irish Influence

Spelling	Irish Word	Meaning in English	Example
Ail	Faill	Cliff	Ailwee
Ard	Árd	High, Height	Killard
Ane	Éin	Bird	Derrynane
Anna, Annagh	Eanach	Marsh	Annalong, Annagh Head
Bal, Bally	Baile	Town	Balintoy, Ballycastle
Ban, Bawn, Fin	Bán	White, Fair, Pale	Banderg Bay, Kilbane Head, Inishbofin
Barnog	Bárnóg	Barnacle	Inishbarnog
Bel, beal	Béal	Mouth, where a river opens into a lake or the sea	Belfast, Bealnalicka
Beg	Beag	Small	Bunbeg, Inishdegil Beg
Boy	Buí	Yellow	Bertraghboy Bay
Brack, breaga	Breach	Trout (so, speckled, or spread out ?)	Aillebrack, Trawbreaga
Bun	Bun	Bottom	Buncrana
Caher	Cathair	Seat, Fort	Caherdaniel
Carrow, Carra	Ceathrú	Literally a quarter, i.e. division of land	Carraroe, Carrowteigue
Carrig, Carrick	Carraig	Rocks	Carrigaholt, Carrickgaddy
Cuan, coon	Cuan	Safe harbour	Cuan, Coonanna
Cool, Cul	Cúl	Back, behind	Kilcoole, Culdrennan
Derg	Dearg	Red	Belderg
Derry	Doire	Oak forest	Londonderry, Derrybeg
Drum	Druim	Hill, ridge	Drumcliff, Dundrum
Duff, Duv, Doo	Dubh	Black	Duvillaun, Inishduff, Doogort

Dun, Doon	Dún	Fort	Dundrum, Knockadoon
-een	-ín	Small, diminutive version	Rusheen Island
Fad	Fada	Long	Carrickfadda
Free, Freagh	Fraoch	Heather	Freaghillaun, Inishfree
Gael, Gall	Gael, Gall	Gaelic, English (speaking)	Gaelteacht, Maghernagall
Garv	Garbh	Rough	Garvan Isles, Garvillaun
Glas, Glass	Glas	Green	Ardglass, Glassilawn
Gorm	Gorm	Blue	
Gub	Gob	Point (of land)	Gubalennaun
Inis, Inish, Illaun	Inis, Oileán	Island	Iniscoo, Inishglora, Inish-vickillaun,
Keel	Caol	Narrow	Inishkeel, Killary
Keeragh	Caorach	Sheep	Inishkeeragh
Kill	Cill	Church, Graveyard	Killiney, Killard, Kilrush
Killeen	Cillín	(Unbaptised) children's graveyard	Killeenaran
Kin	Ceann	Head (opposite of Mouth) of a bay	Kinvara, Kinsale, Kincaslough
Knock	Cnoc	Hill	Knockadoon
Lea	Liath	Grey	Lea Rock
League	Liach		Slieve League
Lis	Líos	Fort	Liscannor
Long	Long	Ship	Annalong
Maan, Mean	Meán	Middle	Inismaan, Inishmeane
Magher, Maghera, Magharee	Machaire	Machair, a common coastal sand dune system	Magheroarty, Magher-amore, Magharee Islands
Mweel	Maol	Bald, bare	Mweelrea
Mor, more	Mór	Big	Inishdegil More
Muck	Muc	Pig	Portmuck, Muckross Head
Oilean, Oileain	Oileán, Oileáin	Island, Islands	Oileán an Anama
Owey, ooey	Uaimh	Cave	Owey, Slievetooey
Port,	Port	Port	Portnablagh
Ros, rush, rin, ran-nagh	Ros, rinn, Ran-nach	Point (of land)	Rosslare, Portrush, Querrin, Ringaskiddy, Rannag
Roe	Rua	Red	Carraroe
Roan	Rón	Seal	Roaninish
Sal	Sál	Salt, salty	Gweesalia, Saltee, Kinsale
Slieve	Sliabh	Mountain	Slievemore
Stag, Stac	Stac	High pointed rock, also a reek (of turf)	Stags of Broadhaven, Stackport
Tor	Tór	Tor, rock tower	Toralayadan
Tra	Trá	Strand	Tramore
Turk	Toirc	Boar	Inishturk

Index

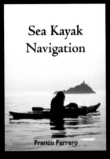
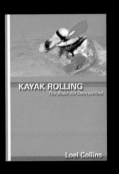

Ocean Paddles

Www.roughstuff.ie
Mill Lane, Palmerstown
Dublin 20
Ireland
+353 1 6264363
+353 1 6864876
+353 87 2596012
Mark@roughstuff.ie

Strength
Matters!!

..A LIFE LESS >.ORDINARY

TOLLYMORE
MOUNTAIN CENTRE

If you're looking for something different in your life then you've found it at the Tollymore Mountain Centre. Set in a superb wooded background with quick access to the County Down coast, we offer a wide range of courses and guiding to suit all levels of skills.

SCNI's National Outdoor Centre

Full range of skills, instructor and coaching courses

Sea and Surf safaris

West Coast island hopping

Guided expeditions to Europe and North America

Highly qualified coaches and instructors

supported by

LENDAL

SPORTS
COUNCIL NORTHERN IRELAND
making sport happen for you

Tollymore Mountain Centre, Bryansford, Newcastle, Co. Down BT33 0PT

T. 028 4372 2158
E. admin@tollymoremc.com
W. www.tollymoremc.com

you weren't designed to go here ...

but your kayak was

VALLEY

Valley Canoe Products - Colwick - Nottingham NG4 2JT   UK - 0115 9614995

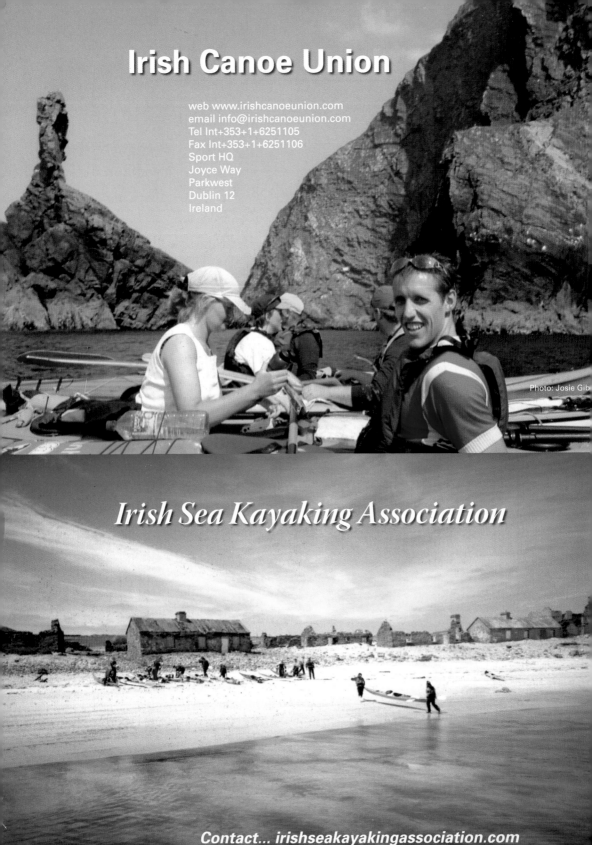

Irish Canoe Union

web www.irishcanoeunion.com
email info@irishcanoeunion.com
Tel Int+353+1+6251105
Fax Int+353+1+6251106
Sport HQ
Joyce Way
Parkwest
Dublin 12
Ireland

Photo: Josie Gib

Irish Sea Kayaking Association

Contact... irishseakayakingassociation.com

Photo: Dave Walsh